MUSIC MAKES YOUR CHILD SMARTER

By Philip Sheppard

SCHIRMER
TRADE
BOOKS

a part of the Music Sales Group
New York / London / Paris / Copenhagen / Sydney / Madrid / Berlin / Tokyo /

Schirmer Trade Books
A Division of Music Sales Corporation, New York

Exclusive Distributors:
Music Sales Corporation
257 Park Avenue South, New York, NY 10010 USA
Music Sales Limited
14-15 Berners Street, London W1T 3LJ England
Music Sales Pty. Limited
120 Rothschild Street, Rosebery, Sydney, NSW 2018, Australia

Order No. OP51689
International Standard Book Number: 978-0-8256-7331-3

Printed in the United States of America

Cover Design: Stacy Boge
Illustrations: Berni Georges
Brass instrument images courtesy of Besson Musical Instruments Ltd.
Double Bass image courtesy of Concord Group (www.concordgroup.com)
Harp image courtesy of Pilgrim Harps (www.pilgrimharps.co.uk)

Contents

On the CD

CD tracklisting

[1] Specially recorded for this book at the Royal Academy of Music, London, July 2005. Piano: Belinda Mikhaïl and Shu-Wei Tseng Cello: Philip Sheppard

[2] Specifically recorded for this book at The Fitzwilliams Centre, Beaconsfield, August 2005.
Children's chorus: Antonia Sheppard, Elena Sheppard, Madeline Lillich, Simone Pillai, Emily Lue-Fong, Tallulah Thomas ('Hop Little Bunnies' solo), Finn Mason, Eddie Mason, Bella Mullarkey, Olivia Flashman, Harriet Flashman

[3] Composed and produced by Mike Sheppard. For further information on Mike Sheppard's compositions please visit the composer's section at www.artemismusic.com

Introduction

Music and your child

Most parents – even those without any knowledge or experience of music – know that music-making is 'a good thing': the combination of self-expression, discipline, fun, and working with others in a positive way is a winning combination, and one to which they want their children exposed. This book aims to reinforce that sentiment, and to discover what really happens when your child makes music.

Can music really make your child smarter? I was sceptical at first, but now that I've explored all the evidence I can confidently say three things:

1. Music can have a profound, positive effect on your child's mental and physical development.

2. Every child is musical.

3. Listening to music is beneficial, but making music is better still.

This book comes in two parts. The first part looks at the scientific evidence behind the claim that music makes your child smarter, and the second part is a practical guide – organized by age group – to making music with your child. The way we react to music has a profound effect on the way we develop socially, physically, and mentally, and making music can build learning ability, cognitive functions, social competence, language, personal confidence, and emotional control.

Of all the tools we are born with, I believe that music is the single most important one for developing mental ability. The desire we all share, to a greater or lesser extent, to make music is a unique, somewhat inexplicable characteristic of being human.

You don't need musical training to be your child's best, most inspiring music teacher – and your home is the perfect place for learning. Who knows – helping your child discover music could even bring out the musician inside you! As you'll discover in the following chapters, every child is born with a huge range of innate skills that can be stimulated and developed by different musical activities. From birth, children have musical skills that rival the skills of even the greatest professional musicians.

This book is intended to be both practical and theoretical: I've collated the most important pieces of scientific research and anecdotal evidence, and I've compared that evidence with my own experiences of teaching toddlers and children. As a parent and a musician, I want to expose my children to musical games and exercises that are entertaining, but I also want those games to have a positive effect on their mental growth, coordination, and creativity.

Over the many years that I have been teaching, I have collected a wide range of traditional music games, and you'll find many of them in this book – together with many that I have created myself. They are all proven exercises that are catalysts for creative music-making, and they help children develop the musical skills they are born with – as well as enhance the skills they acquire through interacting with other people and with their environment. The CD that accompanies this book is packed with music that will help you get the most out of these games and exercises. You might not feel remotely musical, but you really can be your child's greatest music teacher. I hope the exercises unlock some of your own skills, too!

I grew up in a musical environment where I developed a deep love for all sorts of music. Although I am classically trained, I do not believe that any one type of music is better than another: Musical snobbery has no place in this book. What I do believe is that active involvement in music – all kinds of music – can have incredible benefits for babies, toddlers, young children, and their parents. However, I remain cynical about the claims that listening to 'worthy' music can be a quick fix that boosts IQ levels. There are certainly benefits from listening to music, but the real benefits come from making music, from being active rather than passive.

So why do some people believe that passive activities – listening to Mozart, for example – can boost intelligence? In many cases the science has been misunderstood, or exaggerated by people keen to sell products to parents. There's also a great focus on classic IQ tests, which only measure a very small area of a child's abilities. When I use the words 'smart' or 'intelligent' I am not referring to a child's score in IQ tests: I am referring to the all-round abilities that help a child to learn new skills, facts, and functions efficiently, as well as acquiring the ability to express themselves clearly and emotionally, to be socially adept and confident.

I know from my own experience that children engage and develop skills at an incredible rate when they use all of their senses during the learning process. Children learn more quickly when they feel a sense of ownership, and when they have creative input: The pride a child feels when they hear their ideas in a piece of music is extraordinary and highly contagious.

We are all predisposed to be musical, and your child is born musical! I believe that:

- **Music can dramatically improve physiological and mental coordination, which makes it an extremely effective catalyst for learning and development.**

- **Moving to music is a primal reaction that is at the very core of our development.**

- **Physical movement to music can stimulate mental development.**

- **Music plays a critical role in all periods of accelerated childhood development.**

- **Music can be a crucial tool in the development of attentive listening, absorption, and comprehension skills.**

In other words: music really can make a child smarter. In this book you'll find lots of detailed information about the different stages of your child's development and how you can use music in each of those stages.

Introduction

Your child was born musical, and should be given every opportunity to explore and develop his or her musical skills. Music helps mental development, promotes high-level coordination skills, engenders many social skills, enables creativity, and boosts confidence, and it can also be beneficial for your health! Music is the perfect vehicle for learning and every child should experience the sheer joy that music can bring.

Chapter 1

PART ONE: Can music make my child smarter?

First let's deal with some of the most frequently asked questions regarding music, children, and intelligence. From here we'll go on to examine the scientific evidence for these claims in an attempt to answer the question, 'Can music make my child smarter?'

Are children innately musical?

Children are born with an incredible array of musical abilities including acute sensitivity to pitch, extraordinary rhythmic skills, and the ability to discern subtle differences.

How can music affect intelligence?

Intelligence is the capacity to learn and understand new things and making music helps that process. It helps with language and social skills, encourages creativity and has a positive effect on the mental, physical, and social aspects of childhood development.

Can music shape the way a child's brain functions and grows?

Music affects the way the brain develops: Adult musicians' brains show clear differences from those of non-musicians, particularly in areas relating to listening, language, and the connection between the two sides of the brain.

How can music affect my child's mental and physical coordination?

Learning to play music improves fine motor control and coordination, provides a framework for learning new skills, and helps to reinforce 'inhibitory controls.' These controls help children gain mastery over their spontaneous reactions. Many forms of musicianship rely on very advanced coordination between the brain and the body. It is no accident that children's rhymes, songs, and fingerplays exist in all cultures: They're very sophisticated tools for learning and development.

Is there a 'Mozart Effect'?

We are led to believe that playing Mozart to babies develops their spatial awareness. I would argue that this actually has no effect whatsoever – but getting involved in active music-making does seem to have a real effect on a host of spatial processing skills. Playing an instrument develops a sophisticated repertoire of such abilities.

Does music improve children's memory skills?

Musicians use many forms of memory when practicing, performing, improvising, and composing. Music can be an incredible vehicle for retaining vast amounts of associated information. We are genetically predisposed to remember long, complicated musical sequences in a much more efficient manner than that we employ to recall text.

Does music help children's language skills?

Music is the language we are born with to enable us to learn how to communicate and eventually speak in a mother tongue. The very essence of musical phrasing is inextricably linked to the patterns of pre-speech and common speech. These patterns form the foundation for nearly all conscious language acquisition. There are strong similarities between the way our brains process speech and the way we interpret music.

How can music help children understand math and science?

Music, by its very nature, is an expressive combination of mathematics and physics. Because music is built from components that can be described in mathematical terms, it can be an excellent tool for teaching mathematical concepts. Music helps us to understand and use ideas that could otherwise remain highly abstract. Some of the greatest mathematical minds have helped us understand how musical elements are constructed; conversely, composers have created incredible works entirely from mathematical constructions. The spatial reasoning skills advanced by instrumental training can help process complex algebraic functions.

How can music boost social skills?

Our first communications are musical dialogues with our parents. These help us as young children to develop language skills and to 'find our voice.' Music helps us form associations with others and to define those things that set us apart from others too.

Children love to bond with parents and friends through music, and eventually come to assert their individual tastes and differences through such means by the time they reach adolescence. Music enables us to create sonic expressions of our cultural identity and therefore helps to define our own personal heritage, and, by extension, our 'place' in the world.

Can music benefit a child's health?

Music has been shown to reduce certain stress-causing hormones in the body, and it also triggers the brain's pleasure-giving neurotransmitters, known as endorphins. When endorphins are released, they result in feelings of well-being and happiness. A happy child can result in a healthy child! From a bodily fitness viewpoint, music can be a catalyst for many types of physical activity. Young children instinctively move to music, which can therefore be used as a tool for physical exercise and coordination activities.

Should I be playing classical music to my child?

You should be playing music that you love, whether classical or not. More importantly, you should make music with your child. The greatest benefits can be drawn from active music-making rather than passive listening activities. Listening exercises certainly have a place, but children learn a huge amount from the process of making and creating music themselves.

Should my child play an instrument?

Playing an instrument has so many benefits for children. Learning to play can unlock advanced coordination skills, help to focus attention, develops abstract reasoning and affect memory skills. More importantly, an instrument can give children the means to express themselves confidently, as well as giving them the opportunity to form groups with others. This may be a string quartet, a rock band, a choir, or an ensemble of bottles and shakers; it doesn't matter, because all of these groups have great social benefits and can assist in general development. In this book there are many instruments you can make together with your child, as well as advice on buying instruments and formal tuition. If children choose an instrument themselves they are likely to be more committed than if they have the decision made for them.

Can my child compose music?

Yes – we all have the ability to create music. You can compose too! There are many games and exercises in this book that will help unlock these abilities. Children gain a huge amount of pride from creating their own musical works, however modest. For children, a sense of ownership is one of the keys to successful learning. If a child can exercise creative decisions and free will and hear the effects for themselves, they are likely to become totally involved in the process.

How can music help children express themselves?

Children can create musical expressions of emotions and musical representations of literal and abstract concepts. It is therefore a unique system for communicating complex ideas and emotions. One of the drawbacks of being a child is coping with the fact that adults think they know so much! Not being able to have a say in most areas of life can be very frustrating. Music can provide the perfect outlet for children to tell adults what to do and how to do it, without the situation ever getting out of control!

Chapter 2

Everyone is musical

Everybody is born musical: babies absorb music before they are even born, and we seem to be genetically predisposed to making music. Music is in our genes!

Music and evolution

According to recent research, singing has a biological foundation and could in fact be an essential evolutionary function. The scientist Bruce Richman believes that humans essentially use three different forms of vocal expression:

• laughing, sighing, crying, and tutting;

• speech;

• singing.

He believes that singing 'served as an evolutionary transitional state between primate-like vocalizations and speech.' In other words, it's how we learn to communicate. Before children can talk, parents communicate using sing-song language and this musical communication helps to develop the child's language skills. Music has an effect on all of us and it doesn't just affect humans: Its power extends to the animal kingdom, too. The psychologist Jaak Panksepp showed that even chickens demonstrate physical responses to music – they ruffled their feathers at a Pink Floyd track, demonstrating a (no pun intended) goosebump response to the musical gestures of "The Final Cut!" It seems that animals may also experience the rush and tingles that music can trigger in humans when we are moved by a piece of music. Many animals use what we would perceive to be 'musical' signals for attracting mates. Chimpanzees 'chorus' together for two reasons: To defend their territory and to attract single females to their colony. Just like us, animals use music as a way of forming communities, marking their territory, and communicating with others.

Music in the womb

Babies are born with an exceptional range of sophisticated musical skills. They have acute levels of sensitivity to different pitches, different rhythms and pulses, and have the ability to discriminate between different timbres – and their musical education begins in the womb. Before its birth, a baby acquires a huge range of information about music: its tone, pitch, rhythm, and timbre (the 'color' of certain sounds). By the time the baby is born, it can distinguish between important voices, and it quickly learns to interpret the emotional content of speech. Babies initially express themselves musically, but even when they begin to use words they use musical inflections – pitch, intonation, and rhythm – to give precise meaning to those words. These are the core elements of music.

Reflexes

Babies are amazing: a newborn already possesses an amazing range of reflexes that are essential to survival. For example:

• **A baby will display a walking or pedalling action if held upright with their feet just touching the floor.**

• **They will grab hold of anything that touches their palms.**

• **They will flinch and grab upwards if startled by a loud noise.**

• **Only two months after birth, a baby will begin to stare intently at his or her parents and try to match facial expressions.**

• **They will also attempt to face any new noise as a danger reflex.**

After the first few months there is a transition from reflex actions to controlled 'fine' and 'gross' motor movements.

Aural skills

From soon after birth, a baby may try to seek the direction of a sound to locate its source. They are particularly attuned to seek out the sound of their mother's voice. Even at one week of age, it has been shown that many babies can distinguish the sound of their mother's voice as distinct among other voices. They can pick it out from a roomful of other voices.

By three months they will have learned to turn physically and face sounds – especially vocal sounds – directed towards them.

Rhythm

Our bodies are packed with time-related systems. We have built-in pulses, body clocks, and great rhythmic awareness and ability. That's because we need a sense of rhythm to help cope with time structures and sequences of events.

In the 1940s the cognitive psychologist Paul Fraisse conducted a major study into what was named 'preferred timing', and his study was supplemented in the 1970s by Mari Reiss Jones at Ohio State University. Fraisse's research suggested – and Jones' research stated – that we all have an internal metronome: a body clock. This internal body clock controls all kinds of things. It sets the pace at which you walk, the speed of your heartbeat, how quickly you breathe, and how long you sleep. Our body clocks are similar: For example, if you tap your fingers on a tabletop, there's a very good chance that you'll tap every six-tenths of a second. It's fascinating stuff. Most adults walk at a rate of 117 steps per minute; the average stride differs between men and women, but the rate of stride tends to be identical. In classical music terminology, *andante* literally translates as 'walking pace' and is around 110 to 120 beats per minute.

The combination of your body clock and music is a powerful one. The hornpipe was designed to help sailors raise an anchor in time with one another; marching music is used to coordinate vast numbers of soldiers;

chain-gang songs helped prisoners coordinate their labors. All of these things have a natural pulse, a preferred timing at which the activity works at its most economical and its most efficient, and the music reflects that timing.

Of course, many of these preferred timings are actually the speeds at which our bodies carry out physical tasks most comfortably. There are obvious natural rates of movement for walking, marching, swinging a sledgehammer, or pulling a heavy rope. To some extent, our 'sense of pulse' is often comprised of physical sensations that translate themselves into easily memorable rhythms.

It is easy to assume therefore that we develop a sense of rhythm and pulse with age and physical practice. However, it does appear that we are born with many body clocks already active. At two months old, a child can distinguish its mother tongue purely from rhythmic information. In a piece of research carried out by the French researcher Frank Ramus, babies were able to distinguish their home language from other languages when converted into monotone, monosyllabic rhythm patterns.

It appears that babies can recognize the pulse of a language as well as its pitches and melodic contours. This is an incredibly sophisticated ability. Frank Ramus believes that sensitivity to rhythm in young babies may be an essential tool for the acquisition of language.

To be able to perceive rhythm so accurately, we must be born with a strong natural sense of pulse – if we didn't have one, we'd have nothing to compare other rhythms with. We can record tempos, pulses, and rhythms in our memory and, with practice, we can replicate these patterns with great accuracy. Practicing music enables children to develop strong rhythmic consistency. Accurate timekeeping and pulse memory are essential skills for any musician.

Accents

By ten months babies will be able to distinguish between their 'home' accent and other regional accents in their own language. Around this time babies come to comprehend that their names actually refer to them! Name songs can help to reinforce this information and are therefore a useful aid for developing a child's sense of self.

There are 150 different vocal components, the building blocks of every single human language on earth. Babies are born with the ability to distinguish between all 150.

Synesthesia

The word *synesthesia* is constructed from two Greek words; *syn* meaning together, and *aisthesis* meaning perception. A baby's brain has strong links between the regions that process visual information and those that process aural information. Color and music, light and sound are linked together and processed in an extraordinary manner. This is because babies experience all incoming stimuli through the limbic system.

These associations rapidly die away for most of us, but the phenomenon lingers on in some people, manifesting itself in adult synesthesia. An adult with this condition may experience associated textures with numerals or may hear music as certain colors.

Richard Cytowic articulated this extraordinary natural phenomenon in his book, *The Man Who Tasted Shapes*. He cites that babies experience everything in a multi-sensory manner. Any incoming stimulus, whether light, sound, or taste creates an experience across all of the senses. As we grow older the senses become more distinct – our brains would soon become overloaded if we experienced every sensation in every part of our brain at the same time – but when a baby hears music it doesn't just hear It: It sees it, feels it, tastes it, and possibly even smells it! Because of this sensory extravaganza, music can create very rich, very powerful sensations in very young children.

It's a skill we can recapture, too. Highly skilled musicians tend to be able to reconnect these multi-sensory responses in order to communicate musical ideas imaginatively – although thankfully they can turn the sensory overload off again before going home on the bus!

Pitch

Pitch is the technical term that musicians use for how high or low a note is. One of the ways babies identify their mothers is by recognizing the pitch of their voices. Babies have incredibly acute pitch abilities when they are born. At five months an infant can discriminate differences in pitch of less than a semitone (a semitone is the smallest gap, or *interval*, to use its correct name, between two notes – play any note on the piano, then play the closest one to it, whether black or white, and you have just played an interval of a semitone). This enables them to pick out very specific melodic information, and is the key to interpreting subtle vocal inflections.

It is widely believed that children are born with a sense of absolute pitch – this is the ability to accurately recall musical notes and keys. (This is sometimes referred to as perfect pitch.) If this is true, and I personally believe it is, it means that babies possess a level of pitch skills that would challenge the greatest musician!

I think it is essential to tap into these advanced pitch abilities early on as they are critical for future music-making. I have absolute pitch, and find it useful for tuning instruments without having to refer to another pitch, for identifying the chords in a piece of music and for transcribing melodies and harmonies quickly. I still find it a perplexing ability, though. I identify pitches and frequencies by mentally playing back the sound of an 'A' in my head and comparing it to what I am hearing. The strange thing is that the 'A' sound I hear is that of a violin string being bowed slightly awkwardly. When I was very young, I used to sleep in the room next to my mother's violin teaching room. I am sure that the pitch I have in my head is the sound of one of her violin pupils tuning up at the beginning of a lesson!

> *When at school, I learned the frequencies of the notes in a scale and had enormous fun tricking my physics teacher into thinking I had some form of psychic ability by correctly identifying oscilloscope frequencies without being able to see the meter. I was just listening to the notes and working the numbers out from the pitches. Not a very difficult stunt to pull, but very confusing if you can't see how it is done.*

Research has shown that musicians who possess absolute pitch generally began their instrumental studies before the age of seven. This indicates that the ability is retained at a point when the brain is still fairly flexible.

Children can sometimes display this ability when they are very young by singing back a favorite song at exactly the pitch at which they heard it first. As with many forms of neurological development, advanced pitch abilities are likely to develop if frequently stimulated. Regularly singing to your child and playing and listening to music together can help maintain some of the incredible pitch abilities they are born with.

I don't believe that perfect pitch can be taught later in life – despite commercially available courses that happily advertize to the contrary! Having absolute pitch is by no means essential for music-making, and it is only found in a minority of people. However, it is certainly a useful skill. We'll discover more about perfect pitch in Chapter 8.

Eidetic memory

Many researchers believe that babies are also born with eidetic memory. This is the ability to memorize visual information with great photographic accuracy. As with absolute pitch, this is an ability that frequently diminishes with age unless engaged and exercised.

As we have discovered, babies are born with an incredible array of musical abilities. Retaining, encouraging, and developing these skills is one of the keys to training different forms of intelligence.

Chapter 3

Play and playing

Children are born to play. From six months of age, babies enjoy playing peek-a-boo; and as every parent knows, children are naturally – and spontaneously – creative. They interact effortlessly with one another, and they are naturally sociable; when young children are placed together in a group, they will quickly begin to play.

I recently ran two projects in New York, over two consecutive days. The first project was for primary-age schoolchildren, and the second was for adult musicians, but the objective was essentially the same: to devise group compositions and perform them at the end of each day. The music would emerge from exercises and games played throughout the day, and would be created entirely by the participants in each day's project.

When the children arrived, they were already playing games: finger-plays, clapping rhymes, skipping, and tag. The games were mostly very traditional (some of them date back to medieval times) and it was very easy to convert these forms of play into small creative exercises.

The adults were more nervous. When they arrived on day two, they made polite small talk. A hierarchy emerged: Everyone discussed who did what in the outside world, establishing each other's economic, professional, and social standing. It took a lot longer to get the adults into creative mode, because all of their interaction had been rather formal and governed by their sense of social conduct.

Of course, it would have been strange if the adults had started playing games spontaneously – but I couldn't help pointing out that a similar class in the UK had spent a good twenty minutes discussing the weather. Children play two kinds of games: formalized games and improvised games. They like to create their own rules, roles, and codes of play, and these codes and rules often have direct parallels with musical forms. Indeed, many composers have used the structure of games as the inspiration for their compositions.

So what makes a good game? A good game nearly always involves the resolution of problems or conflicts that are established at the beginning of the game. The same thing happens in classical composition, where an opening theme is often juxtaposed with a contrasting subject: The themes are offset against one another until a point of resolution is reached.

The difference between playing and gameplay is richly debatable: if I run around a tree as fast as possible, am I playing or is it a game? Maybe it's only a game if I am racing against someone else. In music, improvising is similar to running around a tree for the sheer fun of it; composition, turning a spontaneous idea into something with a structure, is racing around the tree against someone else. When children play creative games, they are creating situations or environments where they can assume new roles, try new concepts, and indulge in flights of imagination. It's easy to see that making music offers exactly the same things.

Children relish playing games. They're in control, they can implement their own ideas and they can play at leadership and teamwork. If these inherent instincts are fully engaged when exploring music with your children, they can be hooked for life!

The importance of improvisation

Later in this book we'll put a great deal of emphasis on creative, improvisation-based activities. These can really help to stimulate learning by mirroring the processes through which the brain learns speech. The way children learn language is incredibly organic. It evolves naturally through a very complicated yet efficient set of tools. Adults instinctively fuel this extraordinary process – often subconsciously – during their natural interactions and improvisations with their children.

Learning language and learning music are parallel, mirrored processes in the brain – although sadly, formal music training doesn't always tap into the same creative powerhouse of brain activity associated with learning a mother tongue. But it should.

- Children understand sophisticated linguistic patterns long before they begin to master the process of reading and writing.

- Children can understand and experiment with sophisticated musical concepts long before they can master music-reading skills.

When children first begin to experiment with reading, they will often take a newly acquired word and play with it relentlessly. They may try working it into different sentences or patterns, or they may try using it in nonsense rhymes until it finds a place naturally in their own vocabulary.

> *One evening, my five-year-old daughter brought a reading book home from school that had a new word cleverly worked into its storyline. I felt a strange mixture of emotions the next morning when the set of magnetic letters that live on the fridge greeted me with:*

dAd iS fAT anD sTupId

> *The new word had very definitely joined the vocabulary that she felt comfortable with, despite my protestations...*

In most school systems, young children are now encouraged to make up highly imaginative short stories as a tool to advance their command of a language. If the spelling and grammar isn't quite accurate, it can be refined at a later stage; the crucial process is the act of composing, which enables children to become confident in written and verbal communication skills.

Unfortunately, in conventional classical music training, composition sometimes doesn't even get a trial run. The activities of creative play, composition, reading, and learning a new repertoire are often kept strictly separated:

> *As a nine-year-old cello student I was told in no uncertain terms by my teacher that I should not compose or improvise, as it would be very bad for my playing.*

I now know as a professional player, writer, and teacher that encouraging students to improvise and compose can help them discover their innate musical personality. It can also greatly refine technical skills and lead to a much greater understanding of key repertoire.

We are all born with creativity, a desire to play with objects, ideas, skills, and concepts until they become second nature – and yet we often stifle these abilities through very conservative methods of learning. In many cases, pupils are taught to play from sheet music before they have learned how to express themselves with their instrument. As a result, the pupil can only play if there is sheet music on the stand. I'm not suggesting that music on the printed page isn't important – it's a key component of learning and performing many kinds of music – but for many instrumental teachers it becomes the primary source of musical material for their students. Why should this be?

I believe that teaching music from the page up is counterproductive, and that it can in fact limit a child's intellectual and emotional development. After all, when a child is experimenting with initial conversation skills, we don't issue them with a phrasebook: Doing so would obviously stop a natural process dead in its tracks.

Children will begin a life-long love affair with music if they develop a sense of ownership for the materials they play. Through creative musical play, children can acquire an understanding and a real love of composed music. I believe children should be taught existing compositions from the earliest opportunity – in tandem with pieces of their own creative work.

After a workshop one of my students in Harlem wrote:

'I like writing music, writing music makes me feel really important.'

Many classical teachers that I train are initially very scared at the thought of improvising, particularly in front of other people. This is totally understandable, as many of them have never been shown how, and they have a lot to lose.

Playing with the voice

When you're a young child learning to sing, it's a hugely enjoyable process – and it's driven by your own curiosity. You choose songs for their appeal, not just in some quest for technical ability. Your vocal strength, dexterity, and technique all spring from the process of singing for fun.

Children tend to learn songs by ear rather than from the page, and they often choose the songs. Children naturally display a high level of musical discrimination, and they can be very opinionated about what they like and dislike. This is an essential part of developing their own identity.

The songs children demand time after time tend to follow set patterns at different developmental stages. Each of these sets of songs serves a very natural process, and enhances specific sets of skills that are essential to mental and physical development. By engaging in musical play, it is possible to advance children's development very dramatically. Unfortunately in Western music the 'playing' is sometimes removed from the playing of music! Children learn when their sense of curiosity is fully engaged. They learn most when this is satisfied within a seemingly recreational context – in other words, when they're having fun.

Chapter 4

You are musical

How many times have you heard someone say, 'I'm not musical,' 'I'm tone deaf,' or 'I don't have a musical bone in my body?' The truth is that we are all born with the capacity to make music: We all have musical instincts and skills, and all we need is a little encouragement. To help your child pursue musical activities, it's vital that you come to recognize your own musical ability – and where possible, draw it out, develop, and enjoy it.

Humans experience music as a kind of 'supra' language, a language that can convey meaning beyond mere words. Music can express very complex emotional messages, and the weight of new evidence suggests that there really is a biological imperative for making music. It's in our genes.

Music is just a system where we translate vibrations into sounds, which in turn form patterns and structures. We have an emotional, mental, and physical response to these structures, and we attach context and meaning to them.

Music has become a vehicle for expression and communication and we deliberately use it to manipulate our moods. We use it to gear ourselves up for a battle or a big night out, to seduce a partner, to make us cry, to comfort others, to calm a child, to celebrate weddings, or to mark the end of a life.

Being 'musical' isn't just about playing an instrument. It could apply to vocal skills or to the way you respond to a piece of music. You're much more musical than you think you are. You might not think that you know very much about musical phrasing, but the way you shape your sentences when you talk is musical. These are patterns and structures you learned before birth, and they form one of the key links between verbal meaning and melody.

Perhaps you are unsure about your melodic skills, or your sense of pitch. But according to recent research, almost everyone has a very acute sense of pitch.

If you feel you are 'tone deaf,' it's possible that you just didn't learn to connect meaning and melody at an early age.

It doesn't take much to shake your confidence in your abilities, whether it's in the arts or in sport – especially when you're young. A throwaway comment from a friend, teacher, or even a parent can collide with a lack of self-confidence and create a long-term effect. It might reinforce the notion that you're not musical, that you can't sing, that you have two left feet, or that you aren't athletic. These labels often become absolute truths that we accept and never question, and you may find that you often use such terms to define yourself. It's a curious human trait that we often promote our shortcomings – real or imagined – over our abilities.

Of course, these superstitions can prevent people from even attempting to experiment with music. They may feel that they'll only confirm what they already know – but I can honestly say that I have never met anybody who could be described as 'unmusical.'

There are certainly adults who haven't explored even a fraction of their musical potential, but that doesn't mean they're unmusical; it means they haven't seen a glimpse of the 'musician inside.' If you feel you're one of those people, I hope that some of the exercises you'll find in later sections of this book will reveal your hidden talents!

I still have the school report that stated that I would never be good at sports. It meant that by the age of seven I was encouraged by my teachers to give up one of my dreams. The irony is that I now teach advanced instrumental coordination skills that focus on all of the same bodily and mental systems essential for participating in sports.

Getting involved

Whenever I run creative music projects for children, the parents want to watch – but they definitely don't want to join in. This is only natural: Many of the processes used in creative work center around simple games, which aren't necessarily a very 'grown-up' thing to do.

When I get parents involved, they soon stop worrying about what they look or sound like because they're enjoying themselves. The main fear for an adult in such a situation is that they may look foolish, or may get a musical activity wrong. However, by the end of a music session, the parents are often utterly absorbed in the performance without feeling even slightly self-conscious. For an hour or so, they're allowed to act with the same freedom and creativity they had as children. It is wonderful to see sensible, grown-up, professional people throw themselves into something they thought they couldn't, wouldn't, and probably shouldn't do!

Reawakening such senses and accepting that you have musical abilities is essential if you want to make your child enthusiastic about making music. As children we learn most things through play, so you have to be comfortable with communicating sophisticated musical activities through entertaining games – without worrying about how you look or sound!

> *I'm not a professional chef, but that doesn't mean I live on fast food: I might feel that my cooking isn't wonderful, but I enjoy the process – and sometimes the results are even edible! Most of us have the same attitude – so why is it that when it comes to music, we feel intimidated or inhibited at the very thought of trying to sing, play, or create music?*

You might argue that food is essential and that music is not. Of course, I would disagree: We all need music and we all use music – and not always by choice.

I believe that everyone needs music, and that everyone needs to make music. Listening to the radio, playing CDs, and going to concerts all offer instant gratification, but they won't necessarily deliver the benefits of actively making music.

So, accept that you are musical — trust me on this! Don't be nervous or too self-conscious, and remember that every great musician started as a beginner too. You're simply discovering the abilities you already have. You might not become a concert pianist, but you'll have a lot of fun. Music is in your genes, and discovering its potential in you is a critical factor in the process of educating your children.

- We are all predisposed to express ourselves through the use of musical gestures.

- We all initially converse with melodic fragments.

- When vocabulary is acquired, these musical skills give precise yet infinitely subtle meaning to the phrases being spoken.

- The musical inflections of speech convey the speaker's true meaning.

- We are able to process and use sophisticated melodic, rhythmic, and timbral information. These are the core elements of all forms of music.

- Music is the tool we use for the acquisition of our initial language skills.

Chapter 5

Be your child's greatest music teacher

This book is all about sharing musical concepts with your children, and the exercises, games, and activities you'll find in later chapters are designed for musicians and non-musicians alike. That means you'll be your child's very first music teacher.

Yes, you!

You have the capacity to be your child's greatest, most inspiring music teacher – even if you haven't had any musical training yourself. You may think that you're not even remotely musical, but I hope that Chapter 4 has persuaded you otherwise!

Encourage your child...

Dr. Edwin Gordon is a leading expert in the theory of musical learning and he believes that every child possesses 'musical aptitude.' This can be defined as a child's innate potential to learn music. Children are born with an incredible range of musical skills. Their sense of pitch, rhythm, and tonal awareness can and should be encouraged as enthusiastically as possible.

...but don't be a pushy parent!

For a parent, the biggest challenge is in guiding your child from aptitude to achievement – without pushing too hard and removing all the fun from the process. Children can be put off music if parents or teachers are too ambitious.

I have met very many young musicians who, thanks to long hours of practice and intensive coaching, have become technically proficient on their instrument. They can play fantastically, accurately, and with great ability, but without necessarily communicating any sense of joy or love for the music that they are playing. Remember, music is all about expression and emotion.

If a child chooses to pursue their musical dreams, then they should have the encouragement and teaching to inspire them musically and technically to achieve high levels not just of performance, but of expression.

Be inspiring

There are many inspirational teachers. They encourage children's love of music while refining their technical skills. Unfortunately there are also many teachers who teach by rote, and who are not in love with what they are doing. Music teaching should be imaginative, challenging, and most of all, creative.

A study conducted by Moore, Burland, and Davidson at the University of East London monitored the ongoing musical activities of 257 children. The researchers found that children who maintained interest in playing an instrument had:

• started at an early age;

• had a great deal of parental support;

• begun their studies with teachers who were friendly but not very technically able.

The research also covered children who had made the transition to being musicians later in life. The successful musicians had teachers who were 'not too relaxed' and also 'not too pushy.' The students had also had to do substantial amounts of practice!

The most successful adult performers were not necessarily those who did the most practice. In fact, the successful musicians were:

• those who took part in more concert activities in childhood;

• those who did more improvisation;

• those who had mothers at home in their early years.

In other words, creative music-making combined with good parental support will help your child retain and nurture their love of music. By encouraging your child's musicality, you will be nurturing the development of their intelligence too. You can be an inspiring musical influence by encouraging creative play, by building music into everyday routines, by helping technical aptitude, and by framing musical activities in an imaginative manner. Music should never, ever be a chore.

But I don't know much about classical music!

We are led to believe as parents that it is our duty to expose our children to 'good,' highbrow, classical music from the age of minus–nine months if we want them to be the next Nobel prizewinner! The majority of the research into the effects of music on childhood development focuses on western classical music: Music that was composed from the mid-18th century to the beginning of the 19th century.

But what about non-western music? And what about the roots of rock 'n' roll, soul music, jazz, electronica, and so forth? What about the music you can compose with your child? Has this less value and fewer positive effects than classical music? Of course not!

There's a great deal of snobbery about the relative values of different kinds of music, but the truth is that there's a huge amount of dreary classical music that doesn't have even a fraction of the energy you'll find in a good nursery rhyme. For me, music that is enjoyable, stimulating, and effective tends to be full of energy, passion, and commitment. That could be a lament by Purcell or a funk track by James Brown!

Songs my mother taught me

Some of the most famous musical educators – composers such as Zoltan Kodaly or Carl Orff – didn't suggest that western European classical music should be the central focus of musical education. In their opinion, the music that has emerged organically from a child's own culture and environment holds the key to true musical and personal development.

Music with lyrics in a child's mother tongue seems to encourage language skills and expression, as well as helping to balance a child's social skills. Folk music is by its very nature a balanced synthesis of lyrics and music, a perfect combination of meaning and melody.

Music and text evolve from one another and are inextricably linked. The rhythm of the melody emerges from the syllables of the lyrics and the lyrics are led by the direction of the melody. This perfect partnership of words and music reflects the parallel processes that the brain uses to acquire language skills and musicianship.

Start with music you like

Music that you enjoy – as opposed to music that you think you ought to enjoy – provides the best material for listening activities, musical games, and exercises for your child. Because you already have an emotional connection with the music, that will inevitably rub off on your child.

Children are very sensitive to their parents' likes and dislikes. An unborn child will already have acquired aural and chemical information about their mother's listening habits.

Music to try

If you'd like a few pointers towards other kinds of music you might enjoy sharing with your children, we've provided some comprehensive lists in later chapters that you can link to specific games and activities. You'll also find some interesting pieces of music on the CD that you may not have heard before.

I believe it's a mistake to take part in music-related activities simply because you want to improve brain function. After all, you don't play sports just to build muscles!

Brain functions may well be enhanced by active participation in music-making, but I see that as a great side-effect rather than a goal in itself. The skills your child gains from music lead to greater self-confidence, better language skills, fine motor control, spacial and temporal awareness, and heightened creativity.

Chapter 6

Active music-making, not passive

The message of this book is that engaging children in active music-making will help them acquire many mental, physical, and social skills, all of which are key elements of their future intelligence and well-being. Of course, listening to music is good for you too – in much the same way that watching a football game can make you excited or relaxed – but playing music, like playing football, is better still.

Listening to music can alter your mood: It can elevate you, make you sad, make you think; help you remember, mourn, celebrate, or forget. It can provoke unconscious physical reactions and can initiate movement. It can help people bond in social situations, and it can help people articulate feelings of love, religious rapture, celebration, or sorrow. It can be used to unify heavy labor – whether factory work, working in the fields, or on a boat – and it often moves us more profoundly than words alone. It can help us concentrate or work more efficiently, and listening to live music can also have tangible health benefits.

Despite this, I believe that listening to classical music in the hope that it will boost your children's brainpower is misguided. It certainly won't do any harm, but I doubt it will have much of an effect on test scores either. However, I do believe that involvement in active music-making can have dramatic effects. This doesn't necessarily mean playing instruments or performing musical exercises, either: There are many techniques for active listening that can deliver real benefits.

Player or listener?

The majority of the modern music industry is focused on the reception of music: We're encouraged to be music consumers. That's not a bad thing, but it's easy to lose sight of music's origins as a social activity. Of course you can derive huge pleasure from listening actively, but that's no match for the experience of actually making music.

It's easy to take CDs and the radio for granted, but recordings are a relatively recent phenomenon: Even sheet music and musical notation are recent arrivals. Concerts where audiences sit and listen quietly are new, too: Many classical pieces from the 18th century are designed to cover the noise of rowdy audiences and attempt to get their attention.

Most cultures use music for marking significant events, recording social history, lulling children to sleep, waging war, marrying, and mourning the dead. Singing to an audience may well have emerged as a way of imparting sagas over the tribal fire; music is a great vehicle for recording vast amounts of information, and textual memory is often less efficient. (See the music and memory section on page 73 for more details.)

But doesn't listening to Mozart make children smarter?

Many people believe so. To understand the Mozart Effect, though, we need to step back a few years. According to research carried out in 1989, when musicians mentally rehearse pieces of music, very precise patterns of brain activity can be observed. The following year, physicists Gordon Shaw, Xiaodan Leng, and Eric Wright decided to look at these patterns in a novel manner: They analyzed the brain activity and translated it into musical notes. They were surprised to discover that the resulting sounds – it wasn't quite music – shared some features with the patterns you'll find in classical and baroque music. It was an amazing discovery, and the scientists proposed that music is a kind of 'pre-language' that can be used to flex and exercise the brain, helping it to perform complex thought processes more efficiently.

By 1993, Shaw was beginning to wonder: what would happen if the sounds were played back to the brain? Shaw teamed up with cellist Frances Rauscher and they devised a series of experiments to discover whether exposure to Mozart's music could make the brain work more efficiently.

The Mozart Effect

Rauscher and Shaw asked 79 people to complete some exercises which required them to visualize the results of cutting and folding pieces of paper. They weren't allowed to use props; instead, they had to do the whole exercise mentally. It's a well-known exercise, extracted from an IQ test known as the Stanford-Binet test.

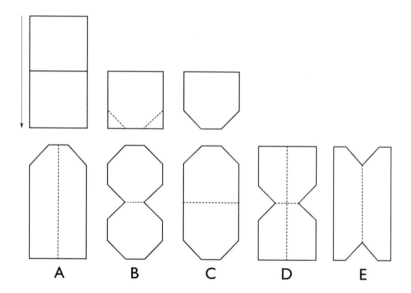

The researchers asked the participants to perform the test, recorded the results, and then split the participants into three groups. The first group was exposed to ten minutes of Mozart's "Sonata For Two Pianos" (K. 448); the second group listened to repetitive, minimalist music; and the third group sat in silence for ten minutes.

The participants were then asked to repeat the paper cutting and folding test.

The results were startling:

- The group who listened to minimalist music scored 11% higher than before;

- The group who sat in silence scored 14% higher than before;

- The group who listened to Mozart scored an incredible 62% higher than before.

It was an amazing result, but unfortunately the results didn't last for long: the increased abilities displayed by the 'Mozart' group wore off rather quickly. It seemed that the 'Mozart Effect' only lasted for ten to fifteen minutes.

Try this at home

Why not try this test yourself, or with your child?

Look at the diagram on page 41. The top line of the diagram gives instructions for folding a piece of paper. The second line gives five possible shapes for the finished folded piece of paper. Which one is the correct shape?

Now listen to TRACK 1 on the CD that accompanies this book – it's an excerpt from the same Mozart Sonata that was used in the original experiment. Now repeat the exercise. Did you experience the Mozart Effect?

(The correct answer for this exercise is 'C'.)

Wolfgang's rats

The Mozart Effect was certainly fascinating, but it didn't last for long. What would happen if people were bombarded with the same piece of miracle Mozart? A follow-up study in 1998 (Rauscher/Robinson/Jens) tried to find out. It would have been difficult to find any students who'd be willing to participate in the study: It required them to be exposed to the same D major sonata by Mozart for 12 hours a day, from before birth to 12 months of age. Luckily for the students, the researchers decided to use rats instead of people.

The rats were split into two groups. The first group was constantly exposed to Mozart and the second group was kept in a more normal environment. The rats were then given a task – not paper folding, of course, but navigating their way through a maze.

The result? The rats that had been bombarded with Mozart found their way around the maze much more quickly and accurately than the less-cultured rats. The scientists suggested that Mozart's music corresponded to the rhythms and patterns of the brain, which are supposedly linked to intelligence. This, they believed, helped the rats complete their task more quickly – although they couldn't single out any one element of the music as a critical factor in this process.

As you'd expect, a lot of people got very excited. Many people believed that if you simply played a carefully structured CD to a child, you could actually increase their intelligence: The genius of Mozart would somehow rub off on the children. Best of all, Mozart's work was out of copyright – so the record companies wouldn't have to give him any money!

Naturally, companies saw this as a license to print money and a huge industry erupted, fuelled by increasingly hysterical media coverage. Before long, CDs with titles such as *Baby Mozart* began to appear in stores. In no time at all, it had become a one-billion-dollar industry: The Baby Genius industry.

Houston, we have a problem

Whenever anything exciting emerges from the world of science, there's always a race to build on the research or to discredit it entirely – and in the case of the Mozart Effect, there were millions of dollars at stake. There was just one problem: When Harvard psychologist Christopher Chabris analyzed the results of sixteen different follow-up studies – studies that involved hundreds of participants – he discovered that nobody had been able to reproduce the Mozart Effect.

So why did the rats run through the maze more quickly? Nobody knows for sure. Maybe they navigated faster because the music cheered them up, or perhaps the noise excited or frightened them. Or perhaps the rats who didn't listen to Mozart were bored, and couldn't be bothered running around a maze. It's certainly strange that the higher-performing rats were played Mozart before they were born: Unlike humans, rats are deaf until some time after birth.

Was the effect due to Mozart or something else? It would certainly have been interesting if one group of rats had been exposed to Mozart and the other group to the music of Mozart's father – or if they'd used other music, such as Bach's algebraic fugues or Miles Davis's forays into be-bop.

Have you ever noticed that at peak times, many shops use fast background music? This is purely to make us walk, shop, and buy faster. At slower times of day, calm music is used to encourage us to browse and proceed more slowly through the shop, spending longer over deciding what to buy. Perhaps listening to Mozart doesn't intellectually stimulate us at all: Like the music in the shops, it just encourages us to move more quickly!

It's important to note that the scientists responsible for the initial studies weren't endorsing the incredible claims made in the media, and they certainly didn't have any financial stake in proving or disproving the Mozart effect. But it's clear that a very lucrative industry had emerged on the basis of a rather shaky premise.

Here's another point to consider: If the music of Mozart is so beneficial, then someone who was exposed to that music for every waking hour of their life must have seen incredible benefits. Yet the man with all this music in his head – Mozart himself – was an unstable, unhealthy person who was notorious for his anti-social behavior. He died in poverty before his thirty-sixth birthday.

Listening to music certainly delivers benefits, but some popular myths have emerged because people – deliberately or otherwise – have misinterpreted scientific research. Does listening to Mozart raise your IQ? Well... does watching the Olympics on TV make you healthier?

Can playing music make my child smarter?

Yes. Studying an instrument involves mastering a wide range of skills and it requires concentration and regular study, comprehension, and communication of sophisticated concepts. Studying an instrument also stimulates fine motor control, breathing, and memory and often requires regular one-on-one coaching or a very low teacher-to-pupil ratio that is rarely experienced in normal schooling.

And that's not all. Active music-making aids mental development and learning, and it can even encourage a growing brain to physically alter its very structure. It builds essential social skills, helps people of all ages define their own identity, creates associations between groups, and helps to forge links between people. It creates great feelings of self-worth and can even have beneficial effects on health. In the next few chapters we'll explore these benefits in detail.

Chapter 7

How active music-making can make your child smarter

It's natural to assume that any theory about music's effects on the brain is a new one, but in fact we've known about the power of music for thousands of years. Great philosophers such as Confucius, Plato, and Pythagoras all discussed the profound and mysterious influence of music upon the body and the mind; in many cases, neuroscience is simply catching up!

Plato said that, 'Music encodes ethical qualities in the human and feeds them back to the soul.' He believed that if children were taught music and gymnastics, all subsequent learning would be derived from those skills. Of course, children need more than just music and gymnastics to thrive, but there's certainly a lot to be said for encouraging children to spend lots of time playing sports as well as practicing musical instruments!

We already know through anecdotal evidence that music is a powerful tool for mental and social development, but there's also a growing body of scientific evidence that proves it.

What do we mean by intelligence?

Many people believe that IQ testing is the best way to assess a child's brainpower, but that's not always the case. While IQ tests are good for assessing some practical skills, it's almost impossible to measure creativity – or at least, it's almost impossible to quantify it. As a result, most of the research into the effects of music on intelligence have focused upon spatial, IQ-style testing.

Much of the information we have about music's beneficial effects is decidedly unscientific. Many musicians and teachers can tell you stories about music working in extraordinary ways, but these stories can't be plotted on a graph or given a score. There's a very real need to devise ways of measuring creativity so that we can more fully understand the amazing work done by educators who use music. While I'm very cynical about the idea of playing Mozart to boost a child's brainpower, I have an unshakeable belief in the importance of music for a child's mental and personal development.

Before we look at how active music-making can actually make your child smarter, it is worth considering what being 'smart' or 'intelligent' really means.

Intelligence is best defined as:

• **the ability to comprehend;**

• **the ability to understand;**

• **the ability to benefit from experience.**

What is IQ?

IQ is short for 'Intelligence Quotient': It's a number that indicates a person's mental ability in relation to other people of similar ages. Every child has a large range of mental abilities and only some of them can be measured with any degree of accuracy in an IQ test. The University of Toronto's Glenn Schellenberg tested a randomly selected sample of children to see whether music could improve their IQ. Pupils were given keyboard or voice lessons, drama lessons, or no lessons at all, and the children took IQ tests before and after the lessons. Compared to the children who were given no lessons at all, the children in the music groups did indeed score slightly higher – but the children who studied drama displayed a surprising increase in their social skills, an increase that didn't apply to the children who studied music instead.

I would argue that Schellenberg's results demonstrate the importance of how music is taught. At my school, music classes were the most boring part of the week for all students – and I loved music!

Thankfully I think there has been a great change in the way music is taught. For example, classroom music is no longer centered exclusively on classical music, but covers a much broader range of pop music. From my observations it also seems to be taught in a much more stimulating manner, with an emphasis on instrumental work and creative composition.

So it seems that music itself may help to improve IQ, but if it is taught well then it can improve social skills too. Other research suggests that musically experienced children also have a higher mental age than other children: the University of Music in Freiburg, Germany, found a very strong correlation between children's mental speed and their musical ability.

IQ isn't everything

As we've already discovered, IQ only measures some of a person's mental abilities. To get a better picture of intelligence, we need to look at multiple intelligences. In 1983, Howard Gardner attempted to find a way to describe all of our key personal skills. He called this theory 'multiple intelligences.' Not everyone agrees with his theory, but it does provide an excellent summary of the skills that can't be measured with something as simple as an IQ test.

Gardner suggests that there are eight kinds of intelligence:

1. Linguistic
2. Logical–mathematical
3. Bodily–kinesthetic
4. Musical
5. Spatial
6. Naturalist
7. Interpersonal
8. Intrapersonal

Through my musical projects, I meet a huge variety of children – and in any group there is always a wide range of different intelligences on display. Here's how I would try to spot these different intelligences in a typical musical activity:

The child who wants to make up lyrics for the songs or who is quick to suggest a title for a made-up piece of music would be showing linguistic intelligence. This is sensitivity to words and their meanings. A child with linguistic intelligence would enjoy wordplays, poems, stories, jokes, and creative writing activities.

The child who wants to conduct the music and who is able to control divisions of the beat while playing would be showing a form of logical-mathematical intelligence. Such children are able to process chains of patterns and sequences in a carefully ordered manner. They are generally interested in making different sounds from one source and are generally relentlessly curious! They will be the children who ask, 'why?' at any given opportunity.

The child who handles instruments skilfully without prior experience, or who creates spontaneous movements to musical stimuli would be displaying bodily-kinesthetic intelligence. This is essentially the ability to use the body confidently and the ability to handle objects dextrously. They will probably be energetic and sporty and will provide plenty of ideas for choreographing movement to musical cues. They will often find the acquisition of instrumental skills easier than other children.

The child who quickly and accurately learns the pitch, melodic structure, rhythms, and timbre from a piece of music is (obviously!) displaying musical intelligence. He or she would be the child who gets fully involved with little need for many explanations of what they are supposed to be doing. Such children really love listening to music and will try to join in at any given opportunity. They will often be successful at accurately replicating music using their voices and they will love recording their voice and playing it back.

The child who can recall the structure of a piece in simple terms is showing spatial intelligence. They will probably use imaginative imagery. They will enjoy learning about the building blocks of music and how notes and motifs fit together to create musical lines and sections of a piece. They will also enjoy music games and puzzles.

The child who wants to make up pieces about animals, or who can describe music in terms of landscape is displaying naturalist intelligence. Children are at their most creative when using the natural world for stimulation. It is hard to think of a project I've been involved with where a jungle creature or dinosaur hasn't found their way into the piece somehow. Developing "naturalist" intelligence may appear far removed from the practice of making music, but of course music itself has emerged from the natural world – possibly as an evolutionary survival tool. Music holds up a mirror to the natural world in which landscapes and the animal kingdom can be represented.

The child who finds it easy to make an ensemble with others and can negotiate musical ideas with others their own age is displaying interpersonal intelligence. This often results in them being natural team players and displaying talents very pertinent to being a great musician, such as being able to work together and perform alongside one another while being able to consider other children's ideas. Such children find it very easy to make friends, for obvious reasons!

The child who is happy to work on a musical idea on their own, or who quietly observes and listens to other ideas may be showing intrapersonal intelligence. Such children can appear withdrawn when they are actually involved internally in musical processes. They use their own feelings to understand other people. One of my young students in New York likes to separate himself from the group for most of the ensemble processes, but always joins in at the last minute once he has seen enough.

How music affects intelligence

By the time they're two years old, most children have developed their own unique combinations of preferences that stimulate and interest them. My oldest daughter, who is five, loves sport, writing stories about animals, and playing with other children. I would say she is bodily-kinesthetic, naturalist, linguistic, interpersonal. This is obviously very long-winded and rather general, and you'll probably pick up on the fact that I didn't include 'musical.' This is simply because I tend to take this for granted in children. (I've never met a child I could describe as unmusical!)

Making music can assist in the development of all of these so-called 'intelligences' by having a positive effect upon:

• **the connections in, and structure of, of the brain**

• **general coordination skills – mental and physical coordination**

• **spatial reasoning skills**

• **memory functions**

• **language skills**

• **math comprehension**

• **personal creativity**

• **social skills**

• **mental and physical health.**

We'll investigate each of these areas in the next few chapters.

Chapter 8

How active music-making affects the brain

"Playing a musical instrument demands extensive procedural and motor learning that results in plastic reorganization of the human brain. These plastic changes seem to include the rapid unmasking of existing connections and the establishment of new ones. Therefore, both functional and structural changes take place in the brains of instrumentalists as they learn to cope with the demands of their activity."

A. Pascual-Leone, Harvard Medical School

Making music can have an effect on both the mental and physiological development of the brain. It appears to help form neural pathways – connections within the brain – by encouraging links between brain cells, and it can promote mental and physical growth. It can also affect certain areas of the brain: For example, the main information channel between the two sides of the brain – known as the corpus callosum – grows larger as a result of musical stimulation. This creates a more efficient connection between the brain's two sides, which in turn means better coordination between the left and the right hemispheres. This can help a range of mental and physical processes including hand coordination and the ability to multi-task.

In order to understand the effect of music on the brain – which starts even before a child is born – we need to understand the way the brain grows and how its two sides differ from one another.

Brain cells

An unborn baby grows an incredible 100,000 nerve cells in the brain every minute, and by the time the brain has matured it will contain more than 100 billion cells. Ninety percent of these cells don't do much; their job is to bond to the neurons, which are the brain cells that do all the work.

Each neuron consists of a central hub, called the nucleus, which is surrounded by a multitude of tendrils that, like spokes on a wheel, radiate in all directions. These tendrils are the brain's wiring system and transmit electrical signals to and from the neuron. The nucleus is essentially a control box that sends signals down the track.

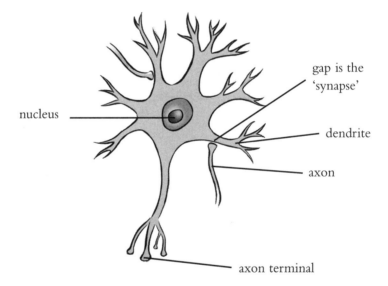

gap is the 'synapse'

nucleus

dendrite

axon

axon terminal

Axons and dendrites

In much the same way that a telephone has a microphone and a speaker, the tendrils in the brain have bits that deal with sending out signals and bits that take care of receiving signals. The senders are known as axons and the receivers are called dendrites.

The number of brain cells you possess is actually less important than how they are wired together.

Synapses

To successfully send a signal, the brain needs to connect an axon to a dendrite. This connection delivers the electrical pulse and is known as a synapse. There isn't actually a physical connection: There is a tiny gap between an axon and a dendrite and this gap is called a synaptic gap.

The message carried along the axon as an electrical pulse is sent to the dendrite by means of a neurotransmitter. If you imagine the axon as a baseball bat and the dendrite as a glove, the neurotransmitter is the baseball.

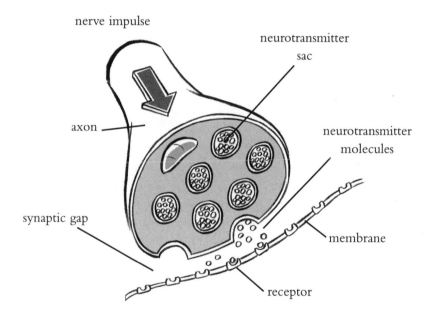

Neurotransmitters

A neurotransmitter is a chemical emitted by a cell and this chemical conveys signals around the brain. There are over 50 different kinds of neurotransmitters and two of the more important ones are glutamate and endorphins. Glutamate is one of the key neurotransmitters involved in developing memory and assisting with learning. Endorphins reduce pain, lower stress levels, and create a sense of calm. The production of endorphins can be stimulated by music. When it reaches the dendrite, the neurotransmitter is converted back into an electrical pulse. Because a neuron can have up to 10,000 connections to nearby cells and because a single electrical pulse can go to any number of these branches, millions of neurons can be triggered by a single impulse. It's like sending the same e-mail to everybody in your address book.

A single neuron can spark a vast amount of activity in the brain, much as a spark can cause a fire or the beat of a butterfly's wing can lead to a hurricane. The result of all this activity might be an emotion, a thought, or an action such as throwing a ball.

Stimulus

When someone in a cartoon has an idea, a lightbulb goes on above their head – and that's not too far from the truth. When the brain reacts to something, it lights up with activity as signals hurtle across the synaptic networks and trigger electrical activity all over the brain. It's no wonder we describe intelligent children as being bright!

It's only very recently that scientists have been able to see evidence of all this activity, through the use of machines such as MRI scanners. A 'functional MRI' scan – it's short for magnetic resonance imaging – can create a picture of brain activity by tracking glucose and oxygen flow to different areas; these chemicals are the fuel used by the brain when it does anything.

Although we're starting to understand the way the brain works, most of the brain is still very mysterious – and one of the big problems with comparing brain activity and intelligence is that nobody really knows what makes one brain more intelligent than another.

It could depend upon:

• the number of cells in the brain,

• the layout of neural networks,

• the density of networks,

• the speed at which brain impulses travel.

Neural 'pruning'

When the brain makes connections between neurons, it drops other connections so that only the stronger links survive. It's a bit like weeding a flower bed to make sure that the weeds don't strangle the plants.

The brain's pruning process is sometimes referred to as Neural Darwinism. During this process the brain learns to replicate patterns it deems to be beneficial for mental and physical functions. Patterns of neural firing that are underused at this stage drop away as their maintenance does not appear to be as important. Such pruning needs to take place; if it didn't happen, the brain wouldn't be able to cope with the sheer amount of information it would have to process. It's through the process of pruning that the fundamental foundations of key thought patterns are laid.

By the time a child reaches the age of six, they possess more neural connections than at any other stage of their life. At this age the pruning process accelerates dramatically as dominant networks assert priority over less-used regions. As the brain reinforces the stronger links and prunes the weaker ones, visible patterns of folds and bulges start to appear. The bulges are called gyri and indicate closely linked networks of neurons; the folds between them are less dynamic areas, and these are known as sulci.

As the streamlining of the brain continues, we can lose some of the abilities we are born with – use it or lose it! If these abilities not exercised, they can become less pronounced – but if we exercise them, they can manifest themselves as almost supernatural abilities.

Left brain, right brain

The popular perception of the brain is that there is a rigid divide between what the left and right sides of the brain do. Some of my colleagues happily define themselves as either 'right-brained' or 'left-brained.' In fact, there is no simple partition between the hemispheres, as most information is processed across both sides of the brain. The two sides of the brain work in parallel, carrying out simultaneous processes – and that means there's an incredible amount of traffic between the two hemispheres.

The main motorway between the two sides of the brain is known as the corpus callosum, and it's a thick bundle of around 200 million nerve fibers. It is at its most active when executing very complex processes, such as speech functions and the processing of visual/spatial information.

The left side of the brain is analytical and deals with factual material in a rational way.

Concerned with perception.

Handles speech, reading, and writing.

Deals with logic.

Deals with arithmetic.

Recognizes words, letters, and numbers.

Deals with literal interpretation of words.

Acts as a 'serial processor' – tracks time and sequences.

Processes auditory information.

Is thought to be the optimistic hemisphere.

If you see something out of the corner of your left eye, it is initially triggering impulses in the right side of your brain as incoming information is registered on the opposite side of the body. Visual, aural, and tactile information enters in this 'crossover' manner and is rapidly disseminated across both hemispheres. In fact, the only information that remains polarized at its entry point is our sense of smell!

If someone is engaged in tasks that require advanced physical and mental coordination, the corpus callosum lights up like a Christmas tree. For example, when someone plays the piano the corpus callosum is coordinating the left and right hands; at the same time, the brain is converting detailed physical information into physical movements and reacting to a vast amount of aural information.

The right side of the brain is often characterized as intuitive and creative.

The 'dreamy' side of the brain.

Concerned with perception.

Deals with visual over verbal information.

Acts as a 'parallel processor.'

Deals with pattern recognition and spatial reasoning.

Handles recognition of faces, objects, and places.

Processes algebra, geometry, visual cues, mental rotation, and mental imagery.

Driven by emotions.

Responsible for the initial processing of musical information.

Is thought to be the pessimistic hemisphere.

The corpus callosum joins the two hemispheres together, acting as a pipeline through which impulses pass in order to cope with tasks that require different parts of the brain to process information in parallel. The temporal lobes deal with sound, the interpretation of spoken languages, and the initial processing of musical information. The frontal lobes deal with analyzing things and making plans.

The musician's brain

Musicians process musical information in a very different way than other people. Essentially, their brains break down sounds in a more analytical way than non-musicians. It appears that adult musicians' brains show distinct patterns, dedicated neural pathways that enable a quick and strong reaction to musical stimuli. Regular musical stimulation reinforces these pathways and the result is increased growth in the sections of the brain that handle musical information.

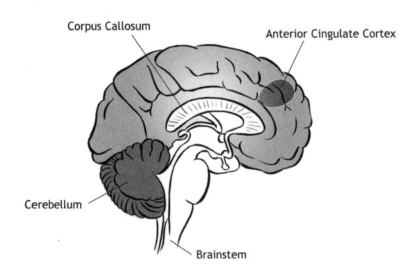

Corpus Callosum

Anterior Cingulate Cortex

Cerebellum

Brainstem

Music isn't processed by a single bit of the brain; Instead, scientists have discovered that music is processed by a widespread set of neural networks, with different areas of the brain working closely together to make sense of things such as melody, harmony, and rhythm.

In 1993, scientists studied musicians' brains to see what happens when they listen to music. The study found that when musicians hear notes played together in simple chords, there's a very specific response in the brain. When a musician hears two notes played together, their brain responds in much the same way that words conjure up mental images. For example, if I type the word 'dog' and you read it, it will probably trigger a picture of a dog in your mind; if I hear the word 'lemon,' I see and smell the fruit in my head – and I actually start to salivate!

Musicians develop similar skills, but with notes and chords rather than words. These skills help them to develop a musical vocabulary – which is essential, because musicians need to process an awful lot of information.

When a cello student plays at a professional level, they need to deal with a massive amount of information. They will be concentrating on the melody, the phrasing, the harmony, the rhythm, the tone, the pulse, and their tuning, and they will have to 'read ahead' if they're using sheet music. The student will also have to concentrate on how their right hand holds the bow and how their left hand shapes the notes; they have to make sure they're sitting properly, that their breathing is controlled and that they are projecting the instrument's sound properly. As if that wasn't enough to worry about, they also have to disguise all of these things and make the performance emotionally moving!

> *"The musician is constantly adjusting decisions on tempo, tone, style, rhythm, phrasing, and feeling – training the brain to become incredibly good at organizing and conducting numerous activities at once. Dedicated practice of this orchestration can have a great payoff for lifelong attentional skills, intelligence, and an ability for self-knowledge and expression."*

John J. Ratey, MD

How musicians' brains are different

The planum temporale is an area of the brain that seems to be connected with literacy, and researchers in Leipzig proved that this area is larger in the brains of musicians than in the brains of non-musicians. A further study, this time in Tokyo, discovered that the planum temporale on the left side of the brain was larger in people who possessed perfect pitch. That's a strange discovery, because it's the right side of the brain, not the left, that handles the majority of information about pitch, melody, and harmony.

Only a small percentage of people have perfect pitch, or absolute pitch as it's sometimes called. Study after study have shown that it's more likely to be present in people who started studying music before the age of seven, and there's a definite cut-off point after which it becomes incredibly difficult to acquire this ability.

The corpus callosum

We mentioned the corpus callosum earlier: It's the brain's motorway, the conduit that's responsible for most of the communication between the left side and the right side of the brain. It plays a crucial role in all kinds of tasks, from holding a conversation to playing the piano with both hands. For example, when you play the piano the corpus callosum is coordinating your left and your right hands, reacting to a huge amount of aural information and converting detailed visual information into physical movements.

Scientists are fascinated by the corpus callosum, and there have been several important studies of this section of musicians' brains. At Mersin University in Turkey, scientists used MRI scans to measure the brain activity of forty people: Twenty of them were professional musicians and twenty of them were non-musicians. The researchers found significant differences between the two groups and concluded:

> *'Our results support the hypothesis that brain morphology is prone to plastic changes caused by environmental factors.'*

In other words, the way in which your brain grows is, to some extent, determined by external factors – in this case, being an active musician.

Another study, this time in Düsseldorf, found similar results. When they scanned the brains of sixty people, they discovered that this shaping, these plastic changes in the brain, occurred in people who had begun their musical adventures before the age of seven.

The auditory cortex

We looked briefly at the auditory cortex earlier in this chapter; this is the part of the brain that's responsible for initiating the analysis of musical material. A number of recent studies found that musicians' brains allocated 25 percent more of this cortex to processing music than non-musicians' brains did.

As we've discovered, it appears that music can affect the way the brain grows, develops, and organizes itself – and it has an effect from a very young age. There is clear evidence of the positive effect playing music has upon the developing brain, and it seems that there are key periods during which the brain is at its most malleable and impressionable.

Chapter 9

How music aids physical and mental coordination

M usic makes us move! When "Here We Go Round The Mulberry Bush" is sung at my local toddler group, the children don't need to be shown how to move to the music: They're already skipping and bouncing around the room! The children naturally find a rhythm that parallels the rhythm of the song.

Children are very skilled at matching movement to sound, images to music and physical movement to visual stimuli. Perhaps children's senses are more connected than adults', in the same way young babies' senses are connected together. Adults certainly tend to pare down their sensory reactions to stimuli, sometimes to the point where we are very literal about what we are hearing, seeing, touching, smelling, or tasting; however, children – and musicians – are more expressive and imaginative. In the case of children that's natural, but in the case of musicians it's an essential skill: musicians have to connect sensory information to emotional and intellectual concepts and to find a way of communicating the results to other people.

One of the tenets of Dalcroze Eurythmics – a very popular system of music education – is that we feel emotions through movement, and that we reveal our emotions through movement, sounds, gestures, and the shape of our bodies. By helping children practice movement to music, we are providing them with a great outlet for expressing their emotions, sometimes at an age when they feel unable to articulate what they feel. Conversely, through musical movement negative emotions can be contained or positively altered.

Children instinctively respond to strong stimuli, and while we have the same responses as adults we tend to be more controlled: I'm sure you sometimes find yourself tapping your foot or your fingers in time to music, but a child may display a whole body reaction to the same song! These movements play a critical role in the way children's coordination systems become 'hard-wired.' Being physically active in this way helps fine-tune the body's motor skills and coordination, which in turn refine mental reflexes and encourage mental development.

Inhibitory controls

When children are very young, music can encourage them to be physically active – but it can also persuade them to sit down and listen quietly. This is when music aids inhibitory controls, which are essentially methods of self-restraint. For example, stopping yourself from interrupting someone else's speech is an inhibitory control, and sitting down to perform a task instead of running around noisily also involves inhibitory controls. This connection between music and inhibitory controls can enable children to focus on learning activities for longer periods.

Of course, music also moves us – and makes us want to move. As children grow up, they demand musical games where they have to react to musical changes: musical chairs, musical statues, and so on. They enjoy being caught out, and these types of game also help to teach important techniques for self-control and self-discipline.

A piece of music can become associated with calm moments, or a musical cue can be learned as a specific movement instruction. For example, one of my favorite workshop games for young children involves moving to music while pretending to be different kinds of beans. Bear with me on this one!

Heavy, resonant music means broad beans, so the children make themselves as wide as possible; fast, short notes are runner beans, so the children run around on tiptoes. No music at all? Frozen beans, so the children stand perfectly still until the music resumes.

My local toddler group had used "Twinkle Twinkle" as a 'quiet moment' song when all the children were encouraged to lie down as if going to sleep to settle them before the end of the session.

> *One week, the leader wanted the toddlers to dance around the room to some slow music while making shapes in the air with silk scarves. All was going well, the children were moving very gracefully around the room in silence. The music was cued in, at which point every child dropped to the floor, motionless, with eyes firmly shut. They would not move until "Twinkle Twinkle" had finished! In just four sessions, the children had learned a conditioned reflex to a piece of music.*

Movement can also power memory functions, which aid the acquisition of linguistic skills and the development of self-awareness.

How movement helps children's physical and mental development

You need a good sense of pitch to learn to speak a language, and you need an inner pulse to control physical movements. As we have already discovered, we are born with many rhythm mechanisms, just as we are all born with an extraordinary sense of pitch. By stimulating these rhythmic mechanisms through musical movement, you can stimulate mental development.

Prenatal listening and postnatal coordination

In 1997, researchers discovered that parental music activities appear to help postnatal coordination and physical skills. In the study (Effects of the Firstart Method – Lafuente), babies *in utero* were exposed to recordings of different musical components that increased in complexity during the pregnancy.

In total, each baby was exposed to between 50 and 90 hours of musical material. The babies exposed to this material seemed to make faster progress in some areas compared to babies who hadn't been exposed to music. Their pre-speech became evident sooner, and there were noticeable differences in hand-eye coordination, visual tracking, facial mirroring, general motor coordination, and the ability to hold their bottle with both hands.

The stages of physical coordination

From the age of just two weeks, babies are already trying to engage with the rhythms of speech and song. They may move their arms and legs in time with the voice of their parent or caregiver, and at one month they begin to notice their hands.

Babies are born with incredible reflexes. They will flinch and grab with their hands when startled – great if you're a baby gorilla! – and they will simulate a walking motion when held upright with their feet touching a flat surface. From the age of one month, a gradual transition begins to turn movements from being reflex actions to being conscious, controlled actions.

When babies notice their hands, they constantly find their fingers and toes fascinating – and they quickly discover that they can conduct the movements of their limbs themselves. This development of bodily movement forms an essential stage in the development of their mental and physical coordination.

From birth, a baby needs to experiment with a huge range of movements in order to build brain and body coordination. They should be encouraged to crawl, to reach for objects, to roll around, to rock to and fro, and to stretch. Using music as a soundtrack to such activities can help you to set the pace of assisted exercises, and will help to create early associations between different kinds of music and movements.

Children react to musical cues without necessarily knowing what they are or what they mean. Babies will sway in time with songs; toddlers like to skip to bouncy music, and they will clap along to strong, march-style beats. On the CD we've included five sample tracks designed to encourage different types of movement:

> TRACK 2: music for skipping
> TRACK 3: music for running

TRACK 4: music for walking (listen for other instructions, including crouching down and stretching up)
TRACK 5: music for marching
TRACK 6: music for resting

Ten-month-old babies may try to imitate other people's movements, and by the time a baby is one year old they will enjoy trying to mirror what their parent is doing – whether that's brushing their teeth or cleaning the floor! This is, therefore, a great time for some motor skills development. Basic movements with songs are especially popular from this point.

From eighteen months, toddlers respond to music in a physical and vocal manner. Basic action songs are favored from this point: Children love stomping, skipping, marching, and beating time to music at this age. By now they are very aware of the beats in a piece and will try to articulate them physically; music with strong beats can trigger such movements subconsciously.

Fingerplays are very important to toddlers, and they find them very entertaining. Fingerplay games are great for refining motor coordination skills, as well as for learning large sets of information.

Children often develop an incredibly natural conducting style by the age of three, without any formal training. They are often capable of tracking or leading a beat, shaping phrases with the contour of their hand gestures, showing emotional content, and indicating dynamic levels. From this age, physical 'warm-up' games can help to build bodily control and motor movement skills in children. These are excellent for building confidence and are essential for acquiring the high levels of coordination necessary to be a musician.

Learning an instrument can really help mental coordination processes. As we discovered in Chapter 8, musicians have enlarged areas of the brain that help to coordinate complex patterns both physically and mentally.

Musical movement and mental gymnastics

There is increasing interest in the use of 'mental gymnastics' to enhance the communication between the two sides of the brain. The exercises in these programs are believed to encourage the body to adjust itself through the use of movement (often to music), and they are believed to help regulate the body's communication systems – which in turn assist overall mental and physical performance.

These exercises seek to stimulate 'cross-reflexes,' the diagonal pathways of communication from one side of the body to the opposite side of the brain. Enhancing these pathways can assist complex thought processes, whole body coordination, depth perception, binaural hearing (balanced between both ears), and help to reduce stress. Exercises often mimic the patterns of movement that the body uses in certain periods of its development. A good example of this is the 'cross crawl,' an exercise that mimics the limb movements of a baby learning to crawl where the arms and legs work in diagonal pairings.

Here's an example of mental gymnastics that you can try: Choose a piece of music whose beat is close to the speed at which you'd walk. Now try touching your left knee with your right elbow by lifting the knee towards the elbow. Alternate this movement with its opposite motion, touching your right knee with your left elbow. This exercise replicates the action of crawling, and is believed to help mental coordination.

The Jaques–Dalcroze system: Eurythmics

The Jaques-Dalcroze system was devised by Swiss composer and pianist Emile Jaques-Dalcroze (1865-1950) and is often known as 'eurythmics.' It focuses on three areas: Rhythmics, which covers rhythm and dynamics through physical movement; Solfège, which focuses on pitch, melody, and harmony through the ear, eye, and voice; and improvisation, which combines the other two elements.

Eurythmics is founded on the notion that rhythm is the primary element of all music, and that the source of all rhythm can be found in the human body; its core philosophy is that the beginning of all music is the translation of human emotions into physical motion.

According to Jaques-Dalcroze, emotions are things we experience physically, through our sensations of muscular contraction and release. We reveal our internal emotions by movement, sound, gesture, and body shape, and these movements are reflex actions, spontaneous actions, or conscious and considered actions. We can express our feelings through breathing, singing, or the use of instruments – and the most important instrument of all is the human body.

Eurythmics stimulates and advances all of the abilities and senses required for musicianship: aural, visual, and tactile sensitivity; knowledge and reasoning skills; and the ability to make informed, emotional, and intellectual judgements. These elements are coordinated by a kinaesthesic sense – that is, the information flow between the mind and body via the nervous system. A skilled eurythmics student will feel that they are thinking with their body and physically flexing and performing with their mind.

Music can regulate a sense of inner pulse through stimulating physical movement. This in turn can advance physical dexterity, develop kinesthetic coordination, and therefore build mental development.

Chapter 10

How music can develop memory

Memory skills are essential for every musician. In addition to recalling pieces of music or remembering the actions involved in playing an instrument, music also involves many forms of intellectual and emotional memory. Memory is the key to learning: We cope with growing up and the challenges of everyday life by remembering our experiences and using those memories to inform our future decisions and processes. By stimulating the development of music-based learning skills, we can help improve future learning ability.

What are memories?

Everything our senses detect is held briefly in the brain, triggering a unique sequence of firing neurons. This stimulus creates a little packet of data that is ready to be converted into a memory.

These little packets of information often trigger related patterns in the brain, and the more powerful our response or the more often these patterns are repeated, the stronger our memory becomes. For example, regular tasks such as walking, tying your shoelaces, or changing the gears in your car are frequently used packets of information, and these are both strong and easy to recall. These are kinesthetic memories, as they concern movement. Music relies heavily on kinesthetic memory: It's essential for playing an instrument.

When you're walking back to your house, you use a different form of memory: visual spatial memory. You are drawing on photographic memories, which you compare with the things you can see. Many musicians use a similar system to navigate around pieces of music that they have memorized, but such memory can be unreliable if it isn't imaginative enough. For example, if you memorize how a page of music looks rather than the images the music suggests when you play it, you'll find it more difficult to remember.

Aural recall, musical memory, and verbal memory

How many pieces of verse or prose can you remember word-perfectly right now? My list contains only eleven small chunks of text that I can accurately recall. These include two poems I learned at school, part of a comedy routine, a couple of prayers, and a few chunks of Shakespeare I learned for some school exams. Your own list may contain more items of text than my own. I hope it does!

Now try to remember some tunes that you like – your favorite pop songs or the records you listened to at college; nursery rhymes, hymns, TV theme tunes, songs you've sung at football games or pieces you've played on a musical instrument. I'd be willing to bet that you don't have enough paper to write down all of these songs; in fact, there are probably thousands of pieces of music stored in your memory!

It's extraordinary that we can hold so much music in our heads, and yet we can't necessarily recall words as easily. Why is it harder to recount sequences of words than sequences of pitches? We appear to be much better at storing music in our brains than we are at storing text.

Sometimes a piece of music – an advertising jingle or an annoying pop song – will get lodged in your head, and it can be very different to shift. These endlessly repeating musical loops in your brain are probably based in a section called the auditory cortex.

It has been suggested that we're born with musical memory skills as a way to store huge amounts of aural information: It's easier to memorize something if it's presented with a melody. One theory suggests that these skills evolved as a way for us to remember our history and pass it on to the next generation in the days before humans invented reading and writing.

When we remember music, we can recall huge amounts of technical data about that music in our brains: We can play back a complete mental recording of it with a high degree of accuracy. Musicians are trained to be very adept at using these skills, and they develop a sensitivity to pitches, accents, and phrasing that means when they recall a piece of music, they can focus on individual instruments and even sounds in their mental recordings.

Too much information?

If we stored every note of music or word we ever heard, we'd have brains full of useless information – so most musical and verbal stimuli aren't stored in our heads. In much the same way that our brains strip away inessential links, we discard musical or verbal information that our brains are unlikely to need again. That's because we're subjected to a constant barrage of stimuli: Visual, aural, olfactory, tactile, and taste. For example, we're exposed to more than 3,000 advertising messages each and every day!

One interesting side-effect of some forms of autism is an over-developed aural memory. This can be linguistic or melodic in nature, and it can manifest itself in extraordinary ways.

> *I was running a composition project with a group of young autistic children a few years ago when one of them, Alex, launched into the script of* The Lion King *including note-perfect renditions of the songs. Not only was he accurate word-for-word, but he was determined to recite the entire film to the class. It transpired that Alex had seen the film the night before for the very first time – and yet he could replicate the entire film word-for-word.*

Of course, there are differences in the way we consume music and consume words: We tend to listen to a favorite piece of music again and again. However, even after multiple readings a book is unlikely to lodge in our brains in the same way that a piece of music will.

Our natural abilities with music mean that musical therapy can be a very effective way to treat people with serious damage to the language centers of their brain. Using a technique called Melodic Intonation Therapy, patients are encouraged to sing rather than speak; the technique has been shown to aid vocal fluency.

Music is also an invaluable learning tool. Many of the exercises in the later parts of this book are list-based and fact-based songs that help young children absorb core information: They could be as simple as the days of the week or the letters of the alphabet. Rhythms and melodies make it much easier to absorb what can otherwise be rather abstract information.

The black box

The brain sometimes works a little like a 'black box' flight recorder. At certain moments of heightened brain activity, a recording is made of all of the sensory information being registered at that point.

In a flash, we record visual, aural, tactile, taste, and smell information – which is why hearing a certain song can trigger an incredibly vivid flashback to an emotional memory such as first love or a great holiday, or a traumatic event such as an accident or the death of a loved one. This can even be the case with pre-natal musical memories.

In one famous case, a mother's pregnancy coincided with the death of a close relative. The mother was listening to Mozart as she grieved – and after her daughter was born, the child appeared to be very disturbed by the same music that had comforted her mother. Doctors concluded that the child had come to associate the music with stressful chemical changes: In other words, the child had developed an association between a specific piece of music and her mother's distress while still in the womb.

Pre-natal musical memories

Thirty-six weeks after conception, an unborn baby is capable of recognizing pieces of music that are played frequently – and those musical memories persist after the child has been born. A study conducted by Peter Hepper of Queen's University in Belfast studied the effects of music on babies in the womb. The participants were moms-to-be who enjoyed watching the Australian soap opera *Neighbours*. Each mom-to-be watched around 300 episodes of the program during her pregnancy, and therefore heard the theme music around 600 times (it's played at the beginning and end of the show).

When the babies were born, researchers tested their reaction to the *Neighbours* theme tune. At two days of age, the babies demonstrated a clear reaction to the tune: Their heart rates slowed down in response to the music. Each baby had associated the tune with a period of relaxation, so every time their mother had sat down to take a break and watch the soap opera, the babies relaxed too. This effect, the researchers found, appeared to be most powerful from 30 weeks after conception.

Musical memory processes

Music is often used as a tool to recover deeply buried memories, acting as a short-circuit to trigger a distant pattern of neural activity.

> *I recently led a social history project for retirees, which was based around wartime 'tea dances' in London. The visiting musicians played Glenn Miller and Cole Porter tunes before interviewing participants about their memories of wartime entertainment. All of the interviewees found themselves talking about times and places they had previously "forgotten." A couple of them recalled fairly outrageous stories about their teenage years – tales that had certainly never been recounted to anyone – and one lady recalled the dance moves she had learned as a chorus girl!*

The music acted as a catalyst and a key to unlock memories that were buried fairly deeply; once revealed, the memories were rich in factual, musical, kinesthetic, and emotional detail.

Excerpts of music can prompt chunks of verbal memory to be recovered. Music seems to be able to accurately and emotionally encode large tracts of information. Indeed, when factual information is set to music, it appears to be lodged in a unique way, to the extent that information can be retrieved more effectively if it is encoded via music.

Research carried out in 1994 by C.M. Colwell studied the effect of combining music with textbook language studies. Twenty-seven kindergarten children were split into three groups. The first group rehearsed information from the textbook in song form, the second group used speech and song, and the final group used spoken text only. In subsequent tests of the children's fluency, the two groups that had used music had improved their reading skills. The researchers concluded that the music had provided a framework on which the children could place the factual information, thus aiding factual recollection and retention of learned material.

A recent study at Hong Kong University also found that children with music training demonstrated better verbal memory than did their counterparts without such training.

Music is an exceptionally efficient vehicle for memory processes. Humans are capable of committing huge libraries of melodic and timbral information to memory. Retention of purely literary information is much harder and more labor-intensive. However, when text-based information is combined with music, it can be learned far quicker and be retained for far longer periods.

The way we acquire linguistic skills is intrinsically linked to musical processes, as we'll discover in the next chapter.

Chapter 11

How music can help language skills

"When we listen to music we don't really know how rich is the semantic information that music carries. The brain computations are just the same for musical and linguistic information."

Stefan Koelsch (Max Planck Institute, Leipzig), quoted in *New Scientist,* February 28, 2004

In 2001, I was working with players from the Academy of St. Martin in the Fields. We spent a week writing a mini-opera with a group of young special-needs students at a London school. One of the children, a nine-year-old autistic child, was uncommunicative at school – but he appeared to be stimulated by what was going on. By the end of the week-long project, he was able to respond to questions if they were sung to him. To everyone's surprise, he was able to respond by singing back. He went on to take a pivotal role in the final performance. This was a dramatic display of just how powerfully music can act as a catalyst for communication. As well as developing our linguistic coordination, it also appears that music is able to unlock elements of our intellect where language alone sometimes fails.

When we process aural information, the brain is adept at deciding what is language and what is music. The processes used in interpreting this information are parallel, and exhibit mirror symmetry in neurological activity. As we discovered earlier, the left and right auditory cortices distinguish between musical information and linguistic data.

The processes used to acquire linguistic skills are largely reliant on the use of musical tools. Prosody and pre-speech are essentially musical interactions. Nursery rhymes serve a serious and crucial role in the development of vocabulary, grammatical concepts, vocal coordination, and comprehension.

Children are thought to process musical and speech skills in similar areas of the brain. One study (Koelsch, Grossmann *et al.*), concluded:

> *"Because children process, in contrast to adults, music in the same hemispheres as they process language, results indicate that children process music and language more similarly than adults. This finding might support the notion of a common origin of music and language in the human brain, and concurs with findings that demonstrate the importance of musical features of speech for the acquisition of language."*

In a study by Anvari and Trainor, strong correlations were displayed between music skills, phonological awareness, and reading development. They concluded that:

> *"...music perception appears to tap auditory mechanisms related to reading that only partially overlap with those related to phonological awareness, suggesting that both linguistic and nonlinguistic general auditory mechanisms are involved in reading."*

The brain uses specialized regions of each hemisphere to process speech and song. As we get older, these appear to become mirrored processes – the auditory cortex is able to judge whether something is spoken or sung. A study conducted at the University of Tübingen in Germany found that when a tune without lyrics was heard, there was a great deal of activity stimulated in the right motor cortex, the right anterior insula, and the left cerebellum, whereas exactly the opposite pattern emerged during speech processing. This pattern shows that we have evolved a mechanism for filtering music and speech into opposite locations, but that they undergo a process that is exactly mirrored.

Key developmental stages

Tuning in

There is a period of 'tuning in,' where the child becomes familiar with the patterns, rhythms, and pitches of language. They soak up colossal amounts of information from their environment. Some scientists believe that this process begins prenatally.

A fascinating study conducted at France's National Agency for Scientific Research explored the sensitivity of very young babies to the rhythmic patterns of their mother tongue. A series of phrases in different languages was used, but the actual words were replaced with the sound 'sa' – spoken in exactly the same rhythm as in the original phrase. Despite the lack of recognizable words, babies were able to distinguish between their mother tongue and a foreign language, even at the age of two months: They were able to discriminate rhythmically between the patterns of the various languages. This displays an already highly sophisticated level of sensitivity to the patterns of a language, its phrase shapes, intonation, and cadences, even when the vocabulary has been removed.

The 'tuning in' period therefore conditions the child to the feel of a language's pitches, phrase structures, timbre, dynamics, and cadences. It is no coincidence that all of these terms are musical!

Babble

A period of attempts at noise and expression called 'babble' or 'prosody' progressed by rewarding with praise, attachment of meanings to formerly abstract sounds, patterns, and pitches.

Think about how you naturally address a newborn baby. You may use short, repeated motifs accompanied by an encouraging facial gesture such as wide eyes and raised eyebrows. You may use short, exaggerated double syllables. These sometimes provoke a reaction, maybe a movement or a vocalization in return.

Babies respond to a range of vocal expression that is delivered at a higher level of intensity than normal speech or song. Infant-directed speech is inherently musical by virtue of its sing-song nature and exaggerated phrase shapes. Being confronted with a baby naturally triggers this behavior in adults, and babies encourage its perpetuation through displaying positive responses. To some extent, our offspring lead us to teach them through a curious mixture of instinct, emotion, and conditioning.

Pre-speech, traditional songs, movement plays, wordplays, and finger games are all sophisticated tools that are often used subconsciously by caregivers. Recognizing the importance of such traditional cultural materials enables you to devise your own stimulating material based on similar techniques and principles.

Why do we sing nursery rhymes?

Nursery rhymes usually feature many close repetitions, double rhymes, and alliterative lyrics, and early words such as 'ma-ma', 'da-da', and 'choo-choo' use a repetition technique that you'll find in almost every culture. This verbal repletion – a kind of elementary 'groove' – finds its way into a huge number of traditional songs, where the first word is repeated as a prompt for the infant to join in. 'Twinkle Twinkle, Little Star' and 'Row, Row, Row Your Boat' are obvious examples of this.

Once a child has mastered simple repetition, a close rhyming repetition is a logical progression: Humpty-Dumpty, Incy-Wincy, Georgie-Porgie, and so on. For example:

> Miss Polly had a dolly who was sick sick sick
> So she phoned for the doctor to come quick quick quick

This is actually a very sophisticated piece! The words have their own beat to the extent that, if you say the words out loud, the song's rhythm will emerge completely accurately. This rhythm is closest in character to a hornpipe, a musical form with an essential practical purpose: It's designed to unify the movements of sailors as they raise a ship's anchor. You can find the whole song on page 204.

In nursery rhymes, the melodic contour of the phrases follows a satisfying series of arch shapes, which musicians refer to as an *anacrusis*. Children really enjoy these arch-shaped phrases – phrases where every ascent has a balancing descent. Many of the most enduring nursery rhymes follow this pattern, where there's a physical ascent followed by a descent or a rapid drop: 'Incy-Wincy Spider', 'Jack And Jill', 'The Grand Old Duke Of York', 'Ten Green Bottles', 'Rock-a-bye Baby'... I like to think that these songs serve an important function in physical development, as they can help ingrain the concept of up and down – and the inevitable falling over that forms a necessary part of learning to stand on your own two feet!

If you look at the lyrics of many nursery rhymes, you'll notice that they contain tension and resolution – and tension and resolution is the key element in most musical forms. The sense of going from a home key and returning is a central technique you'll find in most forms of music, and you'll also find it in the patterns of basic musical phrasing and speech phrasing.

As young children grow, they enjoy playing with the 'feel' of words – articulating complex strings of consonants, using rhythmic repetition, and following melodies. At the early stage of language development, speech essentially is music.

Reading

In 1975, a seven-month study (Hurwitz, Wolff, Bortnick and Kokasj) was conducted to discover whether musical training could improve the reading results in American first-grade schoolchildren.

One group was given a form of musical training called Kodaly Training, while the other children were given no such training. At the end of the survey, the researchers noted that the musically trained children scored around 88 percent in reading tests, while the other children scored 72 percent. In other words, music tuition at a young age appears to help students learn to read.

Experts believe that there are three key stages in learning to read. These stages are:

1. Recognizing words

2. 'Sounding out' – reading aloud

3. Recognizing entire words without having to sound out elements

Music appears to play a key role in the second of these stages. According to reports in *Educational Psychology* (Lamb and Gregory, 1993), children with good pitch skills grasp sounding-out more quickly than children without such skills.

In music, pattern recognition skills are learned through sight-reading. This is the ability to play music fluently without having read or heard the piece before.

Language, expression, and music

One of the most important language skills we possess is the ability to interpret the meaning of a word by the way it sounds: for example, think of the number of different ways you can say the word 'really'. Here are three ways in which the same word has a very different meaning, simply because of the way we say it:

Really? (with a rising pitch)   *Questioning: 'Tell me more.'*

Really? (pitch stays flat)   *Sarcastic or bored.*

Really? (with a falling pitch)   *I don't believe you.*

As you can see, the word is identical each time – but by changing the pitch, we can completely transform the word's meaning. If we say the word with an increasing pitch, it encourages the other person to say more; if we say it flatly, it hardly advances the conversation; and if we use a downwards pitch, it's a guaranteed conversation killer.

The power of phrasing

Every sentence has a key point that we emphasize using direction, pitch, volume, and accent. This may be a syllable within a certain word, or it might be an entire word; it can occur at the beginning of a sentence, at the end, or somewhere in the middle.

Let's take a simple example: 'I want to dance with you.' Depending on our emphasis, that simple phrase can mean several different things:

I want to dance with you	*Don't dance with him! Dance with me!*
I *want* to dance with you	*No, really! I do!*
I want to *dance* with you	*I'm being suggestive, or clearing up confusion.*
I want to dance with *you*	*No, not her! You!*

In any spoken sentence, there is a central peak point which one emphasizes through direction, pitch, volume, and accent. This may be a key syllable within a certain word and can occur at the middle, end, or even beginning of a spoken phrase. It is a crucial skill to make oneself understood.

Music works in exactly the same way: You can draw multiple meanings from the same notes by the way they are expressed.

Time for some jargon: The notes running towards a key note are called anacrusic notes, and the key note itself is called the crusis. The notes that run away from the key note are called the metacrusic notes. Here's an example from The Beatles:

Anacrusis	Crusis	Metacrusis
She loves you	Yeah	Yeah, yeah

It's not unlike the process of hitting a tennis ball. The anacrusis is the swing, the crusis is the moment of impact between the racquet and the ball, and the metacrusis is the remainder of the swing once the ball has been dispatched.

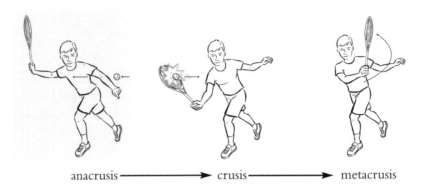

anacrusis ⟶ crusis ⟶ metacrusis

This shape is written through all musical forms of expression from a baby's cry to a Beatles song. By mastering the musical control of such lines, we naturally become sensitive to the expressive potential of controlling such shapes in language skills, and can gain more control of subtle vocal inflections as a result. Many forms of restorative speech therapy use music for just this reason, as we have a built-in comprehension of musical phrase shapes.

In a groundbreaking study, Jaak Panksepp researched these shapes and their connections with language. He discovered that a baby's cries follow the same patterns: When a baby is separated from its mother, its cry has a rising pitch; when the child is reunited with its parent, the pitch subsides. There is a chemical curve, too: A mother's oxytocin levels rise when she is reunited with her child, and this chemical makes her body warmer. This chemical effect adds weight to the feeling of resolution and satisfaction that we associate with the ending of a phrase. As Panksepp noted, 'Music captures something essential about the separation calls of young infants – it hooks directly into the brain's primitive emotional circuits.'

Conveying meaning through phrasing

In one survey, scientists (Koelsch and Friederici) measured the way in which phrasing carries meaning for musicians and non-musicians alike, to the extent that participants knew when a chord change was 'wrong.' They suggested that the ability to acquire knowledge about musical progressions and to process information based on this knowledge is a basic human ability. They also suggested that this ability is of great importance in helping infants and young children to learn language.

Improving writing skills

As children become familiar with a language, their technical grasp of its written components is strengthened through the practice of set exercises, creative writing, and formalized lessons. This obviously has a correlation with the way children learn to play with the structural components of music. However, while we naturally encourage children to experiment with creative writing, there is never the same amount of emphasis placed on the parallel musical processes.

By encouraging musical improvisation and subsequent notation, children can acquire total musical literacy. The notation stage is parallel to basic writing exercises. It is not necessary to teach conventional notation; there is just as much value in letting children devise their own systems of musical symbols and lines. This can really help their planning and organizational skills, and makes them come to grips with the concept of events occurring over a timeframe. Real notation can then be phased in using flashcards and elementary music books – again, parallel processes to those used in literacy.

There are exercises shown in the latter part of this book that will encourage this process, such as graphic notation games and creative drawing to music.

Composition and analysis

In the 19th century, Pierre Broca and Carl Wernicke discovered two major language centers in the brain, and promptly named those centers after themselves. The scientists were able to ascertain that these areas of the brain served distinct purposes: Broca's region is used primarily for speech, and Wernicke's for comprehension.

The area dedicated to comprehension begins to function before the area dedicated to speech, and that can lead to frustration for a young child when they can't express themselves fully. This developmental hiatus – essentially waiting for the speech bit of the brain to catch up with the comprehension bit of the brain – is believed by some scientists to be the culprit behind the 'terrible twos' syndrome.

The neural connections that govern speech development are pre-loaded in the brain, as are the networks that deal with musical stimulus and response. Some commentators have compared these brain systems to the software that comes pre-installed when you buy a new computer. These existing brain systems grow into fully functioning linguistic centers, and vocabulary, grammatical structures, and accents are acquired through experience.

Brain processes:

• Evolve with experience.

• Shape themselves in direct response to their use.

• Rewrite their code to meet the user's needs

Computers don't work that way... yet!

Music gives us language

Music isn't a language: It is a root of language, it can be inspired by language, but it is way beyond language too. All language is musical, and we all become confident linguistically through an extraordinarily sophisticated set of musical tools.

Hearing, interpreting, comprehending, and engaging in dialogue are parallel processes in music and language. Music is always our initial system of communication and prepares the foundation for the building of linguistic skills, speech, comprehension, expression, and vocabularies. Therefore, consciously and unconsciously stimulating children through music will help advance language skills at all stages of childhood development.

Music plays a critical role in the foundations of communication and expression and therefore is critical to our survival and future intelligence.

Chapter 12

How music can improve math ability and spatial reasoning

I was coaching the cello section of the National Youth Orchestra during a summer vacation. During the lunch break, the conversation turned to mathematical puzzles and riddles. I have always been interested in the relationship between music and math and I talked to the students about compositions based on a mathematical concept known as the Fibonacci sequence.

There was something of a polite silence as I tried to remember part of the exact mathematical ratio I was trying to articulate. It transpired that more than a third of the cellists in the orchestra were intending to study mathematics at college rather than music, despite being professional-level cellists, and consequently knew rather a lot more about the subject than I was able to communicate! In fact, a recent survey of university math students in the U.S. showed that 11 percent more of the students had studied music than the national average.

A study by Schmithorst and Holland proposed that:

> '...the correlation between musical training and math proficiency may be associated with improved working memory performance and an increased abstract representation of numerical quantities.'

In an interview in the *New Scientist* magazine, the mathematician Brian Butterworth revealed that in a recent scientific study into the correlation between math and music students, the music students performed better in mathematical testing than the math students. It would have been interesting to see a demonstration of the musicianship skills of the latter group!

Music and mathematics

Studying musical forms can help children understand complicated mathematical and scientific concepts; conversely, studying mathematics can help the comprehension of the physical properties of musical elements such as pitch and overtones. There are some incredible correlations to be found between musical structures, patterns found in the natural world, and complex mathematical phenomena.

Divisions of the beat and fractions

In the simplest terms, musicians use basic mathematical knowledge to play rhythms accurately. Composers generally notate music by using symbols that represent different length values (indicated by the design of the notehead and tail) and different pitch values (depending upon where the notehead is placed on a grid known as the staff).

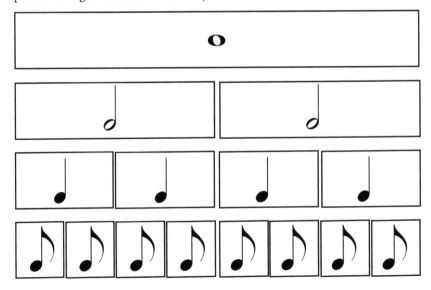

These note lengths are precise proportions of a 'whole note.' In other words, notes operate in the same way as fractions, in so much as they are defined through their relationship to the number one – the 'whole note.'

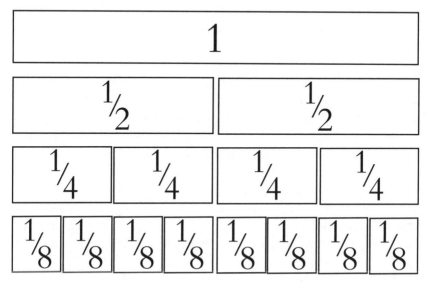

The concept of a half can easily be explained to a child by demonstrating two beats within a single pulse.

In 1999, an experiment for *Neurological Research* magazine set out to research the links between active music study and mathematical learning. Students who had studied fractions using a music-based model, involving divisions of the beat, scored 100 percent higher than their colleagues who were taught in the conventional manner. It appears that by explaining the mathematical concept through a musical model, the students could comprehend the concept through physically feeling and hearing the results of such divisions.

Musical structures can be expressed as fractions, ratios, and proportions.

The mathematics of pitch

As mentioned previously, the pitch of a note is indicated by its placement upon a staff, which acts as a kind of low-to-high matrix. The pitch of a note is represented in mathematical terms by a numerical value, its frequency. In fact, the pitch is the way we perceive the frequency of a note.

Frequency is a measurement of the number of times that the same event happens within a time unit. Sound frequencies are represented by a number that indicates how many times an event happens every second. For instance, the frequency of a violin's 'A' string is normally 440Hz: When it is sounded, it pulses 440 times per second. We perceive this pulsing pattern as a musical note, which we describe in this example as 'A above Middle C.'

Notes that sound comfortable alongside one another often have clear mathematical relationships to one another. For instance, if you hum a note low in pitch, and then hum the same note at a higher pitch (say an octave above), then the frequency of the higher note will be exactly double the number of the first.

Pythagoras and the 'music of the spheres'

Pythagoras believed he had discovered a form of divinity in music. Not only was he a peerless mathematician, he was a musical philosopher too. His precise observations into the way that strings divide into perfect proportions, causing harmonics pleasing to the ear, led to scientific theories that form the foundation of all western harmony. Using vibrating string instruments, Pythagoras demonstrated that by dividing the string into fractional lengths, he could create 'consonant' pitches, that is, notes that fit with one another and are pleasing to the ear.

At this time in history, the planets themselves were believed to correspond to the same musical geometry. As they turned in relation to one another they were thought to create 'the music of the spheres'. Of course, every object vibrates, and every vibration that passes through the air creates a sound, so this is not such a flight of fancy. Plato believed that all matter was composed of vibrating string loops. 'String theory' is something of a hot topic at the moment: Yet again, modern science is catching up with ancient science and philosophy!

Spatial-temporal reasoning

Music can help the kind of reasoning skills used for processing equations and long functions, as it requires thinking in space and time.

Spatial-temporal reasoning involves the ability to resolve three-dimensional puzzles without actually using a physical model. We all use spatial-temporal skills to help us order objects, events, and concepts in time. We use these kinds of skills when playing with jigsaws and board games, and they are an essential component of musicianship. These are essential skills we need to use to cope with everyday life.

When working with young children, I often use short phrases as compositional building blocks. The children can become very proficient at mentally reversing the order of the notes, inverting the figures, or changing the note length relationships.

Let's try a similar exercise right now!

First of all, I want you to recall the first four notes of 'Frère Jacques.' Hum them to yourself at a comfortable pitch. Now picture the contour of the phrase you have just hummed.

It probably looks something like this in your mind:

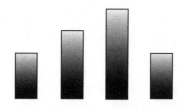

Here's what you have hummed in normal notation:

Now hum the notes in reverse order using your imaginary contour line as a guide. (You will be following the contour in a reverse direction in your head.)

Now try inverting the contour and hum the pattern forwards and then backwards. Congratulations! You've just used a huge amount of spatial temporal reasoning. As a result you've created four different musical themes, any one of which could become a strong piece of music.

I always work without pencil and paper when composing pieces with children, as these creative spatial techniques work their best when visualized mentally and aurally.

Exactly the same skills are used in mental arithmatic, when spatial processing and temporary memory functions are really being tested.

Can active music-making help develop spatial-temporal reasoning?

Scientists have been able to provide compelling evidence to prove that instruction in instruments is an excellent way of stimulating general spatial abilities in young children. Many of the studies have focused on keyboard instruments.

In 1997 a study devised by Frances Rauscher and Gordon Shaw enrolled groups of three-year-olds in either regular group singing classes, basic keyboard, or computer classes. A control group was given no form of special training. All of the participating children had their 'spatial intelligence' measured before and after an eight-month period of research. In the control group, the children's spatial abilities had risen by 6 percent, in line with natural childhood development. However, in the two groups exposed to music, the ability level had risen by an incredible 34 percent.

From this study it was concluded that studying music is believed to greatly aid spatial-temporal intelligence and can therefore be a useful tool in the comprehension and processing of advanced mathematical, analytical, and scientific concepts.

Learning instruments can help spatial–temporal reasoning

Learning an instrument can help enhance spatial-temporal abilities in children. Listening to music often does not produce the same effects, despite early evidence to the contrary. Spatial-temporal abilities are critical for being able to sequence information and ideas, for advancing analysis and reasoning, building higher mathematical skills, refining visual interpretation, and comprehension, as well as helping with planning skills.

A keyboard instrument, such as the piano, presents a spectrum of pitches in a particular prescribed layout. To the developing child, this offers a framework upon which to hang an incredibly complex concept – the division of pitch. Most Western music uses a diatonic division of pitches – (the black and white notes on a keyboard).

On a keyboard instrument, the frequency of the notes ascends from low to high as one plays from left to right. This creates a matrix of spatial location to pitch; in other words, the brain associates a geographical location with a particular note, low sounds on the left, high sounds to the right. This of course has a correlation with the western habit of reading from left to right. The initial 'Mozart Effect' research was centered around the concept that these spatial skills would be enhanced by exposure to a particular piano composition.

When a sequence of notes is sounded in turn on a keyboard, the player is engaging with the dimension of time, as well as movement in space. Music itself is a stunning synthesis of beautiful mathematical and physical laws. There is an incredible balance at work – in the process of making music, one of the highest forms of human expression, we are able to develop skills to help comprehend the very foundations of science.

Chapter 13

How music can help personal creativity

Creativity can be defined as the ability to make new things, to find a new solution to a problem, to find a new way of doing things, to create a new artistic work, or to combine a previously unconnected selection of objects or ideas. Young children are naturally highly creative. They enjoy painting, making up stories, creating sculptures, and spontaneously singing. They indulge in these activities for the sake of doing them, without necessarily worrying how the results will be judged. In short, they find a great deal of joy in their own sense of creativity.

Very young children are capable of developing skills for critical thinking through creative musical activities and play. Children have to exercise thinking skills when making musical decisions and judgments. These can exercise critical functions used in many other mental processes.

What's happening in the brain during creative processes?

When you choose to do something of your own volition, you are exercising free will. This activates the Anterior Cingulate Cortex and the prefrontal cortex – areas of the brain where your perception of 'me' (or rather 'you'!) is located. Thus, when a child makes a creative decision, they are also helping to reinforce their own sense of self-identity.

Balancing technique with spark

As children grow older, they often begin to be more reticent about creative 'play.' As we age, we tend to develop overactive quality controls.

As older children and adults, we begin to learn ways to make our daubings, scribblings, and scraping more skilled. This acquisition of technique is important, but can sometimes be at the cost of the initial sparks of creativity. We can become self-conscious to the point when we actually stop feeling creatively free. The awareness of technical matters makes us believe that we are not actually very good at what we are trying to do, and therefore the results of our artistic efforts are somewhat worthless.

Be encouraging

There are certain critical times when a boost of encouragement can prevent such doubts taking root. I have spoken to so many people who believe that they are 'unartistic,' that they have 'two left feet,' or that they are 'tone-deaf.' In most cases, it is possible to trace this belief back to a defining moment when an ill-placed word halted their potential.

In my opinion, it is unforgivable to tell a young child they cannot sing, paint, or dance. These are the abilities we are all born with that provide a means of communication, consolation, escapism, and expression beyond mere words.

Making music can create a palpable sense of achievement in a young child. Making up a piece of one's own can bring even more marked feelings of self-worth.

Creative outlets

A child may find it difficult to express internal feelings because of a lack of articulation or a sense of self-consciousness. Music can provide a channel for expression and can build confidence through performing in a controlled environment. It can also create situations where a child can be responsible for making creative decisions that have an immediate outcome.

For a child, the act of writing and playing their own music can have a profound effect on the way they come to perceive themselves.

Creating ownership

The crucial factor in creative play is to generate a sense of ownership. Encouraging creative ownership of artistic works can help the process of 'drawing out' introverted children, as well as giving more confident children a positive outlet for their energies with built-in controls.

Teaching an aesthetic sense involves maintaining and encouraging a child's level of curiosity. Children are naturally curious and creative in their learning habits and play. If a child senses that they 'own' a good piece of musical material, it can engender a huge feeling of achievement. 'Ownership' of created material can lead to greater levels of confidence, self-worth, and pride.

How can you encourage creative thinking?

The Torrence Test is a classic measurement system for creative intelligence. It sets tasks that involve thinking of as many uses as possible for a given object. Children who develop lateral thought habits through musical exercises find such tasks highly enjoyable.

A typical question may ask the child to think of as many different uses as they can for an object such as a paperclip, and to draw the resulting ideas in the boxes supplied. They will start with conventional answers and will often get quite imaginative and surreal. One of the best sets of responses I ever saw to such a test involved using the paperclip as a tool for removing stones from horses' shoes, as well as bending the end out straight and using it as a mobile telephone!

Children become very skilled at such tests by practicing similar exercises themselves and can often display witty combinations of ideas and objects. These skills can prove very useful for lateral thinking processes, and certainly improve with practice.

Through practicing a similar exercise using musical gestures, motifs, or ideas, a child can become skilled at perceiving musical ideas from many different angles too. Composers have to create new combinations of melodic and harmonic ideas while only having 12 notes of the scale to choose from, so they have to be very good at such exercises.

Ask a child to think of as many ways of playing this sequence of notes as they can:

CDEGC

They may propose playing it slowly or quickly. They may suggest playing it backwards, or upside down, or both at the same time! These are all techniques that J.S. Bach used when composing some of the most mathematically complex, and yet profoundly beautiful compositions. Of course, your child may suggest playing all the notes together as a chord!

Listen to TRACK 7 on the CD to hear a demonstration of how these five notes can be put together to create a short, but satisfying piece.

Play me a doodle

There is a simple yet incredibly effective exercise you can try with your own child that will encourage their creative play and help develop lateral thought processes. Children enjoy painting or drawing while listening to music. The following exercise is taken from a project I often lead for the Academy of St. Martin in the Fields – a highly skilled chamber orchestra. The orchestra call it 'Play Me A Doodle,' and it forms a key part of many of their education projects.

Young children between four and seven years of age are given large pieces of paper and lots of paints and colored pens. Members of the orchestra proceed to play pieces of music while the children begin to paint and draw.

After about 10 minutes, the pictures are gathered together and a new class starts. Normally there is an even split in the paintings between figurative pictures and abstract compositions.

The pictures are then presented to the full orchestra, who, under direction from the children, have to 'perform' the pictures as if they were reading from a musical score. The results are often very striking, dramatic, and sometimes hilarious.

What is extraordinary for an adult audience to observe is how the children will have very particular ideas about what musical gestures should match which shapes, and how confidently the children throw themselves into expressing these ideas and into conducting the orchestra! At every stage of this process, most adults would feel self-conscious and would question the quality of what they were producing. Children have no such fears!

All composers use such techniques or games to help them compose. In fact, Mozart invented a game for long stagecoach journeys that renders the players' names into elegant little minuets (Unfortunately my name comes out sounding very heavy-footed, which is probably highly appropriate!)

There are many creative games in the second half of this book that can stimulate creative composition and lateral play. They are appropriate for adults and children alike, and work really well – I'm sure of this as I use them all the time myself.

If a child is regularly encouraged to think and act creatively, they can become highly skilled at lateral thought processes and problem-solving.

Creative music-making can help children find out who they are and who they can become.

Chapter 14

How music can help to develop social skills

In every part of the world and in every culture, a crying baby can expect to be sung to and rocked to sleep. This first reaction with a parent or caregiver is critical in a child's formation of character, identity, and sense of self.

Our early social interactions are primarily musical in nature. They take the form of lullabies, nursery songs, action songs, fingerplays, and short repetitive communications. These form the foundation of how we communicate and create an environment in which future language and expression can be nurtured. Singing is a universal feature of any baby's growth and should never be underestimated as a developmental tool.

Music bonds families and defines societies

Music helps children to find their place in the world, to bond with their family, and become entrained in their culture. It's part of the very DNA of any society, and it's an inescapable part of every culture on earth; while it has practical origins, it is spiritual and emotional in its nature.

Music has always been used to articulate a society's identity, its difference from others, its rules, codes, and beliefs. We use national anthems to separate us from other nations and folk music to define our internal cultures. All cultures possess indigenous music, which has often evolved through the need to keep an aural record of historic events. Therefore music helps us impart historical knowledge and gives a sense of cultural perspective.

Music can help build confidence

Music helps children to interact with others at ages when they may be naturally shy. It can have dramatic effects on self-esteem by enforcing a sense of personal identity, and it can be used as a tool for building leadership skills by putting children in positions of creative control and giving them reasons to play, negotiate, and work together.

When children are given an environment in which to play with their creative ideas, they will advance their social skills at an incredible rate. Their sense of self-worth may be strengthened, and their realization that they are naturally creative will remain a positive influence for life.

Music helps people work together

Music can provoke unconscious physical reactions and can initiate movement functions. It can also be a powerful tool, both consciously and subconsciously, to help people work together.

Historically, music has been used to unify laborious tasks, whether gathering in a harvest, pulling up an anchor, hunting for food, rowing a galley, running a production line, or working in a chain gang. In fact, many forms of music have grown from such practical origins, whether Mozart or Motown, Bach or The Beatles. It is important not to forget that music has inextricable links with movement, and that music is rooted in precise, practical, cultural functions.

Even today, music is used in the world of work. I have worked with a number of big businesses who use music to create a sense of community in the workplace and to make their companies more efficient and better places to work.

Music helps us handle our emotions and state of mind

Listening to music can alter your mood: It can elevate, depress, give space for reflection, help you remember, mourn, celebrate, or forget. Music can articulate love or hate, can help us to remember or to forget, and it is often used to mark births, marriages, and deaths.

Music helps us define our individuality and our differences

Music can help us articulate how we perceive ourselves as being different from others. It is an intrinsic part of human nature to seek new stimuli and we often seek separate musical tastes, as well as searching for those we have in common with others. The various youth movements of the last decades – from early rock 'n' rollers to punk, rave, and 'goth' – have all been based first and foremost around music.

By the time children reach adolescence, it is important for them to be able to define their independence by musically asserting their differences – often to the chagrin of their parents!

Music can be a great way to build your child's self-identity, help them acknowledge who they are, show them that they are creative, and demonstrate that what they express musically has great worth.

Active music activities make children socially confident and ready to learn!

Chapter 15

How music can affect health

I used to tour the world as a cellist with Live Music Now, an organization founded by the late Lord Yehudi Menuhin. Our concerts took place in mental healthcare centers, hospices, AIDS wards, and care homes. As a 17-year-old college student, it was shocking to see just how powerful music could be. Not only could it stimulate physical movements, it could temporarily restore speech faculties and provide an outlet for some very pent-up emotions. It made me realize how little I appreciated music, and how easy it is to take music for granted.

Music is dangerous and beautiful! It can actually cause changes in our bodies – physical, mental, and even chemical changes. Music has long been recognized as a powerful therapeutic tool. Many eastern cultures have known its benefits for millennia; yet again, science is catching up and confirming what we already know. For example, the very latest resonance therapies aren't particularly different from Buddhist chanting.

Music and hormones

London's Chelsea and Westminster Hospital conducted a ground-breaking study of the effects of live music and visual arts in a care environment. The results were staggering: Rather than relying on anecdotal evidence, caregivers could now see solid, quantifiable evidence of the positive effects of music.

Imagine this: It is a Wednesday afternoon in a hospital and a harpist is playing in the day-surgery waiting room. This isn't a private clinic – it's an NHS hospital and the harpist is a central part of the hospital's care policy.

Harpists in waiting rooms? According to the Chelsea and Westminster study, when patients were exposed to live music before day surgery, their cortisol levels dropped through the floor – by as much as 40 percent.

Cortisol is a hormone that causes us to feel stress. By reducing levels of cortisol, live music made patients feel better, cut recovery times, and saved money on drugs; as a result of this effect, the hospital policy is to have daily musical performances in public and care environments.

Music and neurotransmitters

Music doesn't just cut levels of 'bad' chemicals; it can boost levels of 'good' chemicals too. Endorphins are neurotransmitters that help to carry impulses around the brain, and they're responsible for making us feel good: They are one of the drugs the body produces naturally to give us pleasurable sensations. Playing music boosts the production of such neurotransmitters.

In addition to making us feel better, music can also help us sleep. This time the culprit is melatonin, which is known to regulate our sleep patterns. A recent study in Florida discovered that music stimulates the production of melatonin.

In the latter part of this book, great emphasis is placed on the need to associate different pieces of music with a baby's daily routine. Lullabies play a particularly important role, because good sleep patterns are very important for readying the mind for learning and maintaining focus. For example, elementary schoolchildren in Taiwan took part in a recent survey where they listened to 45 minutes of restful music before sleeping. The results showed a distinct improvement in the quality and duration of their sleep patterns.

I find that listening to imaginative, calm symphonic music while reading bedtime stories to my own children seems to help their transition from a busy day mode to a profound sleep. In fact Bach wrote his famous 'Goldberg Variations' for just this purpose.

Long-term effects of music on the mind

Music appears to be able to sharpen young minds, making children quick-witted and mentally coordinated. It also appears to have longer-term mental benefits. Research carried out at Manchester University found that musicians are statistically far less likely to suffer senile dementia than other people.

In the U.S., a detailed survey found that college musicians are emotionally healthier than their non-musical peers. They appeared to have more confidence in tests and significantly fewer alcohol-related problems. When I read this study, I had trouble being sure that the same results would emerge from a U.K. survey!

Music can have powerful effects on the health of the body, and therefore has an effect on general mental and physical wellbeing.

Chapter 16

Windows of opportunity

The phrases 'window of opportunity' and 'magic window' have become commonly used buzzwords when discussing early learning. These terms define certain key stages in development during which children are believed to have a huge potential for acquiring a vast array of complex skills. During such times the brain itself is in a very flexible state, able to form complex links and forge patterns of connections for thought processes and tasks. These connections are responsible for analyzing incoming information and mentally and physically coordinating responses, thoughts, and actions.

During these periods, certain levels of intensive stimulation can have an effect on the physical structure of the brain itself. Some remarkable research has shown that active music-making can effect such physical changes in brain structure.

At birth

The largest 'window of opportunity' occurs at birth, when the child possesses the highest level of aptitude and readiness for stimulation and learning. At birth, a baby's brain is processing information purely to cope with bodily regulation, movement, and sensation. These are obviously essential for their immediate survival.

During this time the three parts of the brain that are seen to be most active are:

• the Brain stem – responsible for bodily regulation

• the Thalamus – responsible for sensation

• the Deep Cerebellum – responsible for movement

At this point, the neural pathways in the brain are in their most formative and flexible state. They are developing patterns of firing sequences to cope with common tasks, while constantly forming new links in reaction to new stimuli. Every incoming sensation or feeling, whether centered on sound, sight, smell, touch, or taste, is a stimulus that causes brain activity.

This period is therefore a critical stage in the foundation and growth of intelligence, sensitivity, personality, and 'musicality.' These neurological processes are linking up with the reflexes a baby already possesses at birth. These are reactions displayed from birth that demonstrate extraordinary genetic programming (there is more detail on these reflexes in Chapter 2).

After the first few months, there is a transition from reflex actions to controlled fine and gross motor movements.

In 1987, the Annals of Neurology published findings by three researchers (Chugani–Phelps-Mazziota) that presented groundbreaking data from PET (Positron Emission Tomography) scans of children's brains. The children observed in the research were between five days old and 15 years of age.

When you combine the results of this study with the results of similar studies, a timeline emerges:

• **By the age of two, a child's brain uses the same amount of glucose as an adult brain.**

> '...by the age of three, brains of children are two and a half times more active than the brains of adults and they stay that way for the first decade of life – biologically primed for learning...'
> (White House report)

• **By the age of four, a child's brain uses more than twice the glucose** of an adult brain.

- By the age of six, a child's brain has more neural links than it will ever have at any other point. It uses a huge amount of oxygen and glucose to feed a dramatic period of mental growth and physiological development.

- By the age of nine, the brain levels of glucose metabolism begin to fall.

Areas of the brain that are active require more energy. The source of this energy is glucose; hence it is safe to assume that a huge amount of information is being processed when glucose metabolism levels are high.

Music research

In Düsseldorf, a study of 60 people found that physical changes to the structure and the shape of the brain – caused by active music-making – primarily occurred in people who began musical training before the age of seven.

It seems that at the age of six, children enter a critical year during which the brain chooses the circuits and pathways it considers most important to maintain and develop for the future. This is therefore a great age to introduce quite complex musical coordination exercises, and it is also a great time to consider studying a sophisticated musical instrument.

There does not seem to be a specific cut-off point for key learning periods, though: Developmental phases accelerate and decelerate at particular ages.

Chapter 17

A summary of the benefits of music

Active participation in music assists all forms of personal growth, both mental and physical. It builds many skills essential for everyday life and can aid mental development and learning processes. In fact, it appears that music can encourage the brain to physically alter its very structure as it grows.

Involvement in music helps all ages define their own identities, and music can create associations between groups and helps to forge links between people. In other words, music helps children to build essential social skills.

Music can create great feelings of self-worth – being creative in an artistic discipline can have a profound effect on the way children perceive themselves, and can even benefit health.

Music can change the shape of your brain

Regular participation in musical activities stimulates the development of the brain and improves mental functions.

The very plasticity of the brain, the way it shapes itself, can be positively affected by repeated musical activities. The conduit of information between the two brain hemispheres, the corpus callosum, grows larger as a result of being musically stimulated, and the pathways of communication between areas of the brain are more comprehensively connected together.

Musical activity aids the creation of new synaptic pathways, enabling multi-tasking and general creative thought, and it promotes cognitive development and helps abstract thought processes.

Music promotes language skills

All language is musical, and music itself is a language unbounded by vocabulary. We all become linguistically confident through using an extraordinarily sophisticated set of musical tools related to pitch, rhythm, timbre, and dynamics.

Hearing, interpreting, comprehending, and engaging in dialogue are parallel processes in music and language. Music, though, is always our initial system of communication – our musical 'processors' are the filters through which we learn to make sense of the spoken word – and music prepares the groundwork for the building of linguistic skills, speech, comprehension, expression, and vocabularies.

Therefore, consciously and unconsciously stimulating children through music can help advance language skills at all stages of childhood development.

As well as the obvious benefit in helping to learn language, music also plays a critical role in the foundations of communication and expression, and therefore plays a critical role in the development of character and personality.

Because music is the foundation that underpins the learning of language and comes more naturally at an earlier stage, children can find a means of expression through music well before they become linguistically confident.

Learning an instrument can develop mental functions

Learning to play an instrument can help enhance spatial-temporal abilities in children, where merely listening to music often does not produce the same effects, despite early evidence to the contrary.

Spatial-temporal abilities are critical for being able to sequence information and ideas, for advancing analysis and reasoning, building higher mathematical skills, refining visual interpretation and comprehension, as well as helping with planning skills.

Instrumental study requires determined periods of concentration and regular study, so, on a basic level, it helps to develop self-discipline and time-management techniques. It necessitates comprehension and communication of sophisticated concepts. Instrumental study also stimulates fine motor abilities, regulation of breathing, and extended memory techniques.

Playing music often involves the comprehension and interpretation of musical notation, a highly sophisticated graphic language that is best learned in the context of discovering how to play a musical instrument. Young children learn to read music almost imperceptibly, and quite naturally, as a by-product of learning their way around their chosen instrument. Conversely, adults who try to learn music seem to find it more difficult.

Music stimulates movement and develops physical coordination skills and controls

Children are constantly moving – try keeping your child still, really still, for any length of time and you'll see what I mean – and this is generally a good thing. Movement is the key catalyst for the development of kinesthetic coordination skills, and music is one of the main stimulants to controlled movement. These key kinesthetic coordination skills promote sophisticated mental coordination skills and essential inhibitory controls.

Therefore, music can also help control concentration skills and enables children to focus on learning activities for longer periods.

Music helps develop memory skills for learning and retention

Humans are capable of committing huge libraries of melodic and timbral information to memory. That makes music an exceptionally efficient vehicle for advanced memory functions and processes.

Retention of purely literary information is much harder and more labor-intensive. However, when text-based information is combined with music, it can be learned far quicker and be retained for far longer periods.

Try this quick test: See if you can speak the lyrics of one of your favorite songs without hearing the music, and you'll be amazed at how easy it is to lose your place, forget words or lines, and generally 'lose the plot.' Now try just remembering the song and the lyrics flow naturally along with the music.

Music helps us to understand math and science

Music is an essential tool for teaching sciences, as it naturally expresses the core laws of physics in poetic and emotional forms. A reluctant young scientist can be enthused about the subject when made to realize just how important a role physics plays in music. For example, all properly trained recording engineers have studied the physics of music in great detail and use a whole array of complex meters and measuring devices in their everyday work – they call it a mixing desk!

Music also acts as a great tool for illustrating and teaching complex mathematical concepts to children. Here's just one example: As soon as you start to learn to read music you have to assimilate written rhythms. These are notated by means of mathematical values, and the key to playing these written rhythms correctly is to learn to count. On a more basic level, every rock band in the known universe starts their live performance with '1, 2, 3, 4...' before the band comes crashing in!

Music teaches sophisticated social skills

Music plays a critical role in developing the foundations of personal communication skills and self-expression. It therefore plays a major role in enforcing essential social skills.

Music helps children find their place in the world, bond with their family, and assimilate their culture. Music has always been used to articulate a society's identity; its difference from others, its rules, codes, and beliefs.

Music socially integrates children at ages when they may be naturally shy, and active music-making can increase a child's self esteem. It helps develop a sense of identity and self-confidence, and group skills and teamwork can be learned very effectively through musical models.

Musical activities naturally engender leadership, communication, and team-building skills, and group music-making between people of different ages can promote inter-generational understanding.

Music helps children work together

Music is able to provoke unconscious physical reactions and can initiate movement functions, and it can help people to work together through physical coordination and social empathy.

Music has always been used to unify laborious tasks, whether gathering in a harvest, pulling up an anchor, running a production line, or working in a chain gang. Many forms of music have grown from such practical origins, whether Mozart or Motown, Bach or The Beatles.

Music has inextricable links with movement and it is rooted in precise, practical, cultural functions.

Music can help emotional wellbeing and health

Music can help control moods and can be used to set an appropriate environment or atmosphere for important social functions. Music therapy is deeply effective because music can articulate a huge range of emotions that are sometimes difficult to express using language alone. Music can elevate, depress, give space for reflection, help one remember, mourn, celebrate, or forget.

Music can stimulate the production of pleasure-giving neurotransmitters such as endorphins. Exposure to live music can dramatically lower stress hormones such as cortisol. This means that the body can adjust its own chemical balances through musical intervention rather than through the use of medical drugs.

Music has been proven to stimulate production of the hormone melatonin. Our bodies produce this chemical to enable us to sleep properly. This is possibly one of the reasons why lullabies are so successful for encouraging babies to go to sleep.

A U.S. survey concluded that college musicians are emotionally healthier than their non-musical peers. They reported the musician students generally had more confidence in tests and significantly fewer alcohol-related problems.

Music promotes artistic self-expression and creativity

Creating and playing music brings a great deal of creative satisfaction and pleasure. It can help a child develop an artistic outlook and provides a great means of self-expression. Children are naturally creative in their learning habits and play, and music is a great vehicle for exploring natural creativity as it naturally stimulates a child's sense of imagination and curiosity.

If children create musical material of their own, they often sense a positive feeling of achievement and personal pride. This is obviously invaluable as it can build a positive self-image and personal confidence, as well as developing a feeling of artistic self-worth. Acknowledging, and subsequently enjoying, their own sense of creativity can draw out children who show signs of being introverted.

If a child is regularly encouraged to think and act creatively, they will become more skilled at lateral thinking and problem-solving. Children who develop good lateral thought processes through musical composition exercises find creative intelligence challenges relatively easy and enjoyable.

Through practicing different creative composition exercises, a child can learn to see objects, motifs, or even concepts from many different 'angles' and points of view. This has a positive effect on general problem-solving, advanced mathematics concepts, and personal time management.

Music assists mental development, promotes high-level coordination skills, engenders many social skills, enables creativity and sense of self, and can even be beneficial for your health! Music helps children find out who they are and who they can become.

Chapter 18

PART TWO:
A parent's guide to musical development

When making music with young children, it is really important to set up an environment where creativity can flourish; an environment in which your child feels comfortable and at ease. As a parent, you can really help your child to discover and refine their innate musical skills, whatever your own level of musical expertise. The core elements of any musical activities you explore with your child should be singing, dancing, listening, and playing. These can all be linked together through improvisation, composition, and performance.

The importance of interaction

The emphasis for these activities is always on interaction, rather than instruction. Even the most well-meaning children's music video cannot provide a satisfactory level of interactivity: By its very nature there is no interactive response, so any challenge and stimulus is diminished.

In my view, it is healthiest to encourage a child's natural creativity and help them animate songs and music in their heads. Static images, puppets, and props are useful in this process, and at this stage the emphasis should be on interactivity, playing, and having fun.

A stimulating musical environment

One of the features of human nature that sets us apart from many other animals is our relentless curiosity and our pursuit of new sensation and stimuli. We all have a huge degree of intellectual and artistic curiosity, and an appetite for a constant flow of new sights, sounds, tastes, and smells. It is what makes us play games, paint pictures, travel on vacation, or try the very latest restaurant.

New experiences stimulate a huge degree of brain activity compared to experiences we are already familiar with. We learn to carry out many commonplace tasks automatically, almost subconsciously, unless new elements or challenges are added.

We are hungry for new stimuli for a very good reason: It provides the key to our personal mental growth and development. Music satisfies many of these curiosities and is in itself a tool for psychological and physiological development.

In experiments conducted using animals' brains, applying electrical stimulus to synapses strengthened neural links and made them more responsive. It is believed therefore that children brought up in an environment where their senses receive a high level of stimulus develop many more synaptic links (the bridges between brain cells) than those brought up in a passive environment.

Parents are often made aware of the importance of a stimulating visual environment. Many toys for the crib have bright colors, or sharply contrasting patterns in black and white such as spirals and checks, that can capture a baby's interest. A stimulating musical environment for a young baby could feature the use of lullabies, musical mobiles, nursery rhymes, and interactions with a parent or caregiver where short noises and movements are used.

Conversations and soundplays with a baby rely on contrasting fundamental characteristics of tone (the color of the sound – sometimes referred to as the timbre), pitch (whether the notes are high or low), rhythm, and dynamics (the level of strength, or loudness, of sound). These are some of the core elements of any piece of music you can think of!

Potentially, all sensory learning experiences have the capacity for altering the way the brain organizes itself. New neural links are created with every incoming stimulus. Neural strengthening is essential for learning and reasoning abilities.

Why you should encourage musical activities

• Music is highly effective for drawing children into an activity, both mentally and physically.

• Rituals for learning can be regulated by the use of music.

• Music is a great catalyst for creative ideas – it can provide a comforting structure upon which to project new concepts and reorder existing information.

• Music is sometimes taught by rote. This can distance a child from the very essence of the music, depriving them of the movement and emotion of melody and rhythm.

• Conversely, children can become distressed when presented with too much choice. If you present a child with a few different-colored pencils and a single sheet of paper, they are far more likely to focus on drawing something than if they are presented with a stack of sheets and a huge variety of colors. More importantly, they will enjoy the process far more.

• When writing or improvising music, it is a good idea to set parameters within which the creative work takes place. A good piece can be built from the simplest grain of an idea!

• Creative music-making should incorporate singing, movement, playing instruments (and remember, bashing a tambourine counts as playing an instrument), and listening.

• It should be immensely practical and easy to initiate.

• Successful creative music-making always results when one presents a clear framework with space for children's ideas and a limited set of materials.

Music can be a crucial tool in the development of attentive listening, absorption, and comprehension. As previously discussed, children have a predisposition to be highly creative, and with the right sort of encouragement they are able to compose music with great fluency.

How to use this section of the book

In each age range you will find five different key areas of focus to promote mental and physical development. These include:

• Singing

• Moving

• Listening

• Using instruments

• Creative exercises

Why should I sing with my child?

Singing is the key to our future command of languages. It is the way we initially communicate and sets the pattern for the acquisition of language abilities; through basic melody, we learn subtle inflections of expression long before we acquire a vocabulary. Singing activates parallel brain circuits to those used for speech and the interpretation of speech.

We are all born within a vast heritage of singing and songs, and for each of Shakespeare's *Seven Stages Of Man* there are connected vocal traditions. From the lullaby to the lament, we use singing to mark our progression through life. Singing is always a social activity, even when conducted alone – you connect with yourself when you sing, in a way that talking to yourself really can't do!

Lullabies strengthen the bond between parent and child. A lullaby settles a child through its soft repetitions, the comfort of a familiar caring voice, the gentle rocking motion in synchrony with the word patterns (a motion not unlike the fluctuating movements experienced in the womb) and through the emotions and expressions of love that can be carried in the lyrics (and more importantly, through the emotional pitch of the voice).

Nursery rhymes are the most effective way of rapidly developing your child's vocabulary, grammar, and syntax, as well as imparting valuable lessons about the dangers of falling off things – surely a very important thing to learn when you're moving from crawling to crashing around on your own two feet!

Many nursery songs feature huge lists of information that help to teach information that will be in constant future use. Numbers, days of the week, the alphabet, and so on will be learned quickly and permanently through music.

Fingerplays will help enforce early co-ordination skills, such as the association of abstract groups of things to physical numbers.

Perhaps the most important feature of singing is its ability to bond people together socially. All cultures use group songs to mark significant occasions. A thousand people can sing together and make themselves understood, whereas two people will have trouble being understood if they talk at the same time.

In one of the schools I work in, the entire day-to-day school business is conducted through song, from calling the roll to giving notices in assembly. This may seem ridiculous to an outsider, but the school used to have discipline problems – and those problems have all but disappeared!

Why should my child move?

From birth, babies need to experiment with a huge range of movements in order to build brain and body coordination. They should be encouraged to crawl, to reach for objects, to roll about, to rock to and fro, and to stretch.

It seems that children have an almost Pavlovian reaction to musical stimulus! Music can assist the development of inhibitory controls – the ability to have full command of our movements.

Physical warm-up games help build bodily control and motor movement skills in children – an essential part of confidence-building and vital to the high levels of coordination necessary to be a musician. It is important that children are given the opportunity to practice their 'impulse controls'; this is the ability to trigger and follow their own internal orders.

I frequently use warm-up exercises when working on creative musical projects with large groups of young children. I find that such exercises quickly focus young minds by offering a seemingly simple (yet actually complex) physical challenge, and they definitely trigger a creative mood in the participants. In many Eastern cultures, a physical warm-up in time to music is regarded as an essential component of any educational, creative, or industrial environment.

Young children will often enjoy freely interpreting music through movement. They have little self-consciousness about expressing themselves through dance and are often capable of creating highly artistic spontaneous physical reactions to music. If a child is to begin learning a musical instrument, it is crucial that they have levels of controls in place in order to focus their attention in a lesson.

What you will find in the following chapters:

• **Exercises with babies**

• **Mental exercises**

• **Warm-ups**

The importance of instruments

There is one form of musical activity that, by its very nature, combines many forms of mental and physical development. That activity is, of course, playing a musical instrument. I believe that playing an instrument generates so many coordination challenges and so many neurological stimuli that it should be an essential part of any child's development.

In the following chapters you will find plenty of information on buying instruments for toddlers, advice on the transition to conventional instruments and focused study, and a guide to all kinds of instruments that you can make at home with your children.

Learning an instrument can constitute one of the transitions from music in the home to skills learnt and mastered outside the home environment. Even if you are a skilled instrumentalist yourself, it can be far more effective to have someone else teach your children an instrument. I believe the serious application that is required for the technical mastery of an instrument can detract from the environment of creative play one may have established in the home.

Why listening is vital

I don't believe that children get any smarter simply by listening to music – but I do think that listening can be highly enjoyable, very relaxing, or stimulating and is a useful way to expose your child to the maximum amount of musical influence possible.

Where listening activities are suggested in the following chapters, they tend to be active exercises involving creative thought or play with the music acting as a stimulus to further activities. Children can get wonderfully partisan about what music they want to listen to – even from the age of two. This is a great way for them to feel their individual opinions are having an effect, where they may not in other areas.

The importance of composition and creative activities

Music is the perfect vehicle for unleashing a child's creative instincts. Children are predisposed to learn through play, but when they find themselves in the role of author, composer, or creator they can really flourish!

Children gain a huge sense of pride from the smallest creative gesture – the 'I made that' factor can never be overvalued. If you want a child to learn, if you want them to feel great self-worth, then creating music together can be the answer.

When a child is able to mix ideas together to make an artistic gesture or work of their own, they will draw on everything they already know, and will gain new knowledge in the process.

I have seen children transformed by the confidence that creative music-making can bring. If you show a child that they can compose their own music – and every child can! – they will gain a level of pleasure and confidence that is hard to match in any other area of music study.

Chapter 19

Prenatal: from conception to birth

When a baby is conceived, an incredible chain of events begins: In the early stages of fetal development, a process called neurogenesis begins. This is the formation of the first brain cells and the rudimentary connections between those cells.

• At three weeks, a baby's ears begin to develop.

• At six weeks, a baby's heartbeat can be detected.

• At seven weeks, the main sections of the brain are visible in scans.

• At eight weeks, nerve endings develop on the baby's skin.

• At ten weeks, it is believed that the neurons in the brain start to develop synapses, the links that transmit information between brain cells. The rate of growth at this stage in the baby's development is truly staggering: An unborn baby grows between 100,000 and 250,000 cells every minute.

• At 12 weeks a baby has active nerve endings all over the body.

• At 16 or 17 weeks, a baby has begun to develop his or her hearing skills.

- At 20 weeks, a baby has functional hearing and will demonstrate responses to noise.

- At 24 weeks, the baby's heart rate will change in response to patting and stroking. The baby analyzes sounds, displaying a 'what was that?' response. Loud sounds – particularly sudden loud sounds – will result in an increased heart rate, but when a baby becomes used to a particular sound this response switches off and only new or unexpected sounds will produce the same response.

- At 25 weeks, the brain undergoes a rapid phase of cortex development, although there are still large areas of the brain that have yet to come online.

- By 26 weeks, a baby can hear a range of sounds – albeit fairly muffled ones! – beyond the background noise of the womb itself.

- By 36 weeks, a baby is capable of memorizing pieces of music that it hears frequently, often to the extent that he or she will recognize that music after birth.

Why you should sing to your unborn child

The unborn baby is exposed to a huge range of sounds in the womb. The amniotic fluid surrounding the baby transfers the mother's bodily sounds very effectively – heartbeats, the sound of blood running through veins, digestive sounds, physical movements, the sound of breathing and so on. It's not exactly quiet in there! When a baby is in the womb, sound from the outside world must compete with a level of noise that is surprisingly high. According to research conducted in 1995 (R. M. Abrams), 'airborne' sounds at lower frequencies need to be louder than 60 decibels if they have any chance of being heard above the symphony of gushing, thumps, and gurgles surrounding the child. The volume of a normal conversation is 60-70 decibels; by comparison, a vacuum cleaner tends to run at around 80 decibels.

For an unborn child, one sound rules them all: The sound of their mother's voice, whether speaking or singing. It doesn't sound the same as it does in the outside world, because the sound is transmitted internally as well as externally, but the intonation – the rise and fall, intensity and contour will be crystal clear. The patterns of the mother's speech will already be acclimatizing the baby to the codes of its mother tongue.

To a baby, a mother's voice is:

• **Comforting**

• **Interesting and stimulating**

• **A crucial future reference point**

Lullabies

Every culture uses lullabies to settle babies to sleep. Research some lullabies that may have been used in your own upbringing, and learn some others connected with your own culture. Don't forget that a lullaby can also calm an overstressed parent!

When you're relaxing, listen to a favorite recording and hum along with it. You don't have to be the world's greatest singer or turn in a perfect performance: It's all about helping the baby to grow accustomed to the tone of your voice and to relax along with you. Many mothers-to-be find that this is the point in the day when they notice that the baby begins to get really active. As a starting point we've included a beautiful ballad by Grieg on the accompanying CD – listen to TRACK 8 to hear it.

Recommended further listening

Schubert	'Weigenleid' D.498
James Taylor	'Sweet Baby James'
The Beatles	'Goodnight' (from *The White Album*)
Air	'All I Need'
Lemonjelly	'The Staunton Lick'

Stimulate or settle

Music serves two distinctly different purposes at this stage of development, either to stimulate or to settle.

A stimulating sound is usually interesting or unfamiliar. Such sounds help the early stages of learning, and may help development of synaptic pathways in the brain. A baby's heart rate will change in response to new auditory experiences. For example, it will slow as the baby analyzes a new sound – but loud, sudden sounds will increase the heart rate, and may make the baby flinch. This is primarily a defence mechanism, and it's very noticeable at birth when the baby grabs at thin air in response to sudden noises. This is a reflex essential to survival in the wild, as is the habit of turning towards a sound (the signal of a possible threat) which babies display soon after being born.

When sounds become commonplace, the baby will not react to them as dramatically. Only changes in sound provoke a change in movement or heart rate as babies respond hungrily to novel stimuli. (A baby is already building a library of sound memories that will prove invaluable for helping him or her deal with the monumental challenges of life outside.) For a baby, relaxing sounds are essentially repetitive, familiar and gentle. Of course, these are the key elements of any lullaby.

I feel it is very important at this stage that you do not feel obliged to listen to certain types of music through a sense of obligation. We have compiled various lists of suggested listening, which are presented throughout the book; these are not intended to be mandatory or prescriptive – they are simply a starting point. I have friends who filled their stereos with very worthy classical recordings during pregnancy. There is nothing wrong with this, with one key exception: If a piece of music sets you on edge rather than relaxing you, it sends a clear chemical and emotional message to an unborn child.

Listen to the music you want to listen to, not what you feel you should be playing to the baby. If you are truly relaxed while listening the baby will respond to this and learn the same response. For example, in Chapter 11 I mentioned a survey that proved that babies not only remember music from before they were born, but also learn their mother's reaction to the music too. The research examined the change in heart rate displayed by babies when presented with the music to a soap opera watched frequently by the mothers before the birth of their children.

If you often enjoy a relaxation routine that uses music you like, your baby will learn to associate the sounds with the chemical changes occurring in your body when you relax. For example, you may enjoy listening to jazz while relaxing with a cup of tea – your baby will learn your response to this music as you calm down.

During the last trimester, it is worth introducing the baby to particular songs or tunes that you find relaxing. Sing or play the same material to your unborn child each evening if possible. You may well find that after the baby is born, your baby will remember the song and will settle quickly when she hears it again.

Music and routine

You may want to attempt to devise your listening patterns to match different parts of a daily routine. By setting some clear musical cue points for different times and activities, you may help your baby comprehend and adapt to the different parts of a day. Many systems for helping babies establish regular sleeping and feeding patterns involve creating a pattern to the day that meets their needs, while becoming a comforting routine to follow.

After the baby is born, the music you listened to can help structure transitional activities and care routines. It is most useful for waking and settling, bathing, traveling, and general bonding.

Prenatal listening and postnatal development

In Chapter 9 we discovered that prenatal music activities appear to help postnatal coordination and physical skills. In a scientific study, babies in the womb were exposed to between 50 and 90 hours of musical material; these consisted of short musical elements, such as combinations of notes and short phrases that built in complexity over the duration of the pregnancy.

The babies exposed to these musical elements appeared to be able to make faster progress in certain abilities than a control group. Their prespeech emerged earlier than a control group, as did their hand-to-eye coordination. They learned to mirror facial expressions sooner, and were quicker to hold the bottle with both hands.

If you want to try such techniques, you may want to structure your listening in such a way that it begins with simple repetitive musical elements and builds up to longer, more complex pieces. I would suggest trying music that you may enjoy yourself, where the structures employed in the pieces range from simple to complex. It is also worth trying to source the best possible recordings - I've selected a few CDs below where the players have delivered some truly stunning performances. These are also recordings that you will love, and your children are very likely to enjoy long after they are born!

You could start with piano music by the Italian composer Ludovico Einaudi, such as *Le Onde*. This album is very beautifully paced and ambient. It also has a reputation, in our house, for being a surefire way to calm a newborn baby!

CD:	*Le Onde* by Ludovico Einaudi
Label:	Ricordi 74321397022

You may want to progress to music that has a faster pace and more rapid harmonic changes, such as the 'Keyboard Sonatas' by George Frideric Handel. There is a definitive recording by the jazz pianist Keith Jarrett that is full of an infectious level of vitality.

CD:	*Handel Keyboard Suites* by Keith Jarrett
Label:	ECM 4452982

Carrying on with keyboard instruments, you could build up to foot-tapping ragtime and jazz piano music. My children love music by Scott Joplin, Art Tatum, and Jelly Roll Morton, and I would challenge you not to love it too!

CD:	*Fingerbreaker*
Label:	Decca 4604992

Movement

If you are listening to music and you notice the baby kick, try gently touching the area of impact and saying 'kick, kick, kick!' Some babies 'learn' to join this game and will play along and kick on cue.

Using instruments

If you play an instrument at home, see how the baby reacts when you play. The baby may feel motionless during the music, and may move when you stop. Some instruments send vibrations directly through your body to the baby, and sounds in the middle range of frequencies are likely to reach your child most clearly. Instruments that connect in some way to the body will transfer a great deal of sound; a guitar will carry very well!

Even if a baby cannot hear an instrument, it will feel the vibrations from the instrument. A mother-to-be playing the cello will be giving her baby a huge amount of interesting sonic stimuli! The best instrument of all, though, is your voice. The sound travels internally as well as externally, and is utterly fascinating to an unborn child. As mentioned previously, vocal reference is one of the techniques babies use to bond with their mothers; the more you sing, the better.

Writing your own lullabies

Why not try to make up a lullaby for your baby? Don't be self-conscious about your voice or your performance; to your baby, your voice is a wonderful sound. What you sing doesn't have to scan perfectly or even rhyme – it doesn't even need words! If you find composing a song difficult, here are some pointers to get you started. There are four tracks on the accompanying CD that will help – each one is a simple accompaniment pattern that you can sing along with.

TRACK 9: Lullaby accompaniment 1
TRACK 10: Lullaby accompaniment 2
TRACK 11: Lullaby accompaniment 3
TRACK 12: Lullaby accompaniment 4

When you begin making up your tune, don't try to use too many notes or words. Repetition is the key to a successful lullaby. The more your lullaby repeats patterns of words and phrases, the better. Remember, at this stage babies are lulled by repetitive noises; don't try to compose a complex song with clever lyrics and a difficult tune. A lullaby is not trying to stimulate; it is trying to calm and settle the baby. So keep it simple, quiet, personal, and repetitive!

Let's write a lullaby!

Use the baby's name as a starting point for any lyrical material. First of all, decide which syllable in your child's name has the most emphasis. If the emphasis is on the first syllable, for example Caroline (CAR-o-line), the melody will sound good if it falls away from this point. If the natural emphasis point is later in the name, such as Anastasia (a-na-STA-si-a), build the melodic line up and then let it fall away from the central syllable.

Try speaking the name while you click a beat with your fingers

   Ca – ro -line

Then see what it sounds like if you repeat the name:

   Ca – ro -line, Ca – ro -line

Then build in a simple reference to sleeping:

   Ca – ro -line, Ca – ro -line, go to sleep

Now match the words with a simple melody that follow the rhythms and shapes of the words. In this instance the melodic line falls away each time quite naturally. Try singing your line over one of the accompaniment tracks on the CD.

Now repeat the whole line:

   Ca – ro -line, Ca – ro -line, go to sleep,
   Ca – ro -line, Ca – ro -line, go to sleep.

Make up a third line that is different. It could be another instruction, or an endearment:

Now it's time to close your eyes

The melody for this line could go on a slightly different route from the other lines. In this case I would step to a higher note on 'time,' but aim the phrasing towards 'close.' Now add it to the other lyric and repeat the initial line at the end:

Ca – ro -line, Ca – ro -line, go to sleep,
Ca – ro -line, Ca – ro -line, go to sleep,
Now it's time to close your eyes,
Ca – ro -line, Ca – ro -line, go to sleep.

Try singing with the CD track, until you are happy with its shape. When looking at traditional lullabies you will notice that the melodies are often hypnotically repetitive, the notes cover a small, comfortable vocal range, and the lyrics contain soft consonants.

When trying to settle a baby it is obviously best to keep your voice consistent, use a gentle tone and a small range of notes. Remember that babies are actively stimulated by changes in volume, melody, timbre, and even tempo, so keep it calm and keep it simple!

Incidentally, many composers have written lullabies as 'songs without words,' so if you are really self-conscious about making up lyrics, try listening to these tracks on the accompanying CD:

TRACK 13: 'Cello Lullaby'
TRACK 14: Mendelssohn: 'Song Without Words'

Prenatal music classes

As parents have grown to realize the importance of music in a child's early years, toddler music groups have become commonplace – but there is also an increasing number of prenatal music groups for parents-to-be. These classes are based on the theory that you can bond emotionally with your unborn child through the use of music, and they tend to fall into two camps: Those that promote the use of (primarily classical) recorded music, and those that encourage participants to compose music for the unborn child.

In both cases, the core idea is to perpetuate the use of the music after the baby is born. This is believed to provide a comforting and familiar environment to a young baby, smoothing the extraordinarily dramatic transition from prenatal life to birth.

Chapter 20

Newborn: 0–1 years

When a baby is first born, the contrast between the prenatal environment and the real world is incredible. Music and musical elements play a crucial role in managing the transition, and act as essential components for mental, physical, and social development.

At birth the brain is primarily active in three key regions:

- the brain stem – this regulates the body and its functions;

- the thalamus – this manages sensory information from the environment;

- the deep cerebellum – this determines movement.

In a baby's brain, the neural connections are similar to bundles of uninsulated electrical wiring. As with any electrical circuit, electricity can only be routed correctly once the wires are insulated. The 'insulation' process happens throughout the first year, and is called mylinization.

In earlier chapters we discovered the importance of axons in the brain; in the first year, these axons become coated in a fatty substance that shields them from the surrounding brain networks, enabling them to communicate impulses efficiently. This then allows new neural networks to be formed in response to external stimulation. Music is an excellent source of external stimulation, exciting new combinations of neural activity to light up in the brain.

Singing and the development of pre-speech

From the age of two weeks, babies are already trying to engage with the rhythms of speech and song; at this stage they may move arms and legs in synchrony with the voice of a parent or caregiver. At one month they may begin to play with producing high-pitched intentional sounds.

From two to three months of age, musical 'conversations' with a caregiver can emerge. These are the first signs of musical interaction and are an important component of speech development. You can have long 'conversations' in this manner that contain the features of real dialogue – a baby will start to associate the furrowing of the brow with puzzlement or concern, and will be learning the wide eyes and raised eyebrows that can accompany questioning sounds.

From three months babies often start to experiment with vowel sounds (ooo, eeee, aaa, etc) and cooing sounds. This marks the start of pre-speech vocabulary.

Pitch-matching

Try singing clear, short notes to your baby while maintaining eye contact. Your baby may 'chorus' by finding pitches that fit with your own long notes. At the age of six months, many babies can pitch-match. This is the ability to 'sing back' the note you are singing to them.

Babies learn to converse through this technique. When your baby produces imitative sounds in response to your notes, they are engaging in a dialogue – you are having your first two-way conversations! Early linguistic development is founded upon the use of such games.

Pitch-matching constitutes an essential stage in a baby's development, as it is one of the processes we all use to practice and recognize subtle vocal inflections. Some languages require the speaker to control very fine pitch differences between similar-sounding vocal components to convey entirely different meanings. The listener has to be able to perceive and interpret these subtle pitch differences too. There is a close correlation between these skills and the development of acute musical pitch discernment; indeed, some studies have demonstrated advanced musical pitch recognition skills in speakers of Korean and Japanese, due to the necessity to discern subtle differences in vocal pitches.

Remember, babies are born with an extremely acute sense of pitch, in fact some scientists believe all babies are born with absolute, or perfect, pitch.

Imitation

It is a constant source of wonder to a baby that they can make noises – a lot of noises! Your baby is experimenting with the feel of making sounds. The vocal cords and tongue and mouth shape are all undergoing muscular workouts and experimentation.

Try to get into the habit of imitating the sounds your baby is making so they can hear the effect of their efforts coming back to them. Also, try to prompt your baby with sounds of your own and use facial expressions to match those sounds; you will probably do these things naturally, but it is worth remembering that this is a crucial stage in the development of language and musical sensitivity.

He said 'Dada'!

At around six months of age, your baby may start saying 'dada' and 'mama' to everyone and anyone! Babies are very comfortable with experimenting with pairs of syllables in this way, but may not accurately attribute them to the right object. More of these kinds of words begin to emerge at around seven months – 'gaga, mama, dada, choo choo' and so on.

Try singing highly repetitive songs built around such repetitions – sing along to well-known songs or melodies, using 'ma' or 'pa' so your child can see how you are forming the consonants with your mouth shape.

Clear signaling and signing

By articulating songs with clear signs and gestures, you naturally help a baby with labeling of people and objects with what have been, up to this point, somewhat abstract sounds. From seven months a baby's vocalizations will begin to be more accurately linked to objects. However, it will probably take a few months from this point for a baby to accurately address their parents as mama and dada (when they are around nine months old) – so don't be offended!

First songs

At around seven months a baby can produce spontaneous vocalizations, in which you may discern distinct melodic shapes. Try to sing these back to the baby as accurately as you can with encouraging body language.

At nine months of age babies often demonstrate active responses to familiar songs. A baby will show strong indications of preferred songs by the tone and intensity of their responses. Find ways to respond instantly when you feel your baby is demonstrating preferences.

From ten months, short experimental 'sentences' and vocalizations of linked sounds begin to emerge. Again, these should be responded to with great enthusiasm – babies respond positively when given such encouragement.

Why lullabies are important

All cultures have lullabies! A lullaby is the most natural way to ease a baby to sleep as it uses the comfortable familiarity of your voice and a gentle motion that emulates the more weightless prenatal environment.

A baby is soothed and comforted by being taken back to this state, particularly if you are able to use a melody familiar to the baby from before they were born. A lullaby is the perfect way for a baby to be comforted by a parent's voice without being over-stimulated.

Every culture uses lullabies, and despite language differences they are remarkably similar in their structures, musical contents, and emotional intentions. Here are a few recommendations (the titles alone read like poetry!):

Bye Baby Bunting	UK
Rockabye Baby	UK
Hush Little Baby	USA
Roundup Lullaby	USA
Here Take This Lovely Flower	USA
Come To Your Daddy	Canada
Acalanto	Brazil
Dorme	Brazil
He Punahele	Hawaii
O Can Ye Sell Cushions	Celtic
Sov Du Lilla Videung	Sweden
Sousambella	Greece
Nanita Nana	Spain
Duérmete Mi Niño	Spain
Romansch	Switzerland
C'est La Poulette Grise	France
Schlaf, Kinlein, Schlaf	Germany
Fi La Nana, E Mi Bel Fiol	Italy
Rozinkes Mit Mandlen	Yiddish
Lamma Roohi Bit-Dummak	Lebanon
Bai Bai Bai Bai	Russia
Omo	Nigeria
Nyandolo	Kenya
Thula Thula	South Africa (Zulu song)
Be Still My Child	South Africa
Bébé Kolela Te	Congo (Lingala language)
Do Doi	Indonesia (Sumatra)
Juru Panjar	Indonesia (Bali)
Sakura	Japan
Edo Komoriuta	Japan
Yao Yah Yao	China (Mandarin)

You should try to sing lullabies whenever putting your baby to sleep. A lullaby invariably includes gentle movements. Make sure these co-ordinate with the pulse of the song and that they are very gentle. Sometimes, being looked at while being sung to can overwhelm babies; it can be too much focus and attention all at once!

Of course you shouldn't forget that a lullaby can also be great for calming down an overstressed parent!

Don't be intimidated by the idea of making up your own songs for your child. Writing your own lullaby can be really easy, even if you're convinced that you are not musical – see Chapter 19 for some ideas to get you started (there are accompaniment tracks on the CD to sing along with too, which should help you make up your own lullabies). Here are a couple of traditional lullabies to try with your baby:

'Hush, Little Baby'

> Hush, little baby, don't say a word,
> Mama's going to buy you a mockingbird.
>
> And if that mockingbird don't sing,
> Mama's going to buy you a diamond ring.
>
> And if that diamond ring turns brass,
> Mama's going to buy you a looking glass.
>
> And if that looking glass gets broke,
> Mama's going to buy you a billy goat.
>
> And if that billy goat won't pull,
> Mama's going to buy you a cart and bull.
>
> And if that cart and bull turn over,
> Mama's going to buy you a dog named Rover.
>
> And if that dog named Rover won't bark,
> Mama's going to buy you a horse and cart.
>
> And if that horse and cart fall down,
> You'll still be the sweetest little baby in town.

You can hear a version of this lullaby on TRACK 15 of the accompanying CD – try singing along with it.

'Shenandoah'

Shenandoah, I long to hear you,
Away, you rolling river,
Oh, Shenandoah, I long to hear you,
Away, I'm bound away,
'Cross the wide Missouri.

Shenandoah, I love your daughter,
Away, you rolling river,
I'll take her 'cross the rolling water,
Away, I'm bound away,
'Cross the wide Missouri.

Shenandoah, I long to hear you,
Away, you rolling river,
Oh, Shenandoah, I long to hear you,
Away, I'm bound away,
'Cross the wide Missouri.

There's also a recording of this traditional song on the CD that accompanies this book – listen to TRACK 16 and sing along! It can also be fascinating to listen to how other composers have composed lullabies for their own children – listen to TRACK 17 to hear Schumann's beautiful 'Traumerie' ('Daydream'). Here are some more ideas for further listening:

Brahms	'Lullaby'
Fauré	'Berceuse' Op. 16
The Beatles	'Goodnight' (from *The White Album*)

Making up songs for regular tasks and care routines

Children grow to love songs that are used for routines. These can include bath songs, feeding songs, sleeping songs, game songs, traveling songs, and dressing songs. Because young children often find the concept of time very difficult to understand, these songs help to articulate the structure of the day and are worth building into your baby's daily environment well in advance. It is easier to explain the structure of a day by articulating regular, landmark events rather than time concepts. Music is a great tool for building such structures.

'Task' songs are most effective when they have been introduced very early on. They cover transitional periods – moving from one part of the day to another, changing from bedclothes to daytime clothes, dirty to clean. They become very efficient systems for enforcing good care routines. As your baby grows up, they will remember that a washing song comes after the bathroom song, and that the toothbrush song and pajama songs are connected in some way! Take care to grade the songs so they leave the child in the right physical and mental state for the activity. If you are getting your child ready for bed, you obviously don't want to use something too fast, loud, or bouncy as the high energy levels will have nowhere to dissipate!

Regular activities can be made to fit well-known tunes. For instance, the tune of 'Here We Go Round The Mulberry Bush' is extremely versatile for this purpose. Try to build practical information into the song as well as some facts or daily information. For example:

> This the way we wash our hands
> Wash our hands
> Wash our hands
> This the way we wash our hands
> On a cold and frosty Monday

Or maybe:

> On a lovely sunny Sunday

Or

On a grey and rainy Friday

When your baby is watching you get ready in the morning you could insert more detail about the activity to make the lyrics more sophisticated:

This the way we brush our teeth
Up and down
So they're clean
This the way we brush our teeth
So they're gleaming in the morning.

A seemingly simple song can carry a lot of sophisticated information with just a little creativity. You are enforcing a strong routine; good care habits and fine motor skills while at the same time teaching opposites, days of the week, and the seasons!

Try making songs for other transition activities such as getting dressed, going shopping, waiting for the bus, driving in the car, feeding, or getting ready for bed.

Young children love to have things repeated *ad nauseam*, so, for your own sanity you may want to vary the tunes that you use! For instance, at bedtime try the following words to the tune of 'Teddy Bear Teddy Bear':

'Teddy Bear'

Teddy Bear, Teddy Bear, go upstairs.
Teddy Bear, Teddy Bear, say your prayers.
Teddy Bear, Teddy Bear, switch off the light.
Teddy Bear, Teddy Bear, say Good Night.

Movement songs for your baby

Babies are born with incredible inbuilt reflexes. They will flinch and grab with their hands when startled and will simulate a walking motion when held upright with feet touching a flat surface. From one month old, a gradual transition begins that transfers movements from being reflex actions to being controlled.

From two weeks of age, a baby may try to match their movements to sounds around them. As mentioned previously, babies may move arms and legs in synchrony with the voice of a parent or caregiver. At one month old, babies begin to notice their hands. They are constantly discovering that their fingers and toes are fascinating, and they soon begin to realize that they can actually move these digits themselves.

The development of bodily movement forms an essential stage of mental and physical coordination processes. Physical movements are only controllable with a sense of inner pulse, just as languages can only be mastered with a sense of pitch. As explored earlier in this book, we are born with many rhythm mechanisms already in place, just as we are all born with an extraordinary sense of pitch. Music can help regulate these inner senses of pulse and can therefore help to advance physical dexterity, to develop kinesthetic coordination, and thus assist in building mental development.

So, from birth, babies need to be able to experiment with a huge range of movements to be able to build mental and physical coordination. As babies grow they should be encouraged to crawl, to reach for objects, to roll about, to rock to and fro, and to stretch. Using music as a soundtrack to such activities can help you to pace the rate of assisted movements and exercises, and will help to create early associations between aural cues and related movements.

Children react to musical cues without necessarily having to interpret what they are, or what they mean. Babies will sway in time to songs; toddlers like to skip to bouncy music, and will tend to clap along to strong march-style beats. Ten-month-old babies may try to physically imitate other people's movements. By the time a baby is a year old, they will enjoy trying to mirror what a parent is doing – whether brushing their teeth or cleaning the floor!

This is therefore a great time to teach some motor skill development. Basic movements with songs are especially popular with children from this age.

Music moves us, and makes us want to move. As we grow, we learn to control these instinctive movements. Music is a great tool for refining inhibitory controls – that is, the ability to have full command of one's movements. As children grow up, they enjoy playing music games where the main idea is to react to a musical change of some kind – musical chairs, musical statues, and so on. Children enjoy trying not to get caught out, and this type of play teaches important techniques of self-control and discipline. In later stages, music can be used as a powerful tool for controlling mood and atmosphere without resorting to verbal instructions.

Musical movement exercises for babies

These exercises are for warming up the body, increasing physical awareness, and building general physical and mental co-ordination skills.

'Baby Dance'

Use some calm music for this exercise – we've supplied a sample song on TRACK 18 of the CD. In time to the music, slowly and gently move the baby's arms:

• **up and down, then from side to side, then draw small circles.**

Do the same movements with the legs, and then

• **slowly move the baby's right hand towards their left knee and repeat;**

and repeat with the left hand and right knee. These cross-body movements are thought to assist motor and coordination skills. Many dance companies use these types of exercise at the beginning of rehearsal sessions in order to focus the mind, wake up the connections between different parts of the body, and to sharpen coordination.

Here are the lyrics to 'Baby Dance' for you to sing along with:

'Baby Dance'

We like to start and stop
When we're dancing the day away
We like to start and stop
When we're dancing and playing all day

When we are facing this way we go up and down
And turn to look at you
And when we go dancing round and round
We know just what to do:

Do your dance, do your dance
We stop and start all day
Do your dance, do your dance
We turn in to look your way

We like to twist and turn
When we're dancing the day away
We like to twist and turn
When we're dancing and playing all day

When we are facing this way we go up and down
And turn to look at you
And when we go dancing round and round
We know just what to do:

Do your dance, do your dance
We stop and start all day
Do your dance, do your dance
We turn in to look your way

Music beat

Articulate the beats of a song by clapping or clicking your fingers in time with the pulse. Try to clap with two fingers into the palm of your hand so as not to startle your baby with loud noises! Tap on different parts of the body in rhythm with the song, such as the palms, soles of feet, ears, and nose, etc. You could try singing the following well-known song while articulating the different parts of the body mentioned in the rhyme:

'Head And Shoulders'

> Head and shoulders, knees and toes
> Knees and toes,
> Head and shoulders, knees and toes
> Knees and toes,
> And eyes and ears and mouth and nose,
> Head and shoulders, knees and toes,
> Knees and toes.

Dance together

Hold your baby carefully in your arms while you dance to different styles of music. Take care to support the neck while making any such movements.

Try a wide range of dance music: ragtime, the twist, waltzes, folk dances, marches, reggae music, bebop, salsa, and soul music will all work well. When my oldest daughter first learned to stand, she would very enthusiastically dance by bouncing against my amplifier speaker. However, she would only do this if I was playing rather hardline house music or 1960s soul!

There are three tracks on the accompanying CD for you to experiment with:

TRACK 19: Dance Together 1
TRACK 20: Dance Together 2
TRACK 21: Dance Together 3

Here's some other music you may want to try out:

Bartók	'Romanian Folk Dances'
Tchaikovsky	Anything from *Swan Lake*
Prokofiev	'March Of The Montagues And Capulets' (from *Romeo and Juliet*)
Johann Strauss	'Blue Danube Waltz'
Scott Joplin	'Maple Leaf Rag'
Duke Ellington	'Rocking In Rhythm'
Gene Vincent	'Be Bop A Lula'
Chubby Checker	'The Twist'
James Brown	'I Got You (I Feel Good)'
The Jackson Five	'Rockin' Robin'
Bob Marley	'Get Up, Stand Up'
Chic	'Good Times'
Fatboy Slim	'The Rockafeller Skank'

Interactive songs

Interactive songs involve joining in with movements or sounds at particular points in a song. Babies can easily learn where these cue points occur through repetition. Interactive songs enable a baby or toddler to join in musically while they are still learning to vocalize. They acquire extremely valuable skills through performing such exercises. For instance, the short version of 'Happy And You Know It' is very effective for teaching internal pulse and basic responses.

With a very young baby, you can guide the response by clapping your baby's hands together on cue. Very soon they will enjoy doing this for themselves.

'Happy And You Know It'

If you're happy and you know it, clap your hands! *(clap clap)*
If you're happy and you know it, clap your hands! *(clap clap)*
If you're happy and you know it,
Then you really ought to show it,
If you're happy and you know it, clap your hands! *(clap clap)*

Feel free to invent your own actions to fit this song – for instance you could try stamping your feet. For fine motor coordination you could experiment with;

• **blinking your eyes**

• **wriggling your nose**

• **touching your ears**

Action songs

Marching

These songs use different core rhythmic movements, such as marching, rocking, skipping, and bouncing. In each case, sing the song while leading your baby through the movements. Move your baby's legs in time to the pulse of these songs. When your baby is old enough to support his or her own head weight, help them march around the room with you.

When the baby can sit unsupported from around six months old, they may enjoy banging a basic drum in time with the beats. (Do resist the temptation to use metal saucepans and spoons; after all, an upturned plastic container struck with a wooden spoon is just as satisfying, and will be kinder on your ears!)

'The Grand Old Duke Of York'

The grand old Duke of York
He had ten thousand men
He marched them up to the top of the hill
And marched them down again.
And when they were up, they were up
And when they were down, they were down
And when they were only halfway up,
They were neither up nor down.

'Tom, The Piper's Son'

> Tom, Tom, the piper's son
> Stole a pig and away did run;
> The pig was eat;
> And Tom was beat,
> And Tom ran roaring
> Down the street.

Songs for rocking

Sit on the floor with your legs together, knees raised. Support your baby facing you on your lap. Move your baby gently to and fro to in time to the music. If they are very young, make sure you support the neck properly.

'Row, Row, Row Your Boat'

This is a very well-known song that can have a hypnotic effect on babies. It works best if you gently rock your baby to and fro, forwards and backwards, but can also work especially well when sung at bathtime. You can gently move your baby through the water in time to the song.

> Row, row, row your boat
> Gently down the stream
> Merrily, merrily, merrily, merrily,
> Life is but a dream
>
> Row, row, row your boat
> Gently down the stream
> If you see a crocodile
> Don't forget to scream!

'Seesaw Marjorie Daw'

> Seesaw Marjorie Daw
> Johnny shall have a new master
> He shall earn but a penny a day
> Because he can't work any faster

Songs for bouncing

'Here We Go 'Round The Mulberry Bush'

> Here we go 'round the mulberry bush,
> The mulberry bush, the mulberry bush.
> Here we go 'round the mulberry bush,
> So early in the morning.

The full lyrics for this song can be found on page 216.

'Ring A Ring O' Roses'

This next traditional song can have three different movement patterns; a circular sway, a sneeze movement, and a gentle resting down at the end.

> Ring a ring o' roses,
> A pocket full of posies,
> A-tishoo! A-tishoo!
> We all fall down

'Horsey, Horsey'

To sing this song, sit in a chair, cross your legs and support your baby on your knee. Move your leg in time to the music so your baby gently bounces along with the music.

> Horsey, horsey, don't you stop,
> Just let your feet go clippety clop;
> Your tail goes swish, and the wheels go round –
> Giddy up, we're homeward bound!

Recommended music for quiet times

After all this musical activity you may need to settle your baby down with some gentle, less stimulating tunes! We've included two examples on the CD:

TRACK 22: 'Music For Quiet Times'
TRACK 23: 'Jimbo's Lullaby' – Debussy

Here are some additional recommendations for music that may help the transition from activity to rest.

J.S. Bach   Goldberg Variations
The substantial Goldberg Variations by Bach were composed to cure insomnia – you may find they help lull your baby to sleep too.

Richard Strauss   Metamorphosen
This is a ravishing piece of string music full of wave-like phrase structures and luscious rich harmonies.

Saint-Saëns	'Aquariums'
Rachmaninov	'Vocalise'
Ravel	'Pavane Pour Une Enfant Defunte'
Aaron Copland	Quiet City
Mozart	'Sinfonia Concertante', 2nd Movement
Mahler	'Adagietto' (4th movement of Symphony No. 5)
Delius	'Walk To The Paradise Garden'
Barber	'Adagio For Strings'
Groove Armada	'At The River'
Moby	'Porcelain'
Dusty Springfield	'The Look Of Love'
Pat Metheny	'In Her Family'

Fingerplays

'Fingerplays' are song-based games that use the hands to articulate number-based lyrics as well as to help illustrate actions and characters. They are an invaluable tool for developing incredibly fine coordination and controls, as well as being an unbeatable system for learning facts, lists, and figures. As with many nursery songs, there are frequent references to climbing up and falling down! These songs can help smooth the eventual transition from crawling to cruising and eventually to walking.

Fingerplays help to encode different cultural concepts for counting numbers on the fingers. They also introduce the idea of multiple objects having numerical value. This is something that is easy to take for granted in Western cultures. In Japan for instance, different objects possess totally different types of counting systems. In Taiwan, expressing the number 'ten' is not shown with all fingers extended, it is signed by crossing the index fingers!

Many parents teach their babies basic sign languages. Signing can enable a young child to communicate basic demands before they can articulate themselves verbally.

Fingerplay songs can easily be combined with signing systems such as ASL (American Sign Language), BSL (British Sign Language), or Makaton (a signing system designed to be used with speech).

'This Little Piggy'

This is a good song to distinguish the differences between the fingers.

> This little piggy went to market
> (touch thumb)
> This little piggy stayed at home
> (touch index finger)
> This little piggy had roast beef
> (touch middle finger)
> This little piggy had none
> (touch ring finger)
> And this little piggy cried

(wriggle little finger while describing a circle shape)
'Wee wee wee wee'
All the way home.

'One, Two, Three, Four, Five'

This helps distinguish the fingers and teaches basic number concepts. At first, tap the fingers in turn while singing the numbers. Graduate to gently folding and unfolding the fingers. Eventually children will enjoy trying to do this for themselves.

1... 2... 3... 4... 5... *(While counting on fingers)*
Once I caught a fish alive.
6... 7... 8... 9... 10... *(While counting on the other hand)*
Then I let it go again
Why did you let it go?
Because it bit my finger so!
Which finger did it bite?
This little finger on my right!

Why your baby listens

When babies are born, they are no longer surrounded by the noisy, comforting environment they have grown used to *in utero*. The world outside is much quieter than the environment that cocoons them before birth.

In fact, babies are often settled by what we would consider to be background sounds or 'white' noise. A car engine, a washing machine or the sound of an electric fan can be very comforting to a young baby. It is therefore now possible to buy recordings of the sounds of household appliances on CD to comfort your baby!

Young babies are very sensitive to noise in high registers. They are able to hear harmonics above notes that are way beyond adult perception.

Any note on an instrument is actually a collection of low and high noises grouped together. We perceive these as a single bottom note with a particular texture – it is easy to distinguish between the sound of a flute and that of a trumpet even if they are playing the same note. This is because we hear the harmonics above the bottom note that define the texture of the sound.

For this reason young children can sometimes be quite upset by the sound of high-pitched instruments being played nearby. For instance, a violin has a huge number of upper frequencies present in its basic tone that can be distressing to very young children. We begin to lose our ability to perceive very high notes from only one year of age.

Discriminating sounds

From soon after birth, a baby may try to seek the direction of a sound to locate its source. They are particularly attuned to seek out the sound of their mother's voice. Even at one week of age, it has been shown that many babies can distinguish the sound of their mother's voice as distinct among other voices. They can pick it out from a roomful of other voices. By three months they will physically turn to face a vocal sound.

While in the womb, the baby has already acquired a vast range of information about intonation, pitches, rhythms, and timbre (the color of certain sounds). The color and characteristics of voices that are important to them are very distinct by the time they are born.

The baby is also beginning to learn how to interpret the emotional content of speech patterns. These abilities are at the very core of a baby's innate musicality. Interpreting pitch, rhythm, and timbre are musical skills. This musicianship lies at the heart of the process by which we acquire language skills. Babies are born with the facility to discriminate between all 150 different vocal components that form the building blocks of any human language on earth. When he or she is two months old, a child can distinguish its mother tongue purely from rhythmic information (according to research by Frank Ramus), that is, without any vocabulary or pitch information – this is a phenomenal skill.

At five months an infant can discriminate differences in pitch that are less than a semitone (Olsho, 1984). This will help them pick out very specific melodic information, and is the key to interpreting very subtle vocal inflections. This skill is also essential for being able to sing in tune.

By ten months a baby will be able to distinguish between home accent and regional accent in their own language. Around this time babies also come to comprehend that their name actually refers to them! Name songs can help to reinforce this information and are therefore a useful aid for developing a child's sense of self.

We become intelligent by gathering skills that enable us to learn. Acquiring these skills is utterly dependent upon the development of memories and memory skills. We reference memory to build our knowledge and abilities. Music is an incredible vehicle for large memory tasks and appears to be effective from a very young age. While in the womb, a baby learns to memorize advanced musical information. Research has clearly demonstrated that music introduced after the 30th week of pregnancy can calm a baby's heart rate after they are born – especially if it is associated with a mother's relaxation routine. Babies are incredibly good at memorizing very subtle characteristics of particular pieces of music heard before birth.

Music stimulates many memory functions even before birth, and therefore provides incredible opportunities for early learning. Try to create very detailed songs that carry rich amounts of information. Musical characteristics may well help lyrical content to be stored for later use.

You should try making up songs that repeatedly feature your baby's name, and how it is spelled. Using the letter sounds through the song is a brilliant way of teaching a child how their name is constructed well in advance of them having to learn it. You may find it a good idea to use other essential information such as your address, telephone number, and so on within early songs, as this information will be easily memorized for later use.

Playing with first instruments

My daughter was given a 'babygym' when she was a toddler. It is a contraption with swinging rattles, a truly psychotic light display and an incessant medley of Mozart tunes. The melodies were mangled beyond recognition by the toy's electronic programming. The tunes had missing beats, and a sense of harmony that the most modern of composers would have had problems understanding. I can't help thinking that using it was a more than a little counterproductive...

Babies love musical toys and simple instruments from an early stage. If you are tempted to buy a musical activity center or mobile of any kind, make sure the sounds it makes are as organic as possible; that is, as un–electronic sounding as possible. Wind-up mechanisms often make a more appealing sound as they tend to contain real chiming musical mechanisms; old-fashioned music boxes are great too.

There are some excellent electronic toys available that contain well-produced musical sequences with genuinely stimulating interactive features. Babies can quickly grasp the concept that they need to move an object in some way to make it respond musically. Some of the better 'babygym' products only play tunes and light sequences when moved or struck in some way. This obviously teaches cause-and-effect patterns early on, and it is an important stage in acquiring future instrumental skills.

Introducing basic instruments

From six months, a baby will enjoy using basic instruments. Babies enjoy shaking, rattling, and hitting musical toys with little regard to the resulting noise! They are experimenting with the consequences of their movements and in doing so, are acquiring coordination skills. Rattles are very stimulating for babies, as are bells and shakers. Some musical toys are designed to be wrapped around the wrists; others are for grasping, and can teach basic hand coordination skills.

You should make sure that any instruments you buy sound good, that they are not too loud, and that any effort used to play them is matched with a similar intensity of sound. It is important that the action of making the instrument make a musical noise is reflected in what comes out of it. You're going to be hearing a lot of these instruments too, so it's important that you can cope with the sound they make!

Playing instruments is an excellent way of allowing coordination skills to develop. When you play with your child you are building social interaction skills that will help your child bond with you, and also with their peers when they begin to interact with other babies.

Your baby may enjoy playing instruments in time with favorite nursery songs, pop songs, folk tunes, or classical music. You may want to select music where there are natural gaps for musical events to occur, such as 'Pop Goes The Weasel!' or 'Three Blind Mice,' where there is a strong march beat (such as 'The Grand Old Duke Of York'), or where the instruments you are using correspond to instruments in the tunes – such as bells in a sleigh ride.

Try to encourage your child to play along with your singing, by playing their instruments on the strong beats of the songs. If you are using recordings, don't limit yourself to nursery music. Soul and funk music seem to encourage really accurate drumming.

Certain types of classical dances, folkdances, Motown music, and disco tunes tend to feature 'four to the floor' beats – a strong impact on every beat that is very easy to play with. These particular styles of music evolved for the very reason that they correspond to natural inner pulses to such an extent that it it is very difficult not to tap your foot along in time.

My own children developed a great attachment to 1960s music with a strong beat, by artists such as James Brown and Aretha Franklin that lasts to this day, simply because it was the one type of music that would be sure to get them on their feet!

Recommended listening:

James Brown	'Papa's Got A Brand New Bag'
Aretha Franklin	'Respect'
The Supremes	'Baby Love'
Wilson Pickett	'In The Midnight Hour'

| The Temptations | 'My Girl' |
| Mary Wells | 'My Guy' |

We've also included a track on the CD for you to experiment with – try playing along with the strong beats:

TRACK 20: Playing with first instruments

When your baby can eventually sit up on his or her own, you may want to introduce tuned percussion (also known as pitched percussion), such as xylophones, glockenspiels, or metallophones. Make sure the instrument is suitable – it should have a rich, ringing sound, and the bars that you strike with a beater should not be able to jump off their settings. Obviously it shouldn't have any sharp edges. The beaters used for striking the instrument should be solid and rounded. Make sure the round end cannot be detached with repeated hitting, or even chewing!

Some instruments for older children do have harder edges and corners, so make sure you are buying something that is designed specifically for babies, with safety in mind.

If you are using 'pitched' instruments like a xylophone, experiment with gentle, tonal, classical music to see whether you can play along with notes that match the tunes, and then show your child where these notes are. It is very unlikely that they will repeat patterns with any accuracy, but it is fascinating to note that even young babies have an instinctive preference for certain notes that 'fit' with other notes.

Recommended Listening
Saint -Saëns   'Aquariums' (from *Carnival Of The Animals*)
Notes E and A will fit very well with the beginning section of this piece

Mozart	'Papageno's Aria' from *The Magic Flute*
Mozart	'Horn Concerto' No. 4, 1st Movt.
Steve Reich	'Drumming: Part IV'

Chapter 21

Toddler: 1–3 years

A
t 12 months of age, a baby's brain is already half the size of an adult brain. The Limbic system is developing in the brain, and the primary function of this system is to facilitate free will and choice.

At 18 Months, rapid myelinization (the process of electrical insulation in the neural networks) occurs in the pre-frontal lobes, which creates a sense of self-consciousness. A child can see his or her reflection in a mirror and understand that it is a reflected image rather than another child. At the same time, children begin to understand the concept of numbers. They may say 'more,' or say 'two' when handed a single piece of food or toy.

From 18 months, two separate language areas of the brain also become active. Initially Wernicke's region, which handles comprehension, comes online. This is followed by Broca's region, which is the area that handles general speech skills. There is a short delay between the two different areas becoming functional, which means that it takes time for speech skills to catch up with comprehension abilities. This can be a very frustrating time for toddlers, as they can often feel unable to communicate what they are thinking. However, children love action songs from this point onwards and such songs are a great way of building language skills through movement and music.

By two years of age, a child's brain is using the same amount of glucose as an adult's brain. The glucose is powering thought processes and hence neural development. This is an important period for mental and physical growth and coordination.

Sing!

Between the ages of one and three years, children undergo major mental growth. Music plays a very important role in facilitating this process, and children will begin to demand particular songs as their ability to discriminate becomes stronger and their free will asserts itself. They will begin to experiment and play with patterns of syllables and vowels, while strengthening speech, building vocal muscle tone, and coordinating complex verbal sequences.

At 12 months toddlers will be developing many additional words out of pre-speech vocalizations to add to their previous repertoire, which may have consisted solely of 'mama' and 'dada.' At 14 months toddlers may begin to fit words together in pairs when vocalizing. At a year and a half old, toddlers demand songs to be repeated and appear to love repetitive word patterns.

By two and a half years of age, a toddler will probably be using full sentences in speech and songs. Six months later, songs from the child's surroundings begin to be replicated back in a recognizable form. By this point, children are often very headstrong about songs they do and do not like!

Songs for learning: list and fact songs

These songs will ingrain core information and help to strengthen knowledge of vocabulary for future use. Alphabets, days of the week, and months of the year can all be learned very efficiently to music.

'Alphabet Song'

A – B – C – D – E – F – G
H – I – J – K – L – M – N – O – P
Q – R – S – T – U – V,
W – X – Y and Z
Now I know my A – B – C's
Come and sing along with me!

Listen to TRACK 25 on the accompanying CD for a recording of this song.

'Days Of The Week'

Monday, Tuesday, Wednesday, Thursday
Friday, Saturday Sun-day

'Monday's Child'

Monday's child is fair of face;
Tuesday's child is full of grace;
Wednesday's child is full of woe;
Thursday's child has far to go;
Friday's child is loving and giving;
Saturday's child works hard for a living;
But the child that is born on the Sabbath day,
Is bonny, and blithe, and good, and gay.

'Months Of The Year'

January, February
March and April
May
June
July and August
September, October
November, December

Did you know that 'Here We Go 'Round The Mulberry Bush' also contains the names of all the days of the week? See page 216 for the complete song.

Animal Songs

Children love songs featuring names of animals and their associated actions and noises. Here are some of the best examples your child may enjoy:

'Cows In The Kitchen'

Cows in the kitchen
Moo, moo, moo
Cows in the kitchen
Moo, moo, moo
Cows in the kitchen
Moo, moo, moo
What shall we do Tom Farmer?

Ducks in the dustbin
Quack, quack, quack
Ducks in the dustbin
Quack, quack, quack
Ducks in the dustbin
Quack, quack, quack
What shall we do Tom Farmer?

Cats in the cupboard
Doggies too
Cats in the cupboard
Doggies too
Cats in the cupboard
Doggies too
What shall we do Tom Farmer?

Pigs in the garden
Oink, oink, oink
Pigs in the garden
Oink, oink, oink
Pigs in the garden
Oink, oink, oink
What shall we do Tom Farmer?

Chase them away
Shoo, shoo, shoo
Chase them away
Shoo, shoo, shoo
Chase them away
Shoo, shoo, shoo
That's what we'll do Tom Farmer

Listen to TRACK 26 on the accompanying CD for a recording of this song.

'Old Macdonald Had A Farm'

This song is a great memory exercise. Add an animal sound on every verse:

Old Macdonald had a farm ee-eye, ee-eye oh
And on that farm he had a duck
Ee-eye, ee-eye, oh
With a quack, quack here
And a quack, quack there
Here a quack
There a quack
Everywhere a quack, quack
Old Macdonald had a farm ee-eye, ee-eye oh

Old Macdonald had a farm ee-eye, ee-eye oh
And on that farm he had a cow
Ee-eye, ee-eye oh
With a moo, moo here
And a moo, moo there
Here a moo
There a moo
Everywhere a moo, moo
Quack, quack here
And a quack, quack there
Here a quack
There a quack
Everywhere a quack, quack
Old Macdonald had a farm ee-eye, ee-eye oh

Old Macdonald had a farm ee-eye, ee-eye oh
And on that farm he had a dog
Ee-eye, ee-eye oh
With a woof, woof here
And a woof, woof there
Here a woof
There a woof
Everywhere a woof, woof
Moo, moo here
And a moo, moo there
Here a moo
There a moo
Everywhere a moo, moo
Quack, quack here
And a quack, quack there
Here a quack
There a quack
Everywhere a quack, quack
Old Macdonald had a farm ee-eye, ee-eye oh

Old Macdonald had a farm ee-eye, ee-eye oh
And on that farm he had a pig
Ee-eye, ee-eye oh
With an oink, oink here
And an oink, oink there
Here an oink
There an oink
Everywhere an oink, oink
Woof, woof here
And a woof, woof there
Here a woof
There a woof
Everywhere a woof, woof
Moo, moo here
And a moo, moo there
Here a moo
There a moo
Everywhere a moo, moo

Quack, quack here
And a quack, quack there
Here a quack
There a quack
Everywhere a quack, quack
Old Macdonald had a farm ee-eye, ee-eye oh

You might want to try the following animals too:

cat – meow-meow

sheep – baa-baa

horses – neigh-neigh

'The Animals Went In Two By Two'

This animal song is also great for teaching number concepts. Demonstrate the numbers on fingers as you sing:

The animals went in two by two, Hurrah, Hurrah,
The animals went in two by two, Hurrah, Hurrah,
The animals went in two by two, Hurrah, Hurrah,
The elephant and the kangaroo,
And they all went into the Ark for to get out of the rain.

The animals went in three by three, Hurrah, Hurrah,
The animals went in three by three, Hurrah, Hurrah,
The animals went in three by three, Hurrah, Hurrah,
The butterfly and the bumble-bee,
And they all went into the Ark for to get out of the rain.

The animals went in four by four...
The fat hippopotamus stuck in the door...

The animals went in five by five...
They were so glad to be alive...

The animals went in six by six...
They threw out the monkey because of his tricks...

The animals went in seven by seven...
They thought that they were going to heaven...

The animals went in eight by eight...
Then Noah went to shut the gate...

The animals went in nine by nine...
Then Noah went to cut the line...

The animals went in ten by ten, Hurrah, Hurrah,
The animals went in ten by ten, Hurrah, Hurrah,
The animals went in ten by ten, Hurrah, Hurrah,
If you want any more we can sing it again,
And they all went into the Ark for to get out of the rain.

To tell the story of Noah and the Ark, you could follow this song with 'I Can Sing A Rainbow.'

Surprise songs

Two to three year-olds learn to love anticipation songs with a surprise built in – children like to play at being frightened or surprised! Any song with a crash or a bang works well.

'Round And Round The Garden'

Let your child perform this song and actions with you as the victim – they will love being in control.

Round and round the garden
Like a teddy bear   *(draw circles on the tummy or the palm)*
One step, two steps   *(step with your fingers)*
Tickley under there!   *(tickle gently under the chin or arm)*

'Alice The Camel Has Two Humps'

This is a good song for children to clap along with as it contains some bouncy syncopated rhythms that help develop internal pulse. Also encourage your child to join in with the 'booms' at the end of each verse.

> Alice the Camel has two humps,
> Alice the Camel has two humps,
> Alice the Camel has two humps, so
> Ride Alice, Ride! Boom, Boom, boom.
> Alice the Camel has one hump,
> Alice the Camel has one hump,
> Alice the Camel has one hump
> So ride Alice, Ride! Boom, Boom, Boom.
> Alice the Camel has no humps
> Alice the Camel has no humps,
> Alice the Camel has no humps, so
> Alice is a HORSE!

'Pop Goes The Weasel!'

Encourage your child to clap on the 'pop!'

> Half a pound of tuppenny rice,
> Half a pound of treacle.
> That's the way the money goes,
> Pop goes the weasel!
>
> Up and down the City Road,
> In and out the Eagle,
> That's the way the money goes,
> Pop goes the weasel!
>
> Every night when I go out
> The monkey's on the table.
> Take a stick and knock it off
> Pop goes the weasel!

A penny for a ball of thread
Another for a needle,
That's the way the money goes,
Pop goes the weasel!

All around the cobbler's bench
The monkey chased the people;
The donkey thought 'twas all in fun,
Pop goes the weasel!

'Sausages In A Pan'

Make a noise on the 'bang' by clapping or hitting an instrument.

Five fat sausages sizzling in a pan
All of a sudden one went 'BANG!'

Four fat sausages sizzling in a pan
All of a sudden one went 'BANG!'

Three fat sausages sizzling in a pan
All of a sudden one went 'BANG!'

Two fat sausages sizzling in a pan
All of a sudden one went 'BANG!'

One fat sausage sizzling in a pan
All of a sudden it went 'BANG!'

Listen to TRACK 27 on the accompanying CD for a recording of this song.

Let your children teach you

When your child is very familiar with a song, pretend to get the melody wrong or forget the words you are singing. Your child will quickly pick up the idea of the game and will love putting you right. Children are natural teachers and they enjoy the responsibility of correcting an adult! They don't get many other opportunities, after all.

Move!

At 18 months, children respond to music in a physical and vocal manner; basic action songs are favored from this point. They will also love stomping, skipping, marching, and beating in time to music. They are very aware of the pulse of music by this age and will try to articulate it physically. Music can trigger such movements almost subconsciously.

An adult may find themselves involuntarily tapping a foot in time to a piece of music, where a child may display a whole body reaction. Children can have an incredibly natural conducting style by the age of three, without any formal training. They are often capable of tracking or leading a beat, shaping phrases with the contour of their hand gestures, showing emotional content, and indicating dynamic levels.

One of the tenets of Dalcroze Eurythmics is that we feel emotions through our sensation of muscular contractions and releases, and that the human reveals internal emotions by movement, sound, gesture, and body shape. These fall into three categories: reflex actions, spontaneous actions, and conscious and considered actions.

If we help children practice movement to music frequently, we are providing them with a great outlet for expressing emotions, sometimes at an age when they feel unable to articulate what they feel. Conversely, in expressing oneself through movement to music, emotions can be contained or positively altered.

Being physically active to music in this way helps to fine tune the body's general motor skills and coordination, which in turn refines mental reflexes and development.

At this age, music can provoke children to be physically active, but can also trigger them to sit down and listen quietly.

Music can be very useful in situations where you would like to trigger certain routines or patterns of behavior without using verbal direction. If you regularly sing the same song with your children on the way up to bed, they will happily get into pre-sleep mode when you use it as a cue. The recording of 'Twinkle Twinkle Little Star' on TRACK 28 of the accompanying CD could be used in this way.

Similarly, if you have simple songs to help get washed and dressed in the morning, care routines become easier to manage. Music becomes an excellent tool for handling transition periods smoothly throughout the day. Soon enough, your toddler may learn to initiate some of the songs themselves. You may find yourself being cued to brush your teeth, wash your hands, and so on! Children acquire a great sense of pride from controlling such situations, and music helps them to memorize, structure, and sequence essential tasks.

Sîan Davies, a brilliant children's animateur and leading exponent of the Dalcroze system, uses a system of melodic cues when teaching in a group situation, allowing her very subtly to direct large groups of (sometimes) excitable children without ever raising her voice. If Sîan needs children to stand quietly in their own space before a musical exercise, she simply sounds out the first seven notes of 'London Bridge Is Falling Down.' This has previously been sung by the children with the words 'Find a place and then stand still.' There is always great competition among the children to be the first to respond to the cue correctly. The children quickly react to a descending scale by dropping to a cross-legged sitting position, previously learned as 'Will you please sit down?'

These short melodies are so effective that it is possible never again to have to use the instruction lyrics; one merely sings or plays the appropriate melodic cue on an instrument! Children love turning these exercises around and making up their own cues for adults to respond to. You could try making a very simple version by using a clap to mean 'sit down' and a sung note to mean 'stand up.' Children will enjoy controlling grown-ups through music controls, and it prepares the ground for some sophisticated musical and mental development games.

Movement songs

A song with movement allows a child to 'perform' before their singing voices are fully controllable. This gives them an opportunity to receive praise following a performance despite vocal immaturity or shyness. Children naturally enjoy performing and seem to take the whole process very seriously. I will never forget the occasion when my two-year-old daughter was dancing to a Greek band at a wedding while everyone else was eating. The band finished their number to much applause, at which point she executed a very long, deep bow, clearly acknowledging all the applause for herself...

Movement songs can assist the development of hand-eye co-ordination, and help the child understand how their body moves and functions, as well as teaching left from right.

Don't force your children to sing. They may start by joining you on a chorus; learn to fade your voice out so they take over when the words and melody sound confident. Here are a few examples of songs that work well at this stage:

'Wheels On The Bus'

The wheels on the bus go round and round
Round and round
Round and round
The wheels on the bus go round and round
All day long

The horn on the bus goes beep, beep, beep
Beep, beep, beep
Beep, beep, beep
The horn on the bus goes beep, beep, beep
All day long

The wipers on the bus go swish, swish, swish
Swish, swish, swish
Swish, swish, swish

The wipers on the bus go swish, swish, swish
All day long

The people on the bus go chitter, chatter, chatter
Chitter, chatter, chatter
Chitter, chatter, chatter
The people on the bus go chitter, chatter, chatter
All day long

The baby on the bus goes wah, wah, wah
Wah, wah, wah
Wah, wah, wah
The baby on the bus goes wah, wah, wah
All day long

The bell on the bus goes ding, ding, ding
Ding, ding, ding
Ding, ding, ding
The bell on the bus goes ding, ding, ding
All day long

The wheels on the bus go round and round
Round and round
Round and round
The wheels on the bus go round and round
All day long
All day long

This song naturally lends itself to adaptation. My children love adding animals to the bus: 'The doggies on the bus go woof woof woof', or 'The mice on the bus go nibble nibble nibble'. But their favorite adaptation is, unfortunately, 'The daddies on the bus go snore snore snore...'

'Hop Little Bunnies'

This is a great anticipation action song for older toddlers. The song starts with everyone lying on the floor pretending to sleep. Everyone jumps up on the hopping section, and freezes in position at the end.

See the little bunnies sleeping
Till it's nearly noon
Come and let us gently wake them
With a merry tune
They're so still *(sung slowly)*
Are they ill? *(sung very slowly)*

Hop little bunnies *(suddenly jump up and begin hopping)*
Hop hop hop *(clap and hop at the same time)*
Hop little bunnies
Hop hop hop *(clap)*
Hop little bunnies
Hop hop hop *(clap)*
Hop little bunnies
Hop hop hop *(clap)*

Listen to TRACK 29 on the accompanying CD for a
recording of this song.

'Lou, Lou, Skip To My Lou'

Lou, Lou, skip to my Lou
Lou, Lou, skip to my Lou
Lou, Lou, skip to my Lou
Skip to my Lou, my darlin'!

Lost my partner, what'll I do
Lost my partner, what'll I do
Lost my partner, what'll I do
Skip to my Lou, my darlin'!

Lou, Lou, skip to my Lou
Lou, Lou, skip to my Lou
Lou, Lou, skip to my Lou
Skip to my Lou, my darlin'!

I'll find another one, prettier, too.
I'll find another one, prettier, too.
I'll find another one, prettier, too.
Skip to my Lou, my darlin'!

Lou, Lou, skip to my Lou
Lou, Lou, skip to my Lou
Lou, Lou, skip to my Lou
Skip to my Lou, my darlin'!

Can't get a red bird, blue bird'll do.
Can't get a red bird, blue bird'll do.
Can't get a red bird, blue bird'll do.
Skip to my Lou, my darlin'!

Lou, Lou, skip to my Lou
Lou, Lou, skip to my Lou
Lou, Lou, skip to my Lou
Skip to my Lou, my darlin'!

Flies in the sugarbowl, shoo, shoo, shoo.
Flies in the sugarbowl, shoo, shoo, shoo.
Flies in the sugarbowl, shoo, shoo, shoo.
Skip to my Lou, my darlin'!

Fingerplays

Fingerplays are great musical systems for aiding fine motor skills, as well as reinforcing strong number concepts – a perfect foundation for mathematics.

'One, Two, Buckle My Shoe'

Show the numbers on two sets of fingers, or fingers and toes, and mime the other words.

1... 2... Buckle my shoe	*(lacing motion)*
3... 4... Knock at the door	*(knocking motion)*
5... 6... Pick up sticks	*(gather into your arms)*
7... 8... Lay them straight	*(make straight motions with hands)*
9... 10... A big fat hen	*(make bird wings)*
11... 12... Dig and delve	*(digging motion)*
13... 14... Maids a-courting	*(bat your eyelashes)*
15... 16... Maids in the kitchen	*(stir a pot)*
17... 18... Maids a-waiting	*(yawning motion)*
19... 20... I've had plenty!	*(fling out your arms)*

'Incy, Wincy Spider'

Incy, wincy spider went up the waterspout
('climb' by rotating thumbs to index fingers)
Down came the rain and washed the spider out
(waggle fingers whilst lowering hands, palms facing downwards)
Out came the sun and dried up all the rain
(draw circle shape with hands)
Incy wincy spider went up the spout again.
(repeat index to thumb rotations)

'Mary's At The Cottage Door'

Show the numbers on your fingers and mime the other actions.

One two three four	(count on fingers)
Mary's at the cottage door,	(knock with one hand, mime holding a plate with the other)
Five six seven eight	(count on fingers)
Eating cherries off a plate.	(mime eating cherries from your plate)

'Magpies'

One for sorrow	(mime sad face holding up one finger)
Two for joy,	(smile holding up two)
Three for a girl	(three fingers with...)
Four for a boy,	(four fingers
Five for silver,	(all five fingers spread out)
Six for gold,	(two fists together then move apart spreading all fingers on both hands)
Seven for a secret	(seven fingers on your lips)
Never to be told.	(shake your head)

'This Old Man'

This old man, he played one	(raise one finger)
He played nick-nack on his thumb;	(tap finger on other thumb)
With a nick-nack, paddy wack,	
Give the dog a bone.	(clap hands)
This old man came rolling home.	(roll hands)

This old man, he played two	(raise two fingers)
He played nick-nack on his shoe.	(tap fingers on foot)
With a nick-nack, paddy-wack,	
Give the dog a bone.	(clap hands)
This old man came rolling home.	(roll hands)

Subsequent verses follow the same pattern with the following additions:

Three – on his knee
Four – on the floor
Five – on his side
Six – with some sticks
Seven – up to Heaven
Eight – on his plate
Nine – all the time
Ten – all over again

'One Potato, Two Potato'

Use your fingers for the counting, and sing a higher note with each new number. Alternatively, use this song with the classic hand movements by stacking your fists one on top of the other, hand over hand.

One potato, two potato
Three potato, Four,
Five potato, six potato,
Seven potato, more!

'Ten Green Bottles'

Ten green bottles
Hanging on the wall.
Ten green bottles
Hanging on the wall.
And if one green bottle
Should accidentally fall,   *(hide a finger)*
There'll be...   *(count up the remaining fingers while singing an upwards scale)*

Nine green bottles
Hanging on the wall.

Nine green bottles
Hanging on the wall.
Nine green bottles
Hanging on the wall.
And if one green bottle
Should accidentally fall,   *(hide a finger)*
There'll be...   *(count up the remaining fingers while
singing an upwards scale)*

Eight green bottles
Hanging on the wall.

Sing through the decreasing number of bottles until:

One green bottle
Hanging on the wall.
One green bottle
Hanging on the wall.
If that one green bottle
Should accidentally fall,
There'll be no green bottles
Hanging on the wall.

'Ten Little Fingers'

I have ten little fingers and they all belong to me,
I can make them do things – would you like to see?
I can shut them up tight, I can open them wide,
I can put them together, I can make them all hide.
I can make them jump high,
I can make them jump low.
I can fold them up quietly and hold them just so.

'Five Little Monkeys'

Eliminate a monkey on each repeat.

Five little monkeys
Jumping on the bed   *(five fingers of one hand dance on the other)*
One fell off and broke his head   *(hold your head)*
Mama called the doctor   *(mime making a phone call)*
And the doctor said,
'No more monkeys,
Jumping on the bed.'   *(shake your head and a finger)*

'Here's The Church'

Here's the church,   *(fingers interlocked with fingers inside)*
And here's the steeple.   *(index fingers join in a point)*
Open the door   *(keep fingers together but turn palms up)*
Here are the people.   *(wiggle fingers)*

Singing hands

Some studies have shown that learning sign languages as a baby can lead to higher IQ levels by the age of seven or eight. There are many different language systems including American Sign Language and British Sign Language.

One of the most effective systems is Makaton – a copyrighted language that blends particularly well with singing. In Makaton, core words are signed while you talk or sing – it is not exclusively designed as a language for hearing impairments. (Visit www.makaton.org for more information.)

Signing can be particularly effective when combined with songs and music as it enables totally interactive participation before speech and lyrical singing skills are developed.

'The Paintbox Song'

Here's a song for singing and signing at the same time. It's a fast way to learn the hand symbols for common colors. You may want to experiment with singing the 'Rainbow Song' with hand actions too.

This should be sung to the tune of 'Frère Jacques.'

> Mixing colors
> Mixing colors
> Red and blue
> Red and blue
> Purple on your paintbrush
> Purple on your paintbrush
> Why don't you
> Try it too?
>
> Mixing colors
> Mixing colors
> Yellow and blue
> Yellow and blue
> Green on your paintbrush
> Green on your paintbrush
> Why don't you
> Try it too?
>
> Mixing colors
> Mixing colors
> Red and green
> Red and green
> Brown on your paintbrush
> Brown on your paintbrush
> Why don't you
> Try it too?
>
> Mixing colors
> Mixing colors

Red and white
Red and white
Pink on your paintbrush
Pink on your paintbrush
Why don't you
Try it too?

'Signed Name Song'

Make up a song featuring your child's name where the letters are spelled out within the song. Try sounding out the sequence of letters from your child's first name in a singsong manner followed by their name as a chorus.

So, for instance, if your child's name is 'Thomas,' vocalize:

T H O,
M A S,
Tho-mas
Tho-mas,
T H O,
M A S,
Thomas is my name.

When you are singing the different letters, sign along with ASL (American Sign Language) or BSL (British Sign Language) signs – there's loads of free material on the web that will help you to learn; for ASL check out www.deaflibrary.org and for BSL try www.british-sign.co.uk.

Whenever I have worked with hearing-impaired children on music projects, we have developed shorthand systems of saying names. My friend Mike had his name shortened to:

M – Bike [mimed handlebars]

This was quicker than 'fingerspelling' his whole name. Bike rhymes with Mike and it happens to be the way he likes getting around town, so it was a very logical signed nickname.

Help your child choose their own symbol that represents something they like, an object or an activity. Make up a hand gesture that matches whatever you've chosen, and build it into their song. There is no way that they can forget how to spell their name if you practice this with them a few times. The musical element helps a child memorize the sequence much more accurately than by just using speech or mime.

Now you can sing and sign your child's name together!

Listen

At 12 months many toddlers begin to listen really attentively rather than just hear. They will move their limbs in rhythm to music, and will enjoy making rolling or rocking motions. This is a good stage to introduce music as an accompaniment to storytime. This will really fire up imaginations and enhance the stories more than any video could hope to achieve!

Music for storytime

Telling a story before bedtime serves many purposes. Most importantly, it is one of the few times when the distractions and excitement of the day have abated, leaving a few precious moments when you can settle your child. It is no coincidence that the practice of telling stories late in the evening is prevalent in most world cultures - we're back to the campfire again! You can significantly enhance your child's enjoyment of storytime before sleep by quietly playing music in the background that has connections to what you are reading. This will enhance the natural levels of imagination employed when concentrating on stories, while placing the music in a connected context.

We've included two inspiring pieces of orchestral music on the CD. Why not try writing your own short story to match the changing moods of the music?

TRACK 30: Music For Storytime 1
TRACK 31: Music For Storytime 2

Fairy tales

Fortunately, the great Russian composer Tchaikovsky wrote ballet scores for many of the classic fairy tales. The following pieces represent a small sample of the imaginative and beautiful orchestral music inspired by traditional children's stories. These are ideal for playing in the background while reading at bedtime.

Suggested listening:

Tchaikovsky	'Sleeping Beauty'
Tchaikovsky	Swan Lake
Tchaikovsky	'The Nutcracker'
Adolphe Adam	'Giselle'
Stravinsky	'Petroushka'
Humperdink	'Hansel and Gretel'

For stories about animals, try the following pieces:

Saint Saens	'Carnival Of The Animals'
Ravel	'Mother Goose' suite
Beethoven	'Pastoral Symphony'
Rimsky-Korsakov	'Flight Of The Bumble Bee'
John Willams	'Hedwig's Theme'
The Beatles	'Piggies'

'Tubby The Tuba' is a wonderful story with symphony orchestra accompaniment written by George Kleinsinger. The greatest recording available features Danny Kaye as the narrator.

Buying basic instruments for toddlers

It may seem an obvious thing to say, but you should make sure the instruments that you are intending to buy sound really good, and that any effort required to play them is rewarded with a full, rich sound. Remember, you're going to be hearing a lot of music on these instruments!

Electronic musical toys

Parents are often encouraged to buy electronic music toys for toddlers. I think electronic toys have a great deal to offer, but I would be cautious of introducing them in a musical context. Electronic musical instruments and toys can be counterproductive as they can bypass an important learning factor. Instruments should be tactile. A traditional musical instrument will respond to the playing force in a directly responsive manner. Most electronic children's instruments will make a noise regardless of the way in which they are struck. The physical action of striking, blowing or scraping an instrument should affect the timbre (the texture), the volume, the pitch, and the length of notes. The composer and children's music expert Carl Orff believed that children beginning their musical studies should be encouraged to play instruments that sound good with little expert technique. Consequently, Orff's own teaching method, the Schulwerk system, makes strong use of great-sounding instruments like metallophones, glockenspiels, and wooden xylophones.

Metallophone/xylophone/glockenspiel

These were developed by Orff's associate Karl Maendler in the 1920s and have become standard classroom percussion instruments all over the world. These instruments always sound good when played together, and are mercifully far from the sound of scratchy beginner violins!

These instruments are laid out a little like piano keyboards and help to teach and enforce the idea of the spatial relationships between musical pitches. As explored previously in this book, understanding these concepts can help advance spatial-temporal skills, which in turn aid sophisticated thought processes and complex analysis patterns. In using these instruments one can build small ensemble work with other members of the family or toddlers of a similar age. Playing together will help develop social skills, and helps young children relate to one another within a creative context.

Egg shakers

I often use egg shakers for toddler music projects. They sound great – not too loud or soft – they are very cheap, and they can produce an interesting mixture of sounds. Playing them is harder than it looks at first, and they teach great fine motor movement and advanced coordination skills. You have to relax your physical movements to play them well, and children quickly pick up the technique.

A great advanced technique to teach your children with an egg shaker is the train effect. This is achieved by cupping the hands around the whole egg, with the pointy end facing away from you. Once you have a regular pulse going, try shaking in the following repeating pattern:

closed   closed   open   open

digga   digga   digga   digga

Try this while singing a nursery rhyme with strong beats such as 'Wheels On The Bus,' or 'Old MacDonald.'

Boomwhackers

These are wonderfully simple, great-sounding colorful instruments. Boomwhackers are pieces of plastic tubing that sound different notes depending upon their lengths. You play them by hitting them on the ground, or with a beater or by hitting them against each other. When you use boomwhackers, be sure that it is an environment where there is nothing breakable, and where toddlers will not try to bash each other with them! If you are dancing to a particular piece of music you can easily find ways of working them into the choreographed movements. A good piece for trying this out is the 'Romanian Folk Dances' by Bartók, which feature traditional folk dances – one of them being a stick dance!

Recorders

Recorders are great instruments for two to three year olds as they require the development of fine finger coordination, breathing control, and pitch awareness. They also sound great!

Recorders are very cheap – they can be found for a couple of dollars or less, and come in wild colors to appeal to children.

Making instruments with your children

Making and playing instruments aids muscle development, fine motor skills, and coordination, as well as introducing core science concepts associated with sound production. Playing instruments together is a great social activity, and a wonderful way to share music together, regardless of different skill levels or ages.

Let the children help you to make these instruments! They will have a great sense of ownership and pride if they have helped to build them. Here are some guidelines and ideas for making basic struck instruments, shakers, and plucked instruments.

On TRACK 32 of the CD I've recorded examples of many of the instruments included in this chapter so you can hear just how good they can sound.

Making a drum

Here's what you'll need:

Find a large paper or plastic cylindrical container – a coffee can is perfect, especially if it has a snap-on lid. If not, use some strong greaseproof paper.

Here's how you make it:

Fix the lid or the greaseproof paper to the container and fasten tight with some tape – stretching it as tight as possible.

How you play it:

A wooden spoon makes a great beater – also try playing just using your fingers or palms.

Making shakers

Here's what you'll need:

The plastic containers that come with 35mm film are perfect for these instruments – they are just the right size for small hands. If you can't find one of these you may want to try a baking powder can instead. You will also need small objects such as dry beans, pasta, rice, lentils, or small buttons.

Here's how you make them:

Fill the container one-third full with the dry beans (or alternative material). Don't mix fillings as this won't sound as good. Seal the container tightly and glue shut – make sure the child cannot open the shaker, or they may try to eat the contents.

How you play them:

Shake in time to music. Keep your arm relaxed and loosen your wrist as you play, and it will sound much better.

Claves

Here's what you'll need:

Buy some lengths of dowel, about the thickness of two fingers.

Here's how you make them:

Cut the dowel rods into different lengths between 4 and 10 inches. You may want to paint them bright colors with wood gloss – this will mute their sound a little.

How you play them:

Hold one of the rods as a beater in your dominant hand. Rest the second rod across your other hand from your fingertips to the heel of the palm, it should not be gripped – it should rest in such a way that it resonates a little.

Clip Clops

Here's what you'll need:

Save some clean empty yogurt containers – the bowl-shaped ones are ideal.

How you play them:

Simply play by knocking the open ends together. To get a horseshoes sound effect, swivel one against the other as you strike them together.

Play while singing 'Horsey, Horsey.'

Sandy blocks

Here's what you'll need:

You will need some small blocks of wood, suitable for small hands. The edges should be smoothed into curves. You will also need two pieces of fine-grade sandpaper, the same size as the largest side of the woodblocks.

Here's how you make them:

Glue the pieces of sandpaper to the surface of each wooden block, and paint the wood with durable gloss or varnish.

How you play them:

Rub together lightly in regular tempo! Try accompanying yourselves while singing a march.

Indian cymbals

These are great for developing coordination skills.

Here's what you'll need:

Cocoa tin lids, short length of string.

Here's how you make them:

Punch holes in the tin lids and smooth away any sharp or rough edges. Thread a lid onto each end of the string, and fix tight.

How you play them:

Hold one lid with the string and strike with the other lid held in a similar manner.

Creative music play

Between 18 months and two years of age, you may notice your child making up his or her own little songs. These improvisations probably have regular rhythm patterns and a distinct tonal center.

To encourage this creative phase, try singing songs your child knows really well, but occasionally substitute different words. They will enjoy correcting your mistakes, and will soon get the hang of inserting their own new words. This is a great shortcut to writing your own songs with your children.

Making up songs for regular tasks and care routines

At this age, children will love music that accompanies regular tasks. These include bathing, getting dressed, preparing food, eating, waiting for things, meeting people, going on a walk, and so on. They can easily be encouraged to contribute their own ideas. The use of songs at such times will greatly help to instill routines, and subconsciously triggers behavior patterns and good habits (such as washing hands, brushing teeth, closing eyes at bedtime).

Recording and playing back

Obtain a cheap cassette recorder, hand-held Dictaphone, or get a microphone for your iPod. Record your toddler when he or she is singing, or playing with instruments. Show your child how to sing into the microphone. Play the recordings back and encourage him or her to sing along. Try making up a dance together to go with the recordings, or use the recordings as background music or sound effects when reading stories.

If the recording device has a speed control, experiment with your singing voices when they are played fast or slow. I remember my father showing me as a child a machine at his workplace which could play a 'deep sea' or a 'Mickey Mouse' voice; I found it entrancing and it was many years later that I realized it had been a variable speed dictaphone...

Use melodic instruments to record short patterns one after another on successive sections of tape. Play them back to hear what your whole piece sounds like!

If you have access to sequencing software on a home computer, try importing short sequences of notes from the recordings, and making them into home-made rhythm tracks by looping them.

I have had hours of fun making little dance tunes with my own children using this technique, and they are very proud of the 'singles' that they produce. (Some of the sound effects we've made together have actually found their way onto TV soundtracks I've worked on!)

Different color claps

You have a great musical instrument in your hands alone! There are a wide variety of sounds that can be drawn from even a basic clapping sound. Here are three simple exercises to help you make some new sounds with your hands.

Rain claps

Try to create a stormy rain effect by clapping with one finger into the palm of your other hand, gradually adding fingers, then taking them away again:

One finger
Two fingers
Three fingers
Whole hand
Three fingers
Two fingers
One finger

This is a simple way of demonstrating dynamics, as well as a simple yet fascinating representation of another sound. This exercise works well with a large group of children, particularly if performed with the eyes closed.

Backbeat claps

Try cupping your hands to create a lower-pitched note. Then flatten your hands out as you clap to make a high-pitched sound.

Try cupped hands/flat hands in alternation. You should get a low and high pattern emerging like a rock beat.

Clapping scales

To play an ascending scale of clapped notes, try gradually changing from a cupped shape to a flat shape, gradually opening the hands until they are flat against one another.

Listen to the range of colors you can achieve from this one simple action on TRACK 33 of the accompanying CD. You can also try listening to 'Clapping Music' by Steve Reich.

Joining toddler music groups

You may be considering joining a toddler music group. This can be a great way to introduce your child to a wide range of musical activities.

A toddler music group can also be one of the best environments for your child to develop their social skills. Children at preschool age can be very shy, almost insular when around other young children; only when they reach school age do they really begin to open up and view other children as 'friends.'

A good children's music group can also act as a catalyst for relating music to movement. The groups offer a chance for children to articulate themselves physically and emotionally within a playful environment.

Of course, there are good toddler music groups, and not so good. I have been to sessions where the leaders do not appear to know how to communicate with children, and one gets the feeling that it is just a business. A group should be professional yet highly interactive without being hysterical – after all, you don't want to come out of a session with a child who is so overexcited that he or she cannot be calmed down.

Look for creativity in the way the activities have been devised. Some groups use just taped music and little variation in the sequence of events from week to week. There should be a clearly discernible lesson plan and themes to follow for the duration of the course. They should be active not passive – even where listening activities are part of the sessions, these should be stimulating and interactive. The group leaders should have proper insurance, first-aid training, and background checks where appropriate.

One of my favorite toddler groups is run by two former teachers. They use a clever combination of action songs, storytelling, and puppetry that keeps the children focused and entranced each week. They use a wide range of different instruments with the children, encouraging development of fine motor skills. By the end of the school year, the children have learned more than 150 songs! The children have also become acquainted with other toddlers who are likely to be in the same class when they start at the local school.

If there is no suitable group in your area, it is always worth starting your own informal group with other parents who have children of a similar age to your own. Any musical group activities at this age can have tremendous effects on your toddler's musical development, acquisition of vocabulary, and social skills that will benefit them for years to follow.

There are many high-quality, commercially franchised toddler music groups to consider. Some of the leading organizations are listed on page 325.

Chapter 22

Nursery: 3–5 years

Your child will probably be entering, or about to enter a formal education system. This naturally means that children have to adapt quickly to being able to socialize with a much wider peer group. This coincides with the point at which their brains are two and a half times more active than the brains of adults.

By this age, children have become biologically primed for learning. They are ready to enter a period of exponential development. Every incoming stimulus contributes to their mental and physical coordination.

At the age of four, a child's brain is using more than twice the glucose of an adult brain. This signals a huge degree of neural activity and development.

Sing

Between the ages of three and four, a child's vocal cords gain strength and greater control. By this point, children can normally replicate songs with accurate melody, rhythm, and lyrics. Most children have expanded their vocabulary to around three hundred words.

Songs can strengthen the level of vocal control a child possesses by exercising vocal cords and the muscles employed for singing. Songs at this point should therefore include those that enhance speech technique, expand vocabulary, and build memory skills.

Songs for strengthening speech

'Miss Polly'

This nursery song uses close rhyme brilliantly and is a great way of practicing phonics and articulation. The melodic line is quite sophisticated and assists the development of pitch controls.

> Miss Polly had a dolly
> Who was sick, sick, sick
> So she called for the doctor
> To come quick, quick, quick
> The doctor came
> With his bag and his hat,
> And he knocked at the door
> With a rat-a-tat tat.
>
> He looked at the dolly
> And he shook his head
> And he said 'Miss Polly,
> Put her straight to bed.'
> He wrote on a paper
> For a pill, pill, pill,
> 'I'll be back in the morning
> Yes I will, will, will!'

Listen to TRACK 34 on the accompanying CD for a recording of this song.

'Bubble Said The Kettle'

This song contains an extremely strong inner beat by virtue of its lyrics. For this reason it is excellent for developing a sense of inner pulse. It is also an excellent rhyme for refining vocal control and building speech skills as it exercises contrasting phonic patterns.

> Bubble said the kettle
> Bubble said the pot

Bubble bubble bubble bubble
We are getting hot!
Shall I take you off the fire?
No you need not trouble
This is just the way we talk
Bubble bubble bubble!

Building speech – alliterative songs

'Sing A Song Of Sixpence'

This song is useful for articulation skills:

Sing a song of sixpence,
A pocket full of rye;
Four and twenty blackbirds
Baked in a pie.
When the pie was opened,
They all began to sing.
Now, wasn't that a dainty dish
To set before the King?

The King was in his countinghouse,
Counting out his money;
The Queen was in the parlor
Eating bread and honey.
The maid was in the garden,
Hanging out the clothes.
Along there came a big black bird
And pecked off her nose!

'A Sailor Went To Sea, Sea, Sea'

A Sailor went to sea, sea, sea
To see what he could see, see, see

But all that he could see, see, see
Was the bottom of the deep blue sea, sea, sea.

'There Was An Old Woman Who Swallowed A Fly'

This song is an excellent exercise for phonic development that children are likely to enjoy because of its macabre subject matter! It strengthens memory skills, as it requires recalling a visual sequence – the progressively larger animals.

There was an old woman who swallowed a fly.
I don't know why she swallowed a fly -
Perhaps she'll die!

There was an old woman who swallowed a spider
That wriggled and wriggled and jiggled inside her
She swallowed the spider to catch the fly,
I don't know why she swallowed a fly -
Perhaps she'll die!

There was an old woman who swallowed a bird-
How absurd to swallow a bird!
She swallowed the bird to catch the spider
That wriggled and wriggled and jiggled inside her.
She swallowed the spider to catch the fly,
I don't know why she swallowed a fly -
Perhaps she'll die!

There was an old woman who swallowed a cat
Imagine that! She swallowed a cat.
She swallowed the cat to catch the bird--
How absurd to swallow a bird!
She swallowed the bird to catch the spider
That wriggled and wriggled and jiggled inside her.
She swallowed the spider to catch the fly,
I don't know why she swallowed a fly -
Perhaps she'll die!

There was an old woman who swallowed a dog
Oh, what a hog to swallow a dog!
She swallowed the dog to catch the cat
Imagine that! She swallowed a cat.
She swallowed the cat to catch the bird
How absurd to swallow a bird
She swallowed the bird to catch the spider
That wriggled and wriggled and jiggled inside her.
She swallowed the spider to catch the fly,
I don't know why she swallowed a fly -
Perhaps she'll die!

There was an old woman who swallowed a goat.
She opened her mouth and it went down her throat.
She swallowed the goat to catch the dog-
Oh, what a hog to swallow a dog!
She swallowed the dog to catch the cat.
Imagine that! She swallowed a cat.
She swallowed the cat to catch the bird-
How absurd to swallow a bird!
She swallowed the bird to catch the spider
That wriggled and wriggled and jiggled inside her.
She swallowed the spider to catch the fly,
I don't know why she swallowed a fly -
Perhaps she'll die!

There was an old woman who swallowed a cow--
I don't know how she swallowed a cow!
She swallowed a cow to catch the goat.
She opened her mouth and it went down her throat.
She swallowed the goat to catch the dog--
Oh, what a hog to swallow a dog!
She swallowed the dog to catch the cat.
Imagine that! She swallowed a cat.
She swallowed the cat to catch the bird--
How absurd to swallow a bird!
She swallowed the bird to catch the spider

That wriggled and wriggled and jiggled inside her.
She swallowed the spider to catch the fly,
I don't know why she swallowed a fly -
Perhaps she'll die!

There was an old woman who swallowed a horse...
She died, of course!

Recommended Listening:

Shermann and Shermann   'The Bear Necessities' (from The
                             Jungle Book)
This is an incredible song composed of alliterative, rhythmic
wordplay. It's great for strengthening speech skills and building
vocabulary too.

Cab Calloway   'Minnie The Moocher'
A perfect, highly sophisticated call-and-response song that children
love.

Mozart   Papageno and Papagena's duet (from *The
                             Magic Flute*)

Exploring different emotions in song

You can help your child play with sophisticated ways of expressing
themselves through this very simple exercise. First of all, choose a well-
known song that has a definite character and consistent manner of delivery.
You will be using it to practice exploring some contrasting emotions. Let's
imagine you have settled on 'Twinkle, Twinkle Little Star' as the song to be
used. Sing it through together quite normally to start with. Once you have
done this, suggest, as a game, that it would be fun to pretend to be cross
when you are both singing it. Now when you sing pretend to be scared,
happy, as small as a mouse, as big as an elephant, very hot, very cold, in love.

If you want your child to sing more confidently, and to develop a stronger
voice generally, make suggestions for performance style that are initially
opposite this ideal. So, pretend to sing as if you are very small, shy, and tired.

Then suggest performing as if huge, confident, and full of energy. Because they have just tried the opposite style, they will really try to make an obvious contrast when requested. By demanding the opposite first, you will get a great performance when you reverse the request. See if your child can come up with a fun suggestion too!

Ask your child to sing as if to a very young baby. Many scientific surveys have shown that people naturally project a level of heightened emotion when directing speech or song to a very young baby. The style of communication is very intense and rich with natural phrasing and warmth. This is the same regardless of where you are brought up or your native language.

> I often tell my cello students to perform as if to a young child, as it requires a very instinctively powerful style of playing. It also requires less analysis and a generally more direct manner of musical expression.

It is immensely useful to introduce this concept of elevated speech and song to children, as it will help them to express themselves very directly and develop a powerful set of communication tools.

Movement songs and games

At this age, children begin to develop a strong sense of internal pulse and are capable of completing sophisticated movement patterns while singing. As explored in Chapter 10, these movements form essential learning and memory tools and help articulate the lyrics and message contained in the song.

Musical stairs

Try walking upstairs singing a new note on an ascending scale with each step.

• Try singing using numbers.

• Try using these sounds: doh-re-mi-fah-so-la-ti-doh.

• Use numbers in different languages.

• Step up two steps and see what happens to the pattern when you miss a note out.

Transfer to the floor to play a form of musical hopscotch, then find similar patterns on the keyboard or a xylophone, etc.

Rhythm and tempo creative exercises

If you are not sure about your sense of inner pulse – there's no harm in buying a metronome!

The following exercises should help your children to 'internalize' their sense of pulse. This will help them regulate rhythms, which in turn will help them with many forms of coordination.

Clap it back games

These exercises are great for sharpening aural responses and memory skills. This is essentially a call-and-response activity. First establish a pulse by tapping, stepping, or nodding. Clap a short sequence then invite your child to clap it back to you.

After you have led a few different variations, let your child lead with some ideas of his or her own. If he gets stuck, clap the rhythms of some easy word sequences (the first lines of nursery rhymes can be useful for this exercise). When this exercise is going well, suggest fitting some of the rhythms together, either in a longer sequence, or one on top of another.

Body percussion

Body percussion is the term used to describe rhythm sounds played by hitting parts of the body (obviously not too hard!). For instance, clapping a rhythm while singing at the same time, can help to develop advanced levels of coordination. While singing well-known songs, try to keep a regular beat together by:

• Tapping your chest

• Clapping your hands

• Slapping your thighs

• Stamping your feet

The Thump

To practice coordinating these movements you may want to try putting them in a sequence while singing a song at the same time – the '0' represents a rest beat. Repeat the sequence when you get to the end.

Tap	Tap	Tap	0
Clap	Clap	Clap	0
Slap	Slap	Slap	0
Stamp	Stamp	Stamp	0

Then try:

Tap	Tap	Clap	Clap
Slap	Slap	Stamp	Stamp
Tap	Tap	Clap	Clap
Slap	Slap	Stamp	Stamp

Whole body movement songs

'Tony Chestnut'

Tony Chestnut *appears* to be a simple song – here are the lyrics;

> Tony Chestnut knows I love you
> Tony knows, Tony knows
> Tony Chestnut knows I love you
> That's what Tony knows

This song has a great twist – the words can be interpreted as parts of the body! Here's a diagram to show you how it works:

'toe' 'knee' 'chest'

'nut' 'nose' 'eye'

'love' 'you' 'that's'

Or, in other words:

> Toe-knee Chest-nut nose eye love you
> Toe-knee nose, Toe-knee nose
> Toe-knee Chest-nut nose I love you
> That's what Toe-knee nose

Listen to TRACK 35 on the accompanying CD for a recording of this song.

Don't panic if your child can coordinate this song perfectly while you're getting in a tangle. I found it took me around four times longer to learn the movements for this song than my children!

'Head And Shoulders'

> Head, shoulders, knees and toes,
> Knees and toes.
>
> Head, shoulders, knees and toes,
> Knees and toes.
>
> And eyes, and ears, and mouth,
> And nose.
>
> Head, shoulders, knees and toes,
> Knees and toes.

'Whisky, Frisky, Hippity Hop'

Whisky, frisky, hippity hop,	*(start down low)*
Up he goes to the treetop.	*(hop to standing)*
Whirly, swirly, round and round,	*(turn around)*
Down he scampers to the ground.	*(turn to low position)*
Furly, curly, what a tail,	*(twist hands around)*
Tall as a feather,	*(reach up high)*
Broad as a sail.	*(stretch out wide)*
Where's his supper – in the shell,	*(cup hands)*

Snappity	(stamp)
crackity	(clap)
Out it fell	(roll hand over hand)

'Happy And You Know It'

This is a great song for adapting to your own ideas – anything that can be mimed should be tried. Here are some alterations you may want to try:

If you're happy and you know it, wash your hair
If you're happy and you know it, hop around
If you're happy and you know it, play piano
If you're happy and you know it, tie your shoes

Of course you could make them sillier or a little surreal – children love such displacement jokes:

If you're happy and you know it, eat a cloud
If you're happy and you know it, fold the air
If you're happy and you know it, be a sheep

Children will love suggesting their own ideas and actions. This will stimulate their creativity no end! Here's the song in its proper form:

If you're happy and you know it, clap your hands!
(clap clap)
If you're happy and you know it, clap your hands!
(clap clap)
If you're happy and you know it,
Then you really ought to show it,
If you're happy and you know it, clap your hands!
(clap clap)

If you're happy and you know it, stomp your feet!
(stamp stamp)
If you're happy and you know it, stomp your feet!
(stamp stamp)

If you're happy and you know it,
Then you really ought to show it,
If you're happy and you know it, stomp your feet!
(stamp stamp)

If you're happy and you know it, turn around!
(single turn)
If you're happy and you know it, turn around!
(single turn)
If you're happy and you know it,
Then you really ought to show it,
If you're happy and you know it, turn around!
(single turn)

If you're happy and you know it, do all three!
(clap clap, stamp stamp, turn around)
If you're happy and you know it, do all three!
(clap clap, stamp stamp, turn around)
If you're happy and you know it,
Then you really ought to show it,
If you're happy and you know it, do all three!
(clap clap, stamp stamp, turn around)

'Teddy Bear'

This is a gentle, steady song that contains some great balancing and stretching coordination challenges.

Teddy Bear, Teddy Bear, turn around.
(turn around)
Teddy Bear, Teddy Bear, touch the ground.
(touch fingertips to floor)
Teddy Bear, Teddy Bear, show your shoe.
(raise each foot in turn)
Teddy Bear, Teddy Bear, that will do.
(sit on the floor)

'Peter Works With One Hammer'

This song is excellent for developing inner pulse as it articulates beats through movements cued in the lyrics.

> Peter works with one hammer, one hammer, one hammer
> Peter works with one hammer, this fine day.
> *(1 fist beating)*
>
> Peter works with two hammers, etc.
> *(2 fists beating)*
>
> Peter works with three hammers, etc.
> *(2 fists & 1 foot beating)*
>
> Peter works with four hammers, etc.
> *(2 fists & 2 feet beating)*
>
> Peter works with five hammers, etc.
> *(2 fists & 2 feet & head nodding)*

'Here We Go 'Round The Mulberry Bush'

This is a very old song that uses a full range of movements, using both fine and gross motor skills. It also instills the concept of daily routines (even if they are somewhat dated!) and teaches the sequencing of days of the week. It is also a perfect song to accompany skipping movements – a skill that children naturally enjoy and that refines complex physical movements.

> Here we go 'round the mulberry bush,
> The mulberry bush, the mulberry bush.
> Here we go 'round the mulberry bush,
> On a cold and frosty morning.
>
> This is the way we wash our clothes,
> Wash our clothes, wash our clothes.
> This is the way we wash our clothes,
> So early Monday morning.

This is the way we iron our clothes,
Iron our clothes, iron our clothes.
This is the way we iron our clothes,
So early Tuesday morning.

This is the way we mend our clothes,
Mend our clothes, mend our clothes.
This is the way we mend our clothes,
So early Wednesday morning.

This is the way we sweep the floor,
Sweep the floor, sweep the floor.
This is the way we sweep the floor,
So early Thursday morning.

This is the way we scrub the floor,
Scrub the floor, scrub the floor.
This is the way we scrub the floor,
So early Friday morning.

This is the way we bake our bread,
Bake our bread, bake our bread.
This is the way we bake our bread,
So early Saturday morning.

This is the way we go to church,
Go to church, go to church.
This is the way we go to church,
So early Sunday morning.

Listen to TRACK 36 on the accompanying CD for a recording of this song.

Musical movement games

Physical warm-up games help build bodily control and motor movement skills in children – a vital part of confidence-building and essential to the high levels of co-ordination necessary to be a musician. It is important that children are given the opportunity to practice their 'impulse controls'; this is the ability to trigger and follow one's own internal orders.

I frequently use similar warm-up exercises when working on creative musical projects with large groups of young children. I find they quickly focus young minds by offering a seemingly simple (yet actually complex) physical challenge, and definitely trigger a creative mood in the participants.

At this age, children will often enjoy freely interpreting music through movement. They have little self-consciousness about expressing themselves through dance, and are often capable of creating highly creative spontaneous choreography to music.

The number workout

This exercise promotes coordination skills, awareness of dynamics, and projection techniques. It is a great method of raising a child's focus levels and readiness for other activities, and it helps circulation and flexibility too. The exercise starts very softly and becomes fast and loud, so it is a good way of hyping young children up at the beginning of a creative session. I start every composition workshop I run with this game – it gets everyone in the right frame of mind and can't help but put you in a good mood.

This exercise works brilliantly in a group situation, but is just as effective played in pairs. If playing with a group, stand in a circle formation. If played as a pair, work facing each other. Start by hovering your fingertips above your head.

- **Tap your head lightly eight times while counting up to eight together in a strong whisper. This should be very rhythmic and articulate.**

'head'

- Then tap your shoulders eight times in the same manner, followed by knees and then toes (try not to bend your knees to reach!).

- Then repeat the sequence tapping four times on head, shoulders, knees, and toes while counting together in a firm voice.

'shoulders'

- Next repeat the sequence tapping twice and counting in a loud, exaggerated style.

- Finally repeat the sequence tapping once on head, shoulders, knees, and toes while shouting 'one' on each contact.

'knees'

- With both hands tap the part of the body indicated in rhythm with the spoken numbers. There should be no time taken moving between parts of the body between cycles.

Listen to TRACK 37 on the accompanying CD for a recording of this song.

'toes'

Here are the sequences in a table format.

	Head	Shoulders	Knees	Toes
Stage whisper	12345678	12345678	12345678	12345678
Normal voice	1234	1234	1234	1234
Projected voice	12	12	12	12
Shout	1	1	1	1

Next, try adding some notes to the patterns – try some of these:

12345678: Use a scale – up or down

1234: Use arpeggios – again up or down

12: Use octave leaps

1: Just sing one note

Also try patterns using odd numbers – this can feel harder as it involves less conventional beat groupings.

	Head	Shoulders	Knees	Toes
Stage whisper	1234567	1234567	1234567	1234567
Normal voice	12345	12345	12345	12345
Projected voice	123	123	123	123
Shout	1	1	1	1

We are conditioned to feel beats in multiples of two – we tend to be right-footed in this respect!

Walking, marching, running, and skipping

Walking, marching, stepping, running, and skipping are core speeds in music. Use the examples on the CD (tracks 2–5) for your child to move in time to the music. Start with the feet, then involve the rest of the body too.

Promenade

Here's a good musical exercise that works really well with a group of children and which is great for teaching tempo, pitch recognition, and communication skills. It enforces the idea of music as being a language that can be interpreted, by assigning different reactions to different cues.

There are two game variations below to enhance the exercise once children are comfortable with the idea!

First of all, find a way of making three different musical sounds. You could use three different xylophone notes; low, middle, and high. (To make the game even clearer, I would make the low note very long, the medium note maybe one second long, and the high note should be damped as soon as it is struck.)

The game starts with everyone wandering around in the room in different directions, as if following their own paths.

- **When a low note is struck on the xylophone, then the children have to walk around the room in super-slow motion.**

- **When a middle note is struck, they walk at normal speed.**

- **When the high note is played, they have to walk with short fast steps.**

The game is played in silence so the musical notes are the only audible sounds. The game works best when you vary the order of notes to try to catch the players out. If you want, it can be played as an elimination game, so there is a winner at the end, but this might take the fun out of it.

Variation 1. Promenade and handshake

This enables some great roleplay and miming skills.

When one player 'meets' another player, i.e. when their paths cross, they have to shake hands very earnestly and nod to each other, before moving off in different directions again.

Of course, when the cue note is low, they have to shake hands in super-slow motion and bow very slowly before moving off. Conversely, if the high note has cued the quick walking, the greeting needs to be very fast, as if in a speeded-up piece of film.

Variation 2. Promenade and greeting

In this variation, as well as the slow-motion handshake, the children have to sing 'how do you do?' at the speed and pitch level appropriate to the tempo they are moving at.

Young children love playing this game and it is a great way to get them reacting to musical cues. As they get more sophisticated at playing the different versions of the game, you could try using cue pitches that are closer together, so their pitch memory and awareness is exercised.

Recommended listening:
'Promenade' from *Pictures At An Exhibition* (Mussorgsky)

'Pictures At An Exhibition' brings us to some games that help link music and art.

Art and music games

Reaction dancing

Put on a recording of some music with good beats for dancing. Encourage your child to dance in time to the music, using their whole body to react to the rhythm and melodies. Demonstrate how to draw the 'line' of the melody in the air, showing whether it is smooth or spiky, slow, or fast. When the music is quiet, they could make small movements; they could make large movements for loud dynamics; and they could go up on tiptoes for high notes or go down near the floor for lower notes.

I find that Brahms' 'Cello Sonata In E Minor' works nicely for this exercise – try my recording on TRACK 38 of the accompanying CD.

Interpreting music through art

Children have a very instinctive understanding of the contours of melodic lines. I have been involved in many projects where children have created striking artwork in reaction to hearing music. This is a great thing to encourage, as it helps children to articulate complex moods and express deep emotions without feeling intimidated.

Drawn or painted responses to music can also demonstrate an understanding of structural concepts that can develop and enforce spatial reasoning skills. As explored previously, music is combinations of gestures or architectural forms given context by temporal placement.

Reacting to music in a graphic medium can be very cathartic for children, where they can sometimes feel frustrated by their linguistic skills.

When I attend children's concerts for the Academy of St Martin in the Fields, we help the young participants create big colorful paintings in workshops during the day. The children, from three years of age upwards, work on creating their pictures while members of the orchestra play to them. Later on, in the orchestra's main performance, the orchestra 'reads' some of the pictures as if they were music scores, thus turning them back into very different pieces of music! The children involved always get very excited about hearing the pictures being turned into little chamber symphonies, and often end up conducting the orchestra themselves while their pictures are being used. Every child wants to hear their picture played, and few of them have any fear about jumping up in front of the orchestra and directing a group of very grown-up, professional musicians!

Many well-known artists have drawn inspiration from music, and numerous composers have used artworks as an inspiration. Why not try this exercise at home to see whether your child enjoys connecting the two worlds too!

Drawn to music

Gather some good-sized pieces of art paper and colourful paints. Start painting different pictures while listening to contrasting types of music. You could begin with something smooth and peaceful or ambient such as Vaughan Williams' 'Fantasia On A Theme By Thomas Tallis.'

For a complete contrast try something jagged, angular, spiky, and infectiously rhythmic, such as Leonard Bernstein's 'Symphonic Dances' from *West Side Story*.

Let your child give each of the paintings interesting names, and ask them to describe what is happening in the pictures. For some inspiration you could look together at paintings by Paul Klee, Wassily Kandinsky, or Howard Hodgkin – all artists deeply inspired by music.

When your child is happy with their pictures it is time to reverse the process!

Assemble some simple instruments and organize a 'performance.' The players are going to 'read' the painting as if it were a piece of sheet music. Try following the contours of the picture relating high and low, soft and strong, and types of color to musical gestures. Children enjoy this process, and will often display less inhibition than an adult!

Try reading the 'music' from left to right or from top to bottom, right to left or just flit around the page.

This may feel unrelated to music reading skills, but many contemporary pieces rely upon similar symbolic interpretation. This style of notation is called 'graphic score.'

Graphic notation is a useful concept for children as it encourages them to play naturally with their own forms of notation. It is thrilling when children proudly show you a piece they have composed themselves, written in colorful shapes that probably only they can interpret! This is as important a stage as the first attempts children make at writing little storybooks of their own, and must be encouraged.

Children feel immense pride when they have created something of their own – this sense of ownership is a priceless gift for a child. Self-confidence and the development of an aesthetic sense are very important to learning processes.

You will now have prepared your child for a visit to an art gallery! My children love picking out postcards of paintings they remember from trips to galleries. They enjoy making up stories and little pieces of music to match the images.

Listening activities

Make up stories to existing repertoire

When listening to music with your child, ask them if they can describe what is happening in the music. This will give them a simple boost of creative energy that will put them in a good frame of mind for further mental activities. Pieces of atmospheric, dramatic, and descriptive classical music lend themselves very well to this exercise.

Even young children are able to associate music with characters, landscapes, and moods – help them advance these skills using the following techniques.

Ask questions about the music such as:

• Who or what can you hear in the piece – is it a person, or an animal?

• Where is it? Are we in a forest, or a town?

• Is it a long time ago?

• What time of day is it?

• What are they doing?

• How are they feeling?

• What's the weather like?

• What happens next?

Young children often display an extraordinarily vivid sense of imagination when listening to music. This style of listening is not always encouraged and nurtured as we grow older, and yet it opens up a world of creative thought and wonderful refuge from the mundane.

Try listening to some of these great pieces:

Honegger	'Pacific 231'
Saint-Saëns	'Aquariums' (from *Carnival Of The Animals*)
Vivaldi	*The Four Seasons*
Holst	'Mars' (from *The Planets*)
Mussorgsky	'The Great Gate At Kiev' (from *Pictures At An Exhibition*)
John Williams	*Jaws* Original Soundtrack
John Barry	Theme from *Out Of Africa*
Bernard Herrman	*Vertigo* Original Soundtrack
Ennio Morricone	*The Good, The Bad, & The Ugly* Original Soundtrack
Mike Oldfield	*Tubular Bells*

I regularly work with young children at a project in Harlem. I was stunned when I recently conducted a very unscientific experiment into their perceptive listening skills. My colleagues and I asked the children to close their eyes and imagine that they were at the cinema while we played them a selection of contrasting repertoire. At the end of each piece we asked them to describe what they had seen in their heads. At no point did we give any clues to the titles or subject matter of any of the pieces.

After a waltz, one of the little girls described a ballgown that one of the characters had been wearing in her 'film,' and the other children felt it was a dance from an old-fashioned wedding. But after the next piece, the children pieced together a wonderful description of a vast, hilly landscape where dinosaurs had once lived, but that was now a green and beautiful place. Someone was sad in this beautiful place: A boy who was playing a tune on his whistle. He was playing a tune because someone had died, or he had lost one of his animals.

I was amazed – the piece had been an arrangement of 'The Little Shepherd' by Claude Debussy. The picture they painted with their description was so vivid and rich, that I now always associate with the piece whenever I hear it! We've included a recording of this piece on the CD – you can hear it on TRACK 39.

I believe that music can expose profound feelings that may be hard for a child to articulate verbally, but that can safely be explored through reaction to pieces of music.

Why not:

• **Help your child to write down some of his or her music stories**

• **Encourage him or her to illustrate the stories with colorful pictures**

• **Listen to the music again while reading the stories and looking at the pictures**

This pattern of listening, creating, and then relistening gives a tremendous artistic boost to children.

Here are some other pieces of music they may enjoy at this age:

J. S. Bach	*The Brandenburg Concertos*
Elgar	'Pomp And Circumstance, March No. 1'
Holst	*Brook Green Suite* (contains 'Greensleeves')
Bartók	*Mikrokosmos*
Mussorgsky	'Pictures At An Exhibition'
Mozart	40th Symphony
	Overture to *The Marriage Of Figaro*
	Overture to *The Magic Flute*
Scott Joplin	'The Entertainer'
John Williams	*Catch Me If You Can* (Original Soundtrack)

A few different journeys:

Villa-Lobos	'Little Train Of The Caipira'
Leopold Mozart	'Sleigh Ride'
John Adams	'A Short Ride In A Fast Machine'
John Williams	'The Knight Bus' (from *Harry Potter And The Prisoner Of Azkaban*)
Pat Metheny	'Last Train Home'
Queen	'Bicycle Race'
Kraftwerk	Trans Europe Express
Madness	'I Like Driving In My Car'
Gary Numan	'Cars'

These pieces are about the sea:

Debussy	'La Mer'
Vaughan Williams	'Sea Symphony'

Making instruments

At this age, children are likely to be curious about instruments and new sounds. They also love to get messy making things, so what time could be more perfect for instrument making? Making and playing instruments is great for coordination skills and helps to introduce concepts relating to the physics and science of sound production.

Listen to Track 40 on the accompanying CD to hear some of these instruments demonstrated.

The cardboard strumbox

This is a nice instrument for introducing children to plucked instruments.

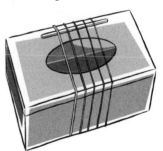

Here's what you'll need:

• shoe box or a strong tissue box

• a large variety of rubber bands.

Here's how you make it:

Make an oval hole in the shoe box lid then stretch the rubber bands around the box so they lie across the oval shaped hole. On one side, insert a pencil or narrow dowel rod underneath the bands. This will lift them off the box on one side, and will make it sound more resonant.

How you play it:

Stretch the rubber bands to different tensions to make the pitch higher or lower. Pluck and strum; experiment with tuning the 'strings' in such a way that they make a tune when you pluck them in order.

Try playing along with almost any simple nursery rhyme, like 'Old MacDonald Had A Farm' or even traditional tunes like 'My Bonnie Lies Over The Ocean.'

The tube kazoo

The tube kazoo is great for learning breath control and pitch technique, and actually making it is good for coordination skills.

Here's what you'll need:

• a strong cardboard tube from a kitchen or bathroom roll

• wax paper

• an elastic band

Here's how you make it:

Fix the wax paper to one end of the tube and fasten tight with the elastic band around the tube. Make a hole halfway up the tube (this makes playing it much easier as it lets the air escape).

How you play it:

Hum through the open end of the tube with your teeth apart, and lips slightly open. This will make a great buzzing sound that will match the pitch of the tune you are humming.

This instrument is great for playing along to music, as it is easy to pitch and makes an interesting sound. You can experiment with using different lengths of tube for this instrument – the card tube from a roll of wrapping paper is particularly effective.

The glass xylophone

This is very easy to make, but it can be very messy if you're not careful! The glass xylophone teaches basic science concepts, composition, and coordination.

Here's what you'll need:

• **eight hi-ball glasses**

• **a plastic jug**

• **a syringe**

• **a small teaspoon.**

Here's how you make it:

Arrange the glasses in a row (I tape the bases down to make sure they don't tip) and give the child a small plastic jug and syringe and instruct them to fill the glasses with varying water levels to create a row of different pitches.

How you play it:

Strike gently with the teaspoon to make melodies; use two spoons for chords.

Introducing other instruments

Keyboard instruments

In addition to xylophone-style pitched instruments, children will probably become interested in keyboard instruments. While it may be a little too early to begin formal lessons, there is no harm in introducing the piano and other keyboard instruments at this point.

If you have a piano or keyboard at home, you can show your child some basic concepts to help their spatial and pitch awareness on the instruments.

Keyboard games

Show your child the low and high notes, and how the fingers can 'walk' up and down the keys. Relate these movements to physical movements, so, for instance, if you are demonstrating an ascending scale, make sure you talk about climbing up the stairs. Show how missing out steps on the stairs makes an interesting melodic shape.

Teach them where Middle C lives, and show them how you can play with two hands at the same time.

Demonstrate how if you play only on the black keys, the notes all fit together in an interesting way. Use the sustain pedal at the same time to make a dreamy, mysterious piece.

If your children enjoy making up their own short note sequences on the keyboard, encourage them to think of a good name for their 'pieces' and see if they can repeat them.

Plate chimes

These are wonderful instruments, a little like chime bars, but much more practical and versatile. They come in all shapes and sizes; the two types I like using are the single, handheld plates, a square chime with a handle – this is played with a beater. The second type of plate chime is constructed from a single metal rectangle, into which different squares have been cut. This instrument has five different notes, tuned in the same way as the black notes on a piano, which are also played with a beater.

Musical table tennis

Children enjoy using plate chimes for playing and composing pieces. The instruments always sound good and are very durable and versatile. During one very memorable music project, the children discovered they could be used to play doubles table tennis. The action of striking the ball with the square chimes made the most wonderful melodic sequence, punctuated by with the rhythmic pulse of the ball hitting the table. All four players had different chime plates as bats, so every combination of shots made a slightly different melodic sequence!

Composers have always been fascinated by games, and have often used them as the inspiration for compositions. Even Mozart was inspired by the rhythm of billiards! Other classical pieces inspired by games and toys include *Jeux* by Maurice Ravel (who also wrote a duo for violin and cello that contains a musical tennis game in its second movement), 'Babes In Toyland' by Victor Herbert and Leopold Mozart's 'Toy Symphony.'

Recording and playing back

House music

To make real home-grown music, try using the place where you live as inspiration! First of all, establish a steady pulse and practice speaking the first line of your address so that it fits into the beats. Repeat this over and over so it feels like a 'groove'. For example, 'Forty-three, Avenue Road' could have a quirky rhythm for 'forty-three' and a pattern of triplets (a group of three) for the word 'Avenue.' With any musical gesture or phrase, additional impact can be gained from making a repeat. Repeat the process for the other lines of the address, paying special attention to the Zip code in the USA).

Try to perform the address, sticking closely to the pulse while repeating each line. You can try this as a call-and-response style game with your child, where he or she sings each line back as a repeat.

Once you are happy with the rhythms you have established, try articulating them together on some of your musical instruments – maybe starting with the drum. You now have a strong rhythm track that could probably benefit from a melody!

Now, encourage your child to try playing the rhythms on a pitched instrument like a xylophone or metallophone. Don't use too many different pitches for the tune; a great tip for making a strong melody is to restrict the number of different notes you use.

Select a note as your 'home' note, and try to start each motif on this pitch. This is obviously easier if the instrument uses different colors for each tone bar, as you can simply 'start on the blue' each time. Try to encourage your child to return to the 'home' note they started on for each phrase and take the melodic line for a walk by using adjacent notes rather than huge leaps.

This can become a very sophisticated musical exercise. In a group situation you can 'layer' the different elements. A key method in composing with young children is to use 'ostinato' technique. An ostinato is a little musical motif that is repeated often as an accompaniment figure. So, in this particular exercise the Zip code could be the underlying accompaniment throughout the piece.

This inspiration from everyday word patterns is a technique used by many well-known composers to create strong rhythmic and melodic material.

Carl Orff, the composer and educator who promoted the use of pitched percussion instruments, is best known for his epic work for choir and orchestra, *Carmina Burana*. Incredibly, many of the themes for this work were drawn from repeated (ostinato) figures devised in children's music workshops.

Of course the key benefit of this particular game is to teach your toddler their home address in such a way that they will never be able to forget it!

Recommended listening:
Ernest Toch   'The Geographical Fugue'
This track features lots of famous place names worked into a great
piece of music that uses only speaking voices.

Tone phone

You can also use the same 'house music' techniques with your home phone
number to create great rhythm patterns and melodies. Using the numbers for
a piece will help ingrain the number indelibly in a young mind – in the same
way that a radio station 'jingle' can lodge itself in your head through frequent
repetition and a clever sequence of notes. Numbers themselves imply
rhythmic values, and can also indicate pitch information too. There are many
ways to render this into musical form.

The simplest way to use a sequence of numbers is to make a melodic chant
with them. Also, don't forget to teach the tune as a fingerplay on the keys of
the phone. The numbers are laid out in a particular manner on a keypad –
this can be easily learnt in combination with musical cues.

How to compose your own songs

You can either start by choosing an existing poem or by making up your
own verses with your child. If you are unsure about coming up with
interesting rhymes, just start by making up a couplet (a two-line rhyming
verse). In a creative situation I tend to suggest themes such as 'favorite
animals' and let the children's imaginations run wild! (They love making
songs about wild creatures – jungle bugs, dinosaurs, sharks, bears, and tigers
always seem popular.)

Children enjoy putting character songs in the first person, and this will
encourage them to play-act and move in character when performing their
pieces.

The following song was made up at a recent nursery-school workshop:

> We are the sharks, and we like eating fish.
> You'd better swim away – or we'll eat you off a dish!

When you have settled on some good lyrics, speak the words over a strong pulse, until they sit really comfortably in the beats. Try to sense the shape of the phrases, and exaggerate the pitch of your voice to highlight these contours as you chant in rhythm. Now fit a melodic line to the phrase shape.

Good songs are often founded on repetition effects. The verse printed above quickly became a call-and-response song when we worked together on the tune.

> **We are the sharks,**
> We are the sharks,
> **And we like eating fish.**
> And we like eating fish.
> **You'd better swim away**
> You'd better swim away
> Or we'll eat you off a dish! *(together)*

Once you have a good little song or two, work out an interesting way to perform your pieces. Try to use strong physical movements, not just with the hands. Use your faces, feet, high and low positions, and simple dance steps. This is a sure-fire way to memorize a song quickly, and provides a very efficient mechanism for recall later on.

A tip...

When trying to recall songs or pieces of music you have composed together, you may find that your children have a much stronger recollection of the material than you! In such a situation, it is a good idea to challenge them that they cannot possibly remember the piece as well as you, and in their no doubt animated response, they will end up teaching it back to you!

Chapter 23

Elementary part 1: 5–7 years

By the time children enter their first years of elementary education, they will be showing distinct musical preferences and will like certain songs, instruments, and even performers over others. They will be gaining the ability to focus consistently for longer periods of time, which means they will be ready for more formalized musical instruction where appropriate.

By six years of age, the brain contains its highest concentration of neural connections, and it has to use a huge amount of oxygen and glucose to feed a dramatic period of mental growth and physiological development. The less-exercised neural networks begin to die away as they receive less stimulation and exercise.

Physiologically and mentally, your child is creating patterns of thinking, behavior, preferences, and abilities that form the foundations of future learning and character. As discussed in Chapter 8, instrumental work can have effects on mental development and the physical growth of certain areas of the brain.

Between the ages of five and seven is often a good time to introduce instrumental instruction, either in a classroom situation or through one-to-one teaching. For more information about choosing the right kind of instrument for your child see Chapter 25.

If instruments do become an important feature of your child's musical life, ensure that you help them maintain their vocal abilities by continuing with vocal games and exercises. Your child's vocal range will be constantly increasing, and his or her vocal technique will improve as the muscles develop and become more controlled. Singing is a major social activity at this point, and it is also an invaluable way to trigger memory function and to stimulate movement exercises.

It is also really important that you help your child to make links between different aspects of their musical activities. For instance, if children are happy making up melodic material in some of the games that follow in this chapter, encourage them to use their instruments to play the results too!

Music and movement

Before any creative activity, it helps to get into the right frame of mind and to warm up both physically and mentally. As movement exercises appear to stimulate both mental and physical coordination processes, there is a real benefit to building these exercises into musical play routines.

The following exercises work very well with slow, gentle music.

Breathing exercise

To establish broad, regular breathing with full breaths and associated physical movements, breathe in while lifting the arms up and then breathe out again on the circular drop.

Standing tall

Stretch your fingertips to the ceiling by standing on tiptoes. Try to keep your fingers as high as you can while you gradually lower heels to the floor. Experiment by adding the arm movements from the previous exercise.

Painting the wall

Choose some music that matches long breathing patterns. With hands pointing downwards and the palms facing the body, raise your hands as if painting a wall with your fingernails. Breathe in very slowly on the way up. When your hands are at eye level, change direction and unfurl your fingers so the palms are facing outwards on the downward stroke.

This exercise is excellent for teaching strong breath control for singing and wind instruments, and it can help develop smooth bowing changes on string instruments.

Elbow and knees

Play some marching-style music and practice touching alternate elbows to the opposite, lifted knees in time to the music.

Hand and heels

This is very similar to the previous exercise, but this time the hand has to touch the opposite, lifted heel behind the body. Use ambient, slow music for this exercise.

Circulation exercise

This exercise is great for waking up sleepy bodies and brains before creative work. From a standing position, bend over and then pat your toes with your hands. Move along the top of your feet and up the front of your legs, then pat the stomach, then the chest, and then from the shoulders to the top of the head. Moving down again pat down the back of the neck, down the back and all the way down the back of the legs until you reach your heels. Once you've finished, repeat the exercise more quickly while trying to keep the movements as fluid as possible.

Try this exercise in time to music, matching the speed of the music whenever it changes.

Circle warm-up

Practice this exercise with some slow music. Balance on one foot by lifting the other foot off the floor, and 'draw' a circle shape in the air with the lifted foot by rotating your ankle. Now try drawing a circle with your knee, then a circular shape with your hips. Swap feet and repeat the sequence.

Shake it out

Find some upbeat music in 'four to the floor' style, such as disco music or an exciting classical march. Encourage your child to move in time to the music – you shouldn't have a problem doing so, as children absolutely love this exercise!

The movements run in a sequence progressing from the fingers to the whole body.

- Shake your hands in time to the music (as if trying to dry them)

- Now shake your elbows too

- Add in your shoulders

- Now move your back too

- And your hips

- And finally your knees (by now your dancing will be fairly wild!)

- Pretend you are at the silliest party in the world and carry on dancing

The promenade

This game is intended to sharpen children's reactions by using a very simple musical signal that triggers a change in the type of activity. Children will walk very slowly or very quickly according to the pattern of claps they hear. When the game is played in a group situation, there is the added challenge of walking in all directions while attempting not to bump into another person!

This exercise will aid the development of spatial awareness and mental planning abilities as well as inhibitory controls.

Body percussion version

Start by walking around

• When you hear one clap you must walk in slow motion

• When you hear two claps you must walk quickly

• When you hear the word 'hey' you must change the direction you are walking

• When you hear a falling 'ooh' sound, you must sit on the floor

This game is also extremely effective when the cues originate from a musical instrument rather than a clap or a vocal cue. Children quickly learn to react physically to signals contained in the melodic material.

Melodic instrumental version

Start by walking around in time to the melody

• When you hear long notes you must walk in slow motion

• When you hear a short note you must walk quickly

• When you hear a skipping rhythm you must change the direction in which you are walking

• When you hear a downward scale you must sit on the floor

You can actually play a tune throughout the game, making special emphasis on the cue points. If you are using a piano, the long notes cue can be when you play with the right pedal sustained. If you are using a melodic percussion instrument, the 'sitting down' cue could be a sweep of downward notes.

Where the game gets really fun for children is when you swap over and let them play for your movements! They will quickly make the connection between cause and effect – they can make you move in a funny way by quickly changing from one cue to another. It goes without saying that this is a great tool for teaching advanced coordination and fine motor skills.

You can also try this game using recorded music, reacting to the melodic elements in the same way. A piece like the 'Overture' to *The Magic Flute* by Mozart has great alternating elements, long chords, fast short notes, and scales up and down. Another idea is to choose music that is slow but contains fast delicate inner parts, such as 'The Snow Is Dancing' by Debussy.

You can help the children devise their own rules for reacting to the music. This naturally enhances their awareness of melodic and rhythmic elements in music and can therefore help to build mental coordination and aural comprehension abilities.

Some variations on the game that you may want to try:

• **As you walk around, draw the melody in the air with your hands**

• **As you walk around in a group, shake hands with others**

• **Try singing H–E–LL–O slow and fast as you meet other people**

Body Signatures

This exercise helps develop a child's sense of self-identity and can help define individual characteristics. It is a great tool for developing physical and mental memory functions and helps link kinesthetic functions to thought processes. It's also a great way to break the ice among a group of children meeting for the first time, and works really well in the context of a party!

The idea is really simple: As you say your name, you perform a movement that fits with it. Everyone copies the speech and movement in response. Some children like to make a dramatic gesture with their hands, do a dance move, or a jump up in the air; others may be more shy at first.

Next, ask everyone to sing their names instead of speaking them and show that you can use your whole body if the movements have been a little inhibited. Again, everyone copies the singing and movement in response.

The final stage involves joining the songs and movements together in a continuous stream of names and moves. This can end up being a really neat piece of choreographed music. For one group of children I worked with recently it became their class theme song and dance, although the last time I saw them my own movement seemed to have evolved into a mime of sitting down and drinking a cup of tea!

Children love making their own 'theme songs' as they help to define and enforce their own personality traits.

Mirror dancing

This is an exercise that will help develop a sense of bodily rhythm relating to music. I use slow classical, reflective (sorry!) pieces for this game.

Stand face to face with your child and explain that they have to act as a mirror, copying everything you do. Try to move in time to the music and make sure your movements reflect the mood of the piece. Start by making small, simple movements; when your child's mirrored moves are accurately matching yours, increase the complexity of your actions.

Once your child has become adept at matching your moves, suggest swapping over and let him or her lead. They will love doing this. Try using more up-tempo movement for a good variation on this exercise.

Musical treasure hunt

The object of this classic game is to locate a hidden object, but in this version all of the clues are hidden in musical elements. In the traditional game, an object is concealed somewhere in a room and a child has to locate it while a controller calls out 'hot' or 'cold' depending on their proximity to the treasure. However, in this version of the game 'hot' and 'cold' are replaced by musical cues. There are of course many musical options for these clues; here are some of the most effective:

Hot	Cold
Fast music	*Slow music*
Loud music	*Soft music*
High pitches	*Low pitches*
Major chord	*Minor chord*
Passionate phrasing	*Boring phrasing*

You can make this game very sophisticated if you wish, and you can teach very subtle musical elements through such techniques. For the loud or soft you could easily use recorded music, but as with many of these games, children react really well when live music is used. You can choose a pattern of notes on a keyboard instrument to control this exercise, use tuned percussion instruments or use your voice instead!

As with the previous exercises, you can have a great time swapping roles. The children will quickly learn subtle variations in musical elements in order to control your movements.

Musical orienteering, or 'human chess'

This is similar to the previous game, but it uses more elements at the same time. The idea is to navigate a course using musical cues. Forwards, backwards, and left and right are represented by predetermined musical elements. We play this game at home using a large rectangular rug, which very helpfully has a chequered pattern! This game can also be great fun if played as a form of 'buff' where the participant is blindfolded – you obviously need to be very careful if trying this version!

I use the following parameters for the musical instructions:

Left	*Low note*
Right	*High note*
Forwards	*Loud note*
Backwards	*Soft note*

You will notice that these parameters correspond with the features of keyboard instruments. By going left, the notes are lower; to the right, the notes are higher.

Reverse musical orienteering

This has nothing to do with walking backwards: It's the reverse of the game we've just looked at. In this version, the child moves in certain directions and you have to respond with the appropriate musical gesture. They will, of course, enjoy trying to catch you out, and as with many of these exercises, there is a great deal to be gained from swapping roles. Let them try to represent your movements with a musical response.

This process helps children understand the relationship between movements and musical gestures. This process is a short step from moving to music more freely. Using some of the stages above, your child can listen to recordings of pieces and respond directly to pitch and dynamics, as well as some of the more textural elements.

Singing

The voice is still your child's best tool for musical expression, even if instruments have entered the scene. Short warm-up games are useful for promoting good technique and provide a good way to give the voice a regular workout.

The four aaahs!

This exercise encourages children to characterize their voices and to 'sing out' while indulging in imaginative storytelling. It also teaches different dynamic levels and strengthens vocal technique. This exercise is great to try at home, and also works nicely in a group situation.

I introduce this game within the context of telling a story that has elements that the children can join in with. In this example, the vocal element that the children join in with at each stage is always the same word; in this case 'AH.' It is presented very differently at each point of the story. Ask your child to suggest a different sound and see if that works too. You will find that any story works best for children if it is a little surreal…

> When I left the house this morning I remembered that I had forgotten to put on any socks.

> 'ah..' *(a short sound, with finger on bottom lip while looking embarrassed)*

> As I got to the bus stop I saw my friend who owes me some money, so I tried to catch his attention.

> 'Aaah.?' *(make a questioning sound as you point at someone else in the room – raise your eyebrows as if attempting to catch their attention)*

> When I got to school, we rehearsed the school play. I play the hero and only have one word to say when I reveal the master criminal with a loud

'Ahaaaaaa!' *(project your voice melodramatically while pointing at an imaginary character in the middle of the room)*

Later that evening it was time to go out to the opera where I saw the best singer in the world in the world's shortest opera. The opera only has one note, a very good note indeed, and it sounds like this:

'AAAAAAAAAAAAAAAHHH'

(sing a clear note for as long as possible with one hand outstretched; children also enjoy making a shaking action with the hand while adding 'vibrato' to the note)

After telling the story, the children can join in with the actions and sounds until you take out the narrative and simply perform the sequence of sounds:

ah   AH   AHaaa!   AAAHHHHHH...

Listen to TRACK 41 on the accompanying CD for a demonstration.

As they become more familiar with the game, transfer it to instruments and illustrate the narrative with sounds too. As the children become familiar with following the exercise, they will enjoy adding their own ideas and suggestions to the story complete with vocal components.

At this age, children like buried clues and sophisticated plays on words as well as mystery, challenge, and trick songs, where previously they may have strongly preferred word plays, rhymes, and alliterative lyrics. Adventure songs like 'We're Going On A Bear Hunt' containing journeys, suspense, and surprises will naturally appeal to children aged five to seven.

Rounds and canons

This is a great time to introduce the idea of sequenced songs such as rounds and canons. A 'round' is a piece of music consisting of a single musical line, which harmonizes with itself when sung in a delayed sequence. This round is sung to the same tune as 'Frère Jacques' – experiment with incorporating hand signs to represent listening, rain, wet, and 'you' mentioned in the lyrics.

Voice one	Voice two	Voice three
I hear thunder		
I hear thunder		
Hark don't you?	I hear thunder	
Hark don't you?	I hear thunder	
Pit-a-patter raindrops	Hark don't you?	I hear thunder
Pit-a-patter raindrops	Hark don't you?	I hear thunder
I'm wet through	Pit-a-patter raindrops	Hark don't you?
So are you	Pit-a-patter raindrops	Hark don't you?
I hear thunder	I'm wet through	Pit-a-patter raindrops
I hear thunder	So are you	Pit-a-patter raindrops
Hark don't you?	I hear thunder	I'm wet through
Hark don't you?	I hear thunder	I'm wet through
Pit-a-patter raindrops	Hark don't you?	I hear thunder
Pit-a-patter raindrops	Hark don't you?	I hear thunder
I'm wet through	Pit-a-patter raindrops	Hark don't you?
So are you	Pit-a-patter raindrops	Hark don't you?

Listen to TRACK 42 on the accompanying CD to hear a recording of the basic tune and then listen to TRACK 43 to hear the round.

Here are some other rounds to try.

'Row, Row, Row Your Boat'

> Row, row, row your boat,
> Gently down the stream,
> Merrily, merrily, merrily, merrily
> Life is but a dream.

Row, row, row your boat,
Gently down the stream,
If you see a crocodile
Don't forget to scream!

'London's Burning'

London's burning
London's burning,
Fetch the engines
Fetch the engines
Fire Fire
Fire Fire
Pour on water
Pour on water

'Frère Jacques'

This is a lovely round, which naturally introduces another language. You may want to try to introduce instruments to represent the bells ringing half way through the song.

Frère Jacques,
Frère Jacques,
Dormez vous?
Dormez vous?
Sonnez les matines,
Sonnez les matines,
Din, din, don!
Din, din, don!

In English this is sung as follows:

'Brother John'

> Are you sleeping,
> Are you sleeping?
> Brother John?
> Brother John?
> Morning bells are ringing,
> Morning bells are ringing,
> Ding ding dong,
> Ding ding dong.

If you enjoy this round, you may be interested to listen to how it appears in a famous piece of classical music. Gustav Mahler uses the tune at the opening of his '1st Symphony' where it appears very low on the double basses and winds its way up the orchestra.

> Further listening:
> Pachelbel   'Canon'
> Bach   'Musical Offering'
> Mozart   'Tafelmusik'

Call-and-response songs

Primary school-age children enjoy call-and-response songs. These are great for developing rhythm, memory, coordination, and fast responses.

'Boom Chicka Boom'

This song is excellent for developing rhythmic and consonant confidence. The line in bold is the call; the non-bold type is the response.

> **Say boom chicka boom!**
> Say boom chicka boom!
> **Say boom chicka boom!**
> Say boom chicka boom!
> **Say boom chickaroka chickaroka chicka boom!**
> Say boom chickaroka chickaroka chicka boom!

Uh-huh!
Uh-huh!
Eeh hee!
Eeh hee!
One more time...
One more time...
Louder!
Louder! *(repeat from the top!)*

Listen to TRACK 44 on the accompanying CD for a recording of this song. Experiment with altering the last word of the verse; we've used words like 'quieter,' 'faster,' 'lower,' and 'higher,' but feel free to come up with your own – the sillier the better.

'Bear In The Woods'

The other day,
The other day,
I saw a bear.
I saw a bear.
Up in the woods
Up in the woods
A-way up there
A-way up there.

(together)
The other day I saw a bear,
Up in the woods a-way up there.

He looked at me
He looked at me,
I looked at him
I looked at him.
He sized up me
He sized up me,
I sized up him
I sized up him.

(together)
He looked at me, I looked at him.
He sized up me, I sized up him.

He said to me
He said to me,
'Why don't you run?
'Why don't you run?
I see you ain't
I see you ain't
Got any gun.'
Got any gun.'

(together)
He said to me, 'Why don't you run?
I see you ain't got any gun.'

And so I ran
And so I ran
Away from there
Away from there.
And right behind
And right behind
Me was that bear
Me was that bear.

(together)
And so I ran away from there
And right behind me was that bear.

In front of me
In front of me,
There was a tree
There was a tree
A great big tree
A great big tree
Oh, Lordy, me!
Oh, Lordy, me!

(together)
In front of me there was a tree.
A great big tree, oh, Lordy me!

The nearest branch
The nearest branch
Was ten feet up.
Was ten feet up.
I had to jump
I had to jump
And trust my luck
And trust my luck.

(together)
The nearest branch was ten feet up,
I had to jump and trust my luck.

And so I jumped
And so I jumped
Into the air
Into the air
And missed that branch
And missed that branch
A-way up there
A-way up there.

(together)
And so I jumped into the air
And missed that branch a-way up there.

Now, don't you fret
Now, don't you fret,
Now, don't you frown
Now, don't you frown.
I caught that branch
I caught that branch
On the way back down
On the way back down.

(together)
Now, don't you fret, now, don't you frown.
I caught that branch on the way back down.

This is the end
This is the end,
There ain't no more
There ain't no more.
Unless I meet
Unless I meet
That bear once more!
That bear once more!

(together)
This is the end, there ain't no more.
Unless I meet that bear once more.

The end, the end
The end, the end,
The end, the end
The end, the end,
The end, the end
The end, the end,
The end, the end

The end, the end,

(together)
The end, the end, the end, the end,
The end, the end, the end, the end,
THE END!!!!

Movement songs

These naturally develop extreme levels of physical and mental coordination, while acting as great warm-up songs. You should still use 'Tony Chestnut' and 'Head And Shoulders,' but the following song is extremely popular with children at this age. It really helps the development of internal pulse and bodily coordination.

'Hello, My Name Is Joe'

Hello, my name is Joe and I work in a button factory
I have a house, and a dog, and a family
One day, my boss came up to me and he said 'Joe, are
   you busy?'
I said, 'No.'
So he said 'Push this lever with your right hand.'
(Move your right hand)

Hello, my name is Joe and I work in a button factory
I have a house, and a dog, and a family
One day, my boss came up to me and he said 'Joe, are
   you busy?'
I said, 'No.'
So he said 'Push this lever with your left hand.'
(Continue moving your right hand, but add the left hand too)

Hello, my name is Joe and I work in a button factory
I have a house, and a dog, and a family
One day, my boss came up to me and he said 'Joe, are
   you busy?'
And I said, 'No.'
So he said 'Push this lever with your right foot.'
(add the right foot to the other movements)

Hello, my name is Joe and I work in a button factory
I have a house, and a dog, and a family
One day, my boss came up to me and he said 'Joe, are
   you busy?'

And I said, 'No.'
So he said 'Push this lever with your left foot.'
(add the left foot to the other movements)

Hello, my name is Joe and I work in a button factory
I have a house, and a dog, and a family
One day, my boss came up to me and he said 'Joe, are
   you busy?'
And I said, 'No.'
So he said 'Bump this lever with your head.'
(nod your head with the other movements)

Hello, my name is Joe and I work in a button factory
I have a house, and a dog, and a family
One day, my boss came up to me and he said 'Joe, are
   you busy?'
And I said, 'Yes!!!'

Of course you can try other characters with interesting jobs, such as 'Hello, my name is Mo and I work in a chocolate factory...'

Listen to TRACK 45 on the accompanying CD for a recording of this song.

Listening projects

Children may now start expressing a preference for particular types of music and performers. It is also the age at which they can generally begin to focus on single activities for extended periods. Consequently, it is a good age to investigate children's concerts. Most arts venues have events especially for children, often with well-known musicians, orchestras, and bands fronted by charismatic presenters. You can always experiment at home by devising your own themed programs – maybe by listening to a section of a piece each night before bedtime, or during story time.

Here are some great pieces of music grouped thematically. You may want to explore these pieces while recounting the stories they are based on, or find stories with similar themes to match their content.

Stories, Tales and Legends:

Rossini	'William Tell Overture'
Offenbach	'Tales Of Hoffmann'
Mozart	*The Magic Flute*
Britten	Noye's Fludde
Stravinsky	Pulcinella
Bernstein	Overture to *Candide*
Richard Strauss	'Till Eulenspeigel'
	'Don Quixote'
John Williams	*Harry Potter* original soundtrack
Mendelssohn	'A Midsummer Night's Dream'
	'Fingal's Cave Overture' (*The Hebrides*)
Tchaikowsky	'1812 Overture'
Sibelius	*Peer Gynt* Suites

Animal stories:

Alan Ridout	'Ferdinand The Bull'
Prokofiev	'Peter And The Wolf'
Schubert	'Trout Quintet'
Saint-Saëns	'Carnival Of The Animals'
Bartók	'The Mosquitos' (violin duos)
Rimsky Korsakov	'Flight Of The Bumblebee'
Vaughan Williams	'The Lark Ascending'
Respighi	'Pines Of Rome' (with recorded nightingale!)

Pieces about childhood:

Bartók	*Für Kinder*
Debussy	*Children's Corner*
Gabriel Fauré	*Dolly Suite*
Arvo Pärt	'Für Aline'
Schumann	*Kinderszenen*
Britten	'Young Person's Guide To The Orchestra'
Chick Corea	*Children's Songs*

Instruments

At this age, children are often capable of replicating simple tunes on tuned percussion instruments or keyboards. This is in line with their natural spatial-temporal pitch awareness. As discussed previously, it is therefore naturally a great point at which to investigate formalized instrument training. For more on this, see Chapter 25, which is dedicated to instruments and such choices.

Meanwhile there are many more instruments you can make at home! Listen to TRACK 46 on the accompanying CD to hear some of these great sounds demonstrated.

The balloon cello

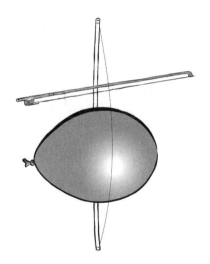

Here's what you'll need:

• a length of pole or dowelling

• a balloon

• a length of fishing line

• ideally, a violin or cello bow

Here's how you make it:

1. Attach the length of fishing line to both ends of the pole, leaving plenty of slack.

2. Inflate the balloon and insert it between the fishing line and the pole, so that the line becomes taut and holds the balloon in place.

3. Pluck or bow the string with a violin or cello bow.

At the end of a performance the player has the option of bursting the balloon!

Strawphone

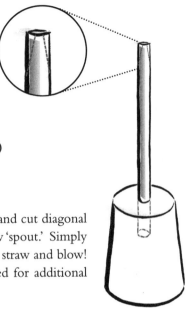

Here's what you'll need:

• a straw

• a paper or plastic cup (optional)

Here's how you make it:

Flatten the end of a drinking straw and cut diagonal strips off both sides to form a narrow 'spout.' Simply place your teeth over the top of the straw and blow! A paper or plastic cup can be added for additional power.

Ghost whirlers

Here's what you'll need:

• a length of ribbed tubing

There's no construction required for this instrument – simply whirl the length of tubing around your head or in a circle in front of you. This sets up a standing wave in the tube, creating a ghostly note, which varies according to the length of the tube. It is wise to make sure that any breakable items are removed from the vicinity when using this instrument!

Bottle choir

Here's what you'll need:

• a variety of different-sized bottles

• a wooden spoon

• a length of wood

• double-sided sticky tape

Here's how you make it:

1. Fix the bottles to the length of wood securely with the double-sided sticky tape.

2. Fill each bottle with a different amount of water to produce a pleasing array of different notes. The more water you add to the bottle, the lower note it will produce.

3. Hit the bottles gently but firmly with the wooden spoon.

high note   low note

Now for some really messy instruments...

Water gong

Here's what you'll need:

• a plastic storage box

• a saucepan lid or metal tray that will fit into the storage box

• a wooden spoon

Here's how you make it:

1. Fill the plastic storage box with water.

2. Tap the lid or tray with the wooden spoon while lowering it into the water. The notes will bend in a very spooky manner!

Plant pot handbells

Here's what you'll need:

• a selection of different earthenware pots

• several short lengths of dowel and a length of strong ribbon.

Here's how you make it:

1. Tie the ribbon to the short length of dowel

2. Feed the piece of dowel through the hole in the bottom of the pot.

3. Suspend upside down and strike gently with a rubber-ended beater or a wooden spoon.

Bendy bowl

Here's what you'll need:

• a metal mixing bowl

• a wooden spoon or beater

Here's how you make it:

1. Put a couple of centimeters of water in the bottom of the bowl.

2. Strike the edge with a large spoon and gently tilt the bowl so the water moves around. This gives a great spooky sound!

Create

This is a version of 'Simon Says' played with music. First, choose a well-known short piece or song such as 'Happy Birthday' or ' Twinkle' and sing it through together normally. Then play 'Simon Says' using Italian musical terms; e.g. 'Simon says sing it *forte*' – sing it loudly.

Here's a chart of some commonly used musical terms with their meanings that you can use for the game:

forte	Loud or strong
piano	Quiet or soft
allegro	Fast
lento	Slow
staccato	Spiky
dolce	Sweetly
legato	Smoothly
tacet	Silent!

There are hundreds of other terms you can teach and use. I use this exercise to teach elements of vocabulary from other languages too.

Games for mental flexibility and coordination

One two three!

Here's an immensely tricky, and yet useful, musical exercise for improving multitasking skills.

Stand facing one another. One of you is person A, the other is person B. You are simply going to count to three together...

A	B
One	Two
Three	One
Two	Three
(keep repeating)	

Listen to TRACK 47 on the accompanying CD to hear a demonstration of this game.

Now try singing your numbers. Any notes will do: You're composing! Try singing your numbers to the notes of a nursery tune as you do this – it is immensely difficult, but a great mental exercise.

The body percussion variation

Imagine that this time you are not allowed to say number two, and it has been replaced by a clap:

A	B
One	Clap
Three	One
Clap	Three

(keep repeating)

Make sure you are breathing well and not clapping stiffly – it is easy to 'lock up' physically while performing this exercise.

This is incredibly difficult, and yet it is a game children love to attempt until they have mastered it. It obviously promotes mental and physical flexibility, and appears to be easier for younger people to master – so be warned!

Language variation

Try changing languages in this exercise! Each player has to speak the numbers in a different language from the other; the result may be:

A	B
Un	Clap
Trois	Eins
Clap	Drei

This is fiendishly difficult but can be mastered when you realize you only have to worry about your own numbers and claps, not the other player's.

For variation – if you can handle any more by this point – try to add other body percussion elements to the exercise too. For example, you could replace 'one' with a stamp and 'three' with a click. You can also try to add melodic elements. Singing an ascending note pattern on successive notes can sound really great, or you could sing a well-known melody note by note.

Thinking about tempo

There are some nice exercises that can lead to interesting conversations with your children. Try taking a well-known uptempo song and sing it really slowly – for instance, try 'If You're Happy And You Know It.' What happens when it's sung really slowly? Singing skipping music slowly (such as 'Here We Go 'Round The Mulberry Bush') has very strange results; conversely, try to sing a lullaby quickly. What would happen to the baby? When you sing a march slowly – does it still work as a march? (We naturally march at around 117 steps per minute, as explained in Chapter 9.)

Animal rhythms

In many forms of traditional music, printed music is rarely used when learning pieces. Complicated rhythms are learnt initially with speech patterns, before being practiced on instruments. This creates a connection between different centers of motor coordination and also ensures the pattern is memorized in a highly effective manner

Many musicians use word patterns to practice and subsequently recall complex rhythmic structures. This game helps to develop rhythmic structures by word substitution.

Make sixteen cards featuring pictures of the following animals – four of each:

Shuffle them and deal them randomly into piles of four cards. Lay each set of cards in a line and say the words as rhythmically as possible. For example, if you've drawn the cards Frog, Spider, Caterpillar, Elephant – you will create the pattern:

Frog, Spider, Caterpillar, Elephant

Rhythms sound more 'musical' if they loop around – so repeat the pattern and emphasize the second line more than the first:

Frog, Spider, Caterpillar, Elephant
Frog, Spider, Caterpillar, Elephant

Each word has a distinct rhythmic shape and emphasis, as well as a natural phrase pattern. These patterns are, of course, inherently musical.

Try performing this chant with a very pronounced beat. It quickly becomes a sort of jungle chant. Be aware of the way in which your voice rises and falls on certain parts of the line and exaggerate these shapes with your child. Draw the rising and falling line with one hand. Imagine a musical line following this shape and try to sing the shape.

Decide on a tune that matches the rise and fall and rhythm of the words and practice singing it. Try clapping the rhythms of two lines at the same time – each player claps their own line. If you have four people, try all your rhythms at the same time.

To make the exercise even more complex, you can add in other animals:

• **Witchety grub**

• **Hippopotamus**

Breakfast music

In this exercise, you rhythmically clap the question: What did you have for breakfast?

And the player or players have to clap their answers prefaced by;

> I had ...

> Toast
> Pancakes
> Cornflakes
> A cup of tea
> A cup of coffee
> Jam and bread
> Bread and butter
> Apple turnover
> Sausages

This pattern can then be repeated, and the result is a double 'call and response' that can be turned into an attractive melody with very little effort.

Homemade salsa

The breakfast exercise leads naturally to a game where one can generate dance rhythms by combining and layering comments about other types of food:

> Peaches – peaches

> I like apples, I like bananas

> When I'm alone, I like to eat my chocolate

When all of these patterns are combined they form a great Latin American rhythm section – just from food rhythms!

Listen to TRACK 48 on the accompanying CD to hear a demonstration of this game.

Animal jazz

If you prefer, you can try making a voice percussion piece out of animal noises that will reinforce inner pulse and rhythmic controls.

With your child, devise some different animal sounds together that have characteristic rhythm patterns. Oink, Ruff, Moo, Woof Woof, Meeeow, and Chitter Chatter will all work well!

Play with different combinations of these sounds. You can get a great 'backbeat' going with this pattern:

oink woof woof, oink woof woof

Then make up a farmyard song to fit over the top of it – or try singing 'Old Macdonald' or 'Cows In The Kitchen' while maintaining the animal sounds.

Chapter 24

Elementary part 2: 7–9 years

B y the age of seven, the reticular formation is developing in the brain. This aids a longer attention span and helps a child focus on single activities for progressively longer periods. Children will be capable of holding long musical sequences in memory, and retrieving them accurately. They will generally be displaying more confidence, particularly in performance situations, and they will make decisions based on strong personal preferences.

This is a great period to focus on children's composition skills, as they will be keen to improvise with ideas and will have developed systems for accurately recording and recalling previous work. Some of these are rooted in traditional notation practices, others are systems they can confidently develop themselves. Encouragement is key: when indulging in creative work, it is critical that children are shown the validity of their efforts as well as being given the tools to replicate successful pieces.

They will be able to express their ideas more confidently on musical instruments and will be able to devise techniques for notation. Increasingly children are able to express and record their ideas by using technological interfaces, whether electronic instruments or software-based sequencing systems. There will probably be a significant amount of music naturally occurring in the school environment and curriculum – the activities suggested in this chapter should supplement these activities.

This is also an ideal age range for regular exposure to live music, as children will be mature enough to attend and enjoy a wide range of music-based performance events.

Going to concerts

There are many opportunities for children to attend concerts of all genres, probably because music promoters have spotted a growth market! Most orchestras now have dedicated education officers and outreach departments: Examples include the New York Philharmonic Orchestra's children's series and the London Symphony Orchestra's 'Discovery' program. In common with many other orchestras and ensembles these offer children's concerts, free performances, online programs, and practical workshops.

Many parents also come to their very first concert by attending these events. Such concerts can be a great way to ease yourself into what sometimes appears to be an intimidating environment. The style in which many concerts are presented has moved on significantly in the last few years to be welcoming, informative, and entertaining.

Your local arts center will probably have a program of events for children that covers many musical styles and events. Funding for the arts often requires a significant percentage of events aimed at the younger audiences, so there is no shortage of opportunities to expose children to great live music-making, composition skills, and even instrument-making.

Making instruments with older children

For older children you can begin to introduce quite sophisticated, science-based instrument-making projects that result in things that sound and look great. There are many instruments you can make together, and they are all based on three core techniques: they are blown, scraped, or hit in order to produce a sound.

I've featured some of the most unusual home-made instruments below. Many of them are very close in nature to key orchestral instruments – listen to some of them demonstrated on TRACK 49.

The balloon bassoon

Here's what you'll need:

• a large balloon

• a strong cardboard tube (from a roll of wrapping paper or, ideally, a small carpet roll)

• masking tape

• a straw

• a strong plastic disposable cup

• a pair of scissors

Here's how you make it:

1. Remove the bottom section of the balloon (the part where you would normally blow to inflate it).

2. Punch a small hole in the bottom of the plastic cup and then carefully remove the base of the cup using the scissors.

3. Stretch the balloon over the wide end of the cup and secure with masking tape.

4. Slide the plastic cup over the end of the tube, with the wide end of the cup nearest the end of the tube. Secure with masking tape, ensuring that the tube stands proud of the cup by about three quarters of an inch, stretching the balloon.

5. Make a small hole in the side of the glass and insert the straw. Make the hole airtight with masking tape.

Experiment with smaller plastic cups and tubes, or with a really long tube, and see how it affects the sound.

Tin-can fiddle

Here's what you'll need:

• a drink can with pull-tab still attached

• section of dowel, .5 inches in diameter

• an eyelet screw

• a guitar string or violin string

Here's how you make it:

1. Screw the eyelet screw into one end of the dowel

2. Insert the other end of the dowel into the can

3. Tie the guitar or violin string to the eyelet at one end, and thread through the hole in the pull-tab at the other end.

4. Tie the string to the pull-tab so that is it is taut.

The tin-can fiddle can be plucked or bowed with a violin bow, or a lollipop stick!

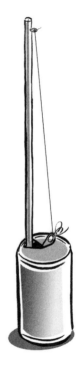

Parsnip/carrot flute

Here's what you'll need:

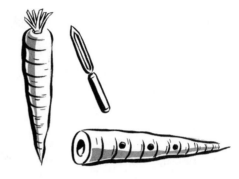

• a carrot or parsnip

• a potato peeler

• an electric drill

Here's how you make it:

1. Peel the potato or carrot.

2. Drill a ½ inch hole right through the centre of the peeled carrot or parsnip.

3. Drill three or four ¼ inch holes down the length of the vegetable.

4. Using the peeler, make the narrow end as narrow and sharp as possible – this is the end you blow through!

Floor whackers

Here's what you'll need:

• a selection of wide plastic pipes

• table tennis paddles, or similar

Here's how you make it:

Simply stand the pipes on the ground and whack them with the table tennis paddles!

Hosepipe horn

Here's what you'll need:

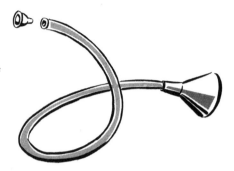

• a length of tubing (hosepipe or similar)

• a funnel

• a mouthpiece (optional)

Here's how you make it:

Attach the funnel to one end of the tubing and blow into the other end. If you have access to a mouthpiece (from a trumpet or similar brass instrument) try inserting this into the other end of the tube.

Body percussion

There are many ways to create effective sounds with your body, from simple claps to beatboxing, where you vocalize complex patterns with explosive consonant sounds. Body percussion is a great vehicle for creative play and composition. There's no equipment to buy, and the only resources necessary are a sense of imagination and a level of coordination. These exercises are a superb way to increase and refine coordination.

One of the greatest benefits drawn from such activities is the development of an internal sense of rhythm. One of the key indicators of confident musicianship is the manifestation of rhythmic confidence and personal accuracy of pulse. As explored in previous chapters, we all display preferred timings: The rates at which we perform common physical and mental tasks are often consistent. However, we don't always use these timings when developing musicianship. Some classically trained musicians have little physical confidence despite being able to play wonderfully; for example, they might not be able to dance in time to the music that they play.

The better your internal sense of pulse, the greater the musical rewards. The following exercises are commonly used by musicians to reconnect with the physical pulse of music; when we join the melodic sense to the physical pulse we are reconnecting with the primal, fundamental elements of all music.

Here are some of the most common body percussion elements:

Hand claps – you can make low notes with your claps by cupping your hands as you hit them together. You can clap with your fingers stretched wide for a higher sound.

Finger clicks – some children find this difficult to do, but will enjoy the challenge of learning how.

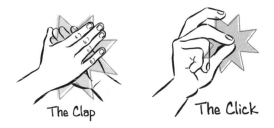

The Clap   The Click

Chest beats – pat your chest with a flat palm to make a 'Doof' sound

Thigh slaps – slap your thigh – right and left

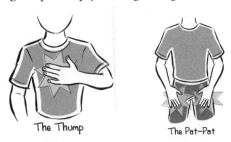

The Thump   The Pat-Pat

Foot stamps – stamp either your left or right foot

To create interesting patterns with some of these elements you can duplicate their names onto a number of cards, making a series of body percussion flashcards. Using these, you can devise great rhythm games where the cards create interesting sequences by being shuffled, dealt, and performed.

The main difficulty in coordinating such patterns is in the transition from one movement to another. With practice, though, you can quickly click, clap, and stamp in sequence!

Here are some patterns for you to try. Remember to keep a regular pulse, and to loop each pattern around. Each box represents a beat, while a zero in a box is a rest pulse.

'Backbeat'

Stamp	clap	0	0
Stamp	clap	0	Clap clap

'Group Chant'

Chest	Click	Chest	Click
Chest	Click	Clap	0

'X beats'

Thigh	Clap	Click	Clap
Thigh	Clap	Click	0

'Oom-pah-pah'

Thigh	clap	Click
Thigh	clap	Click
Thigh	clap	Click
stamp	0	0

When you feel confident with these patterns, you may want to experiment with your multitasking skills by walking, talking, or singing at the same time as playing the rhythms with your body. This is incredibly good for both physical and mental coordination.

Don't forget to make flashcards using the elements listed above.

Listen to TRACK 50 on the accompanying CD to hear a demonstration of a body beat.

Body groove

Chest	Click	Clap	Chest chest
0	Click	Clap	L.Thigh R.thigh

This is a body percussion pattern that really tests physical and mental co-ordination. The result is a strong groove that helps engender an internal pulse and moves the body in a practical, expressive dance pattern that in itself is a musical gesture. You'll notice the pattern works in a fluid pattern of two different circular movements.

Threes and twos

Stamp	Clap	Clap	Stamp	Clap	Clap
Stamp	Clap	Stamp	Clap	Stamp	Clap

This is a great stepping and clapping pattern that works beautifully in canon (delayed sequence) with another person. The pattern explores the relationship between a pattern in two beats and a pattern in three beats occupying the same timeframe.

The pattern repeats around – person A starts on the 1st line, person B on the second.

Body clock claps

Here's an exercise that leads neatly into some cross-curricular work concerning clocks and time. It is an incredible coordination exercise that leads to confident internalization of a pulse.

Get into a relaxed, loose standing position with feet apart. Set up a regular four beat pulse – count 1, 2, 3, 4 aloud.

Practice stepping on 1 and 2, setting up a pattern like this:

left step	right step	0	0
left step	right step	0	0

Keep breathing, and try to keep your body loose. On '3,' try adding a fingersnap in your right hand. The pattern is now:

left step	right step	right click	0
left step	right step	right click	0

On '4,' add a fingersnap in your left hand (if you cannot click your fingers, lightly slap your hand on your thigh instead).

The pattern is now:

left step	right step	right click	left click
left step	right step	right click	left click

Try to execute the sequence without counting the beats out loud. Now move without even thinking of the numbers. If you can do this, you have internalized the pulse!

Let's add the final beat! Try to sense the pulse circulating like the second hand on a clock face. Between your right hand click and your left hand click add a vocal sound as the beat goes past your head – a word like 'Hey!' or a sound like 'Ya' works well.

left step	right step	right click	'hey'	left click
left step	right step	right click	'hey'	left click

Try taking the pulse for a walk, by moving on the steps in each case. You will look like a robot! Try moving those steps smoothly and loosely instead; it should feel more like a dance. Listen to TRACK 51 on the accompanying CD to hear this demonstrated.

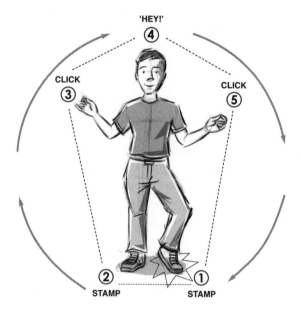

If keeping a steady pulse is a problem, then find a ticking clock in your house and use its steady beat to practice to.

Beat body clock:

Once you have mastered the body clock, you can try 'playing' rhythms and tunes around it. Starting with the left foot, try playing a well-known rhythm around your body, using the steps and clicks and vocal noise in exactly the same sequence, only this time you stick to the adopted rhythmic pattern.

Here's a well-known clapping rhythm often heard at sports events.

In the diagram, the 'X's represent the claps, the 'O's are rests:

XOXOXXXOXXXXOXXO

If you prefer, you could notate the pattern this way:

X	0	X	0
X	X	X	0
X	X	X	X
0	X	X	o

Repeat the sequence four times around the clock pattern. You will notice that each time the pattern cycles, it begins on a different point of the body. The last time through, the sequence begins on the vocal sound.

You can hear this demonstrated on TRACK 52 of the accompanying CD.

Further listening

You may want to play your child some of the following tracks in order to help develop his or her sense of inner pulse through rhythmic movement and physical body percussion. All these tracks contain depictions of wild dances or wild bangs and excitement.

Tchaikovsky	'1812 Overture'
Heinrich Biber	'Battle Symphony'
Stravinsky	'The Rite Of Spring'
Bartók	'Romanian Folk Dances'
Copland	'Hoe Down' from *Rodeo*

Table music

Many composers have experimented with writing pieces that can be played by reading the music upside down as well as the right way up. If you take the pattern above and read it upside down, this is the resulting rhythm:

0	X	X	0
X	X	X	X
0	X	X	X
0	X	0	X

If you clap this while another person claps the music the right way round, it sounds wonderful!

Now try rotating the grid clockwise onto its side:

0	0	X	0
X	X	X	X
0	X	X	X
X	X	X	0

The resulting rhythms also sound fantastic. You can have four clapping patterns that are all completely different, coming from one piece of music.

In Mozart's era, this kind of piece that fits against itself was called 'Tafelmusik,' meaning 'table music.' The sheet music would have been placed on a table between the two musicians and played at the same time.

Obviously the rhythms above can fit together really well. What is incredible is that the pieces that Mozart was writing are melodic – there is a famous example for two violins. The tune fits against itself upside down and backwards! Bach also created a series of pieces in his 'Musical Offering' that play similar tricks.

Further listening:

Mozart	'Tafelmusik'
Bach	'Musical Offering'
Shostakovitch	'Preludes And Fugues'
Steve Reich	'Vermont Counterpoint'
	'Clapping Music'

Musical tic-tac-toe

Play a game of X's and O's with your child. You may end up with something like this:

O	X	X
X	O	O
X	X	O

If we treat the 'X' as a clap and the 'O' as a rest you can read and play the game as a piece of music!

By assigning specific notes to the symbols, you can create a rudimentary melody from the grid. If you rotate the pattern there are three further 'grid pieces' to be found, all of which will fit together if played at the same time.

Fibonacci grooves

Rhythm games can be very useful tools for teaching children to experience and actually feel advanced mathematical concepts. I have used rhythm games to help children memorize sequences such as prime numbers, or the Fibonacci sequence. As both of these mathematical concepts appear in music, it is natural to use music to learn them.

The Fibonacci sequence is constructed from the addition of two preceding integers to create a sum, which is then added to the preceding number. This results in an infinite chain of numbers where the proportional relationship between any three adjacent numbers in the sequence is the same. The beginning of the sequence features the following series of numbers:

2   3   5   8

If one claps the pattern above while accenting the first of each group, you end up with a strong groove with an interesting series of 'kicks.' You can hear this pattern on TRACK 53 of the accompanying CD.

X	X						
X	X	X					
X	X	X	X	X			
X	X	X	X	X	X	X	X

This can be used as the rhythmic backbone to a new piece of music. Composers such as Bartók and Kodaly used the relationship between these numbers to inspire their melodies, harmonies, rhythms, and compositional structures; the relationship also occurs in many famous pieces of visual art where it is commonly referred to as 'The Golden Section.'

Musical signing systems

In previous chapters, I talked extensively about the importance of 'fingerplays' in developing personal coordination and musical skills. In music, the hands can obviously be used to direct musical flow and content – for example, by conducting.

Before written notation systems had been devised, the hands were often used to convey pitch and duration information accurately through the use of sophisticated hand signals. In one system, the thumb touching different parts of the hand could indicate the pitch. I have learned to use a similar system when playing with Indian musicians to synchronize rhythmic locations in long musical sequences.

In the system of music training devised by Zoltan Kodaly, (for more detail see Chapter 26) hand signals very specifically indicate the pitch in relationship to the given key note.

Below are some examples of the common hand signs used to define pitches in what is known as 'tonic solfa.' It is worth teaching these to your child on an ascending scale using both the names (which are sung) and the hand signs, which indicate melodic intent.

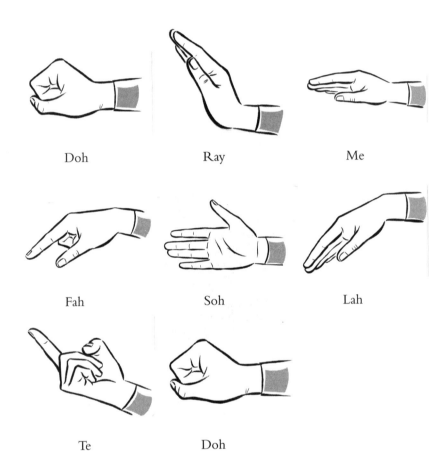

Doh

Ray

Me

Fah

Soh

Lah

Te

Doh

Generating musical material

These are all potentially cross-curricular projects that can trigger some exciting musical ideas and can lead to a lot of follow-up activities. The following exercises show you how to tie together coordination games, musical material, creative play, and cross-curricular learning.

Melodic verse

To generate a melody with an appealing phrase shape and rhythm, it is worth using verse as a source of inspiration. You can use existing poetry or create your own.

When working with children, I try to work their own experiences or feelings into the pieces so they have a sense of ownership of the resulting material. An extremely effective way to do this is to create short couplets about people, things, places, or occasions that mean a lot to them.

Once you have enough of these couplets, you can join them together to make a song. Of course this may end up being rather surreal, but will be all the more memorable and funny as a result.

When I'm feeling short of ideas, I turn to an old writer's trick. I have a box of words printed on magnetic strips that stick on a metallic surface (normally the fridge door!) which are great for generating nonsense poems. Even if a line of verse makes no sense, it can still display a musical shape that can easily be rendered as a melody.

Living score

Children love playing cumulative picture or story games. You've probably played these together in one form or another before. One of my children's favorite games involves the telling of a story together, each player contributing a single word at a time. The story veers off in all directions according to each player's agenda and is always amusing if not always very coherent.

'Living score' is an exercise that is based on the same concept, which never fails to generate interesting melodies, and yet uses free choice and random factors in equal proportion.

Players sit in a circle facing each other with tuned percussion instruments to hand – metallophones, hand chimes, glockenspiels, etc. all work well in this exercise.

To start, each player chooses a single note on their instruments and one player starts by sounding their note once. The player to his or her right plays next, until everyone has played as part of the sequence.

This works well with as few as four players and can be really effective with up to twenty participants. If the sequence of notes sounds interesting, reverse the order by going round the circle in the other direction.

Try swapping places with others to change the order in which the melody notes fall, and get the children to decide which sequence sounds best. They will always have a strong opinion on such matters.

Try to play combinations of the notes at the same time, to see which group chords sound interesting. It is very important to give any good-sounding combination or sequence a catchy name that will act as an aide memoire when trying to recall it. It is quite easy to build a short piece from the sequences, playing them in repeating loops, both forwards and backwards, maybe starting and finishing with a chord played together.

Instrument signatures

If you have access to tuned percussion, it is possible to explore some fairly advanced compositional techniques just by playing simple games.

Using a tuned percussion or keyboard instrument, ask your child to create a three-note pattern on the keys that represents their 'signature.' I often ask children to imagine they are introducing themselves to an alien, that the only language they have in common is music, and that they are allowed to use three different notes, each struck only once.

They may come up with something like this:

D F G

This pattern can be reversed like this:

G F D

This technique is called *retrograde* in classical music, and is a way of extending musical material.

If we add the first phrase to the second, this is the resulting pattern:

D F G G F D

This is a musical palindrome, that is to say it can be played forwards and backwards with the same result.

By turning the first phrase on its head we can create this pattern:

D B A

This is called an *inversion*. (Our initial pattern goes up three letters from the starting note and then up one further letter for the latest note. To invert the pattern, just move in the opposite direction – in this case, down three letternames for the second note and down one further for the last note).

By turning it on its head and reversing it we arrive at this pattern:

D B A A B D

This is known as an *inverted retrograde*.

By adding all of the patterns together, one can create a nicely shaped musical phrase like this:

D F G G F D D B A A B D

This is a technique that all major composers have used at one stage or another, and is a simple way to extend a short idea into a major melodic theme. By adding repeats to some of the patterns, the material can form the basis for an entire piece! If one repeats a short phrase over and over, it is technically known as an *ostinato*. Ostinato techniques are incredibly useful for composition exercises with children, as they constitute regular patterns that can be maintained while other musical material fits over the top. The great German composer and educator Carl Orff based his 'Schulwerk' system of music training on the use of such systems, and through teaching using such systems was inspired to write one of the best-known pieces of classical music, 'Carmina Burana.'

Yes, no, and maybe

This is a game used by theatre companies to generate emotional improvised scenes, but it can easily be adapted to create wonderful melodic question and answer sequences.

Work in a pair; one of you is person A, the other is person B. Person A has to ask person B questions relentlessly, and person B is always going to respond with a forceful 'No!' in response. Try this for a minute or two.

Now swap roles. This time person B has to ask person A questions relentlessly, and person A is always going to respond with an enthusiastic 'Yes!' in response. Again, try for a couple of minutes.

Swap once again.

For the final conversations, person A asks person B questions, but this time, person B always responds with 'Yes, and... (carrying on with the conversation each time)'. You will find it easy to develop a fairly entertaining, if surreal dialogue. After about five questions and answers, stop proceedings and repeat the last question and response over and over. Then apply the following suggestions:

• **Fit the words to a strong pulse.**

• **Exaggerate the phrase shapes of the words.**

• **Now make a more sing-song sound when you speak.**

- Try to sing the question and response while keeping in rhythm.

- If the melodies sound particularly good, try to find them on a pair of musical instruments.

- Practice the question and answer on the instruments and repeat the pattern.

You will by this stage have generated a very organic phrase shape with a satisfying contour that will probably make a great musical lead theme.

If playing this game with many players, join the questions and answers together into scenes. They may not relate to one another at all, but it's an incredibly entertaining and simple way of composing in a group without resorting to pen, paper, or any hint of writer's block!

I recently worked with a group of elementary-age schoolchildren who made up their own short musical by playing this game and structuring the results in a creative way.

Disco freeze

Put on a recording of some music with good beats for dancing. Encourage your child to dance in time to the music, using his or her whole body to react to the rhythm and melodies.

Demonstrate how to draw the 'line' of the melody in the air, showing whether it is smooth or spiky, slow, or fast. When the music is quiet, they should make small movements and make large movements for loud dynamics. Reach up for high notes on tiptoes, and scoop the lower notes from the floor.

Explain that you are going to hold a contest (a little like musical chairs). When you pause the music, players have to stand totally still, holding their positions as if frozen mid-step, until the music starts up again. This can easily be played as a kind of knockout competition.

Strange art gallery

The Disco Freeze can be played with a good variation. This can either be in a pair, or with a group of children.

First of all, split into two teams. One group dances to the music and will freeze when the music stops abruptly. The players who are not frozen walk around as if in a gallery, observing the strange sculptures, i.e. the frozen players! Swap over and repeat the process.

The best sculptures should be pointed out and given witty names – it's best if the children suggest these themselves. This game is always really popular and encourages the children to think laterally and artistically, even though they are playing a party game.

If your children enjoy this game you could find some pictures of well-known sculptures and explore the music that could have inspired them. For example, *Don Giovanni* by Mozart has a statue that comes to life with very dramatic consequences.

See whether the children can make up instrumental music to fit the mood of the people portrayed in stone.

Comic strip

This is one of my favorite musical composition games. This is incredibly good for stimulating imagination, spatial temporal awareness, and lateral thinking.

First, take a favorite image, whether a painting, photo, or drawing and set it on a page with a blank box preceding it, and a blank box following too. It should have the appearance of the central panel of a comic strip with two blank panels on either side.

Your child should be encouraged to describe what they think is happening in the picture – let them run with the ideas! Help them to break the image into foreground, background, atmosphere, and characters. Ask questions to aid the process:

• Who is depicted in the picture?

• What are they doing?

• Where are they?

• What time is it?

• What's the weather like?

• Is it happy, sad, or ambiguous?

Children enjoy making musical sounds to depict the elements listed on the previous page. You can use voices or instruments to create sounds to match the ideas. For instance, if the picture shows a calm sea, make some sounds that gently shift around, maybe with the odd seagull! Children tend to be very good at matching images to musical ideas – they won't find this difficult.

The idea of this exercise is to encourage your child to think about a sequence of events around the displayed image. They should then sketch pictures in the two spare panels – a 'before' and 'after' image, rendering the whole sequence into a kind of comic strip. It could be a boat setting sail in the first panel, and a storm in the third. Then, devise music to match these ideas – so the musical ideas naturally build and develop to match the images in the comic strip.

The great thing about this exercise is that it very naturally encourages children (and adults) to look at paintings or photographs in an entirely different way. The images cease to be frozen moments and take on an entirely new dimension. Adding music to the process makes the images come to life.

> *I ran a project recently where the participants spent the day at the National Gallery in London hearing lectures on different paintings – all of which represented a captured moment. The children then chose which painting to represent musically. The most gratifying part of the process was hearing the children point out things in the paintings to the curators that they themselves had never noticed!*

You might want to try this exercise with a range of very different images. For instance, if you were to choose a landscape, seascape, or urban scene, it is worth 'listening around' to descriptive music.

Recommended listening for musical landscapes:

Richard Strauss	'Alpine Symphony'
Debussy	'La Mer'
Sibelius	'Finlandia'
Saint-Saëns	'Aquariums'

My favorite image to date for this project is 'Rain, steam, and speed' by Turner. It is an almost abstract, stormy, dramatic picture with plenty of space for one's own ideas. There is a great tradition of composed music representing train journeys and speed:

Recommended listening for transport and speed:

Honegger	'Pacific 231'
Villa-Lobos	'Little Train Of The Caipira'
Pat Metheny	'Last Train Home'
John Adams	'A Short Ride In A Fast Machine'

If possible, visit an art gallery and choose some favorite pictures to work with. Buy postcards and use them as the central image in your comic strip. Look up paintings or photographs online – most of the major galleries have online collections. Bear in mind that photos work really well too – you could use some of your own images for this exercise to great effect. If your child enjoys this activity, make them aware of the link to animation, cartoons, and film music. Listen to the music in favorite films to see how the composer can use music to tell a story as effectively as pictures.

You can listen to a wide range of music to explore how composers can represent weather and the seasons.

Recommended listening for weather and the seasons:

Vivaldi   *The Four Seasons*
This famous work features storms, dogs barking, farmers stamping their boots, and many other fabulous musical depictions of weather, people, and animals.

Tchaikovsky   'The Seasons'
A very different take on the times of year!

Peter Sculthorpe   'Port Essington'
In this brilliant Australian piece, the outback gradually invades a dilapidated Victorian spa resort.

Vaughan Williams   'Sinfonia Antarctica'
'Sea Symphony'

Beethoven   'Pastoral Symphony'
A wonderful depiction of springtime, birdcalls, and country landscapes.

Debussy   'Nuages'
Mussorgsky   'A Night On The Bare Mountain'

Here are some online resources for images:

MOMA, the New York Museum of Modern Art has online exhibits here: www.moma.org
Fine Arts Museums of San Francisco has a wonderful set of collections online, with a fully searchable database. This can be found at: www.thinker.org
The National Gallery in London has most of its artworks available online: www.nationalgallery.org.uk
The Tate Gallery has major historic and contemporary British and international collections for view at the following address: www.tate.org.uk

These are other highly recommended places to look for music project ideas for children:

Boowa Kwala
www.boowakwala.com
New York Philharmonic
www.nyphilkids.org
American Symphony Orchestra League
www.playmusic.org
Carnegie Hall
www.listeningadventures.org
Dallas Symphony Orchestra Kids
www.dsokids.com
London Sinfonietta
www.londonsinfonietta.org.uk
London Philharmonic Orchestra
www.lpo.co.uk/education

Chapter 25

Instrument Lessons

At certain points in a child's education, a more formal approach to music training may be appropriate. Your child may benefit from specialized instruction, either in general musicianship or in learning specific musical instruments.

Formalized instrumental training

Studying an instrument requires dedicated periods of concentration and can therefore help children mentally focus for set periods of time. Learning an instrument is also a great way to develop self-discipline and time-management techniques. It requires the comprehension and communication of sophisticated concepts as well as stimulating the development of fine motor abilities.

Instrumental study can help to teach control of physical functions such as the regulation of breathing. It can also refine mental functions such as extended memory techniques.

Learning an instrument normally involves the learning, comprehension, and subsequent interpretation of musical notation, which is in effect a highly sophisticated graphic language!

Studying an instrument naturally leads to playing and performing, whether solo or within ensembles. As a cellist I split my work between solo playing, chamber music, or playing in bands.

Learning an instrument can involve incredibly challenging and technically detailed work, but inevitably leads to a great level of satisfaction by giving one a means by which to express musical ideas, whether for one's own pleasure or for an audience.

When should instruments be introduced?

Many teachers recommend that children should have basic reading skills before starting to learn an instrument. This normally corresponds with the age at which they are able to start focusing for progressively longer periods of time – essential when studying something requiring both technical and expressive concentration. You may have been experimenting together with home-made or purchased instruments, and have reached the point where your child would would benefit from something more formalized. However, you should resist the temptation to rush out and spend a lot of money on equipment if it is only a brief passing interest that is being expressed!

In the pages that follow we present a brief guide to the most common instruments that your child might want to learn. For each one we have given a suggested age for starting formal music lessons and a 'startability' rating (which indicates the ease with which a child can get a satisfactory sound out of the instrument and, therefore, the time taken before a first tune can be played). The easier an instrument is to start, the lower the 'startability' rating. For example, the piano, which requires no special technique to create a sound, gets a rating of one star, whereas the oboe, which is much more difficult to obtain a pleasing sound from, gets a rating of six stars.

Exploring a wide range of instruments

You should encourage your child to try a wide range of instruments before you settle on one in particular. They must love the sound of the instrument and the challenges that it presents; otherwise they will not want to continue playing it after the initial novelty has worn off. Listen together to a wide range of instruments and try to attend as many children's concerts as possible. Many of the major orchestras have community programs that encourage children to try a wide range of instruments at outreach events. This can be a great way to explore the range of instrumental options open to your child.

Don't be pushy!

If a child is forced to play an instrument, they will regard it as a chore rather than a pleasure and will give up at the first opportunity. Your child does not have to play a musical instrument just because of peer pressure (or even parent pressure!). Your child may derive more satisfaction from studying a certain sport seriously. I would also question whether a school environment is necessarily the best environment for instrument instruction. Your child may have to miss parts of their academic lessons in order to attend their instrumental lessons each week. Sometimes schools force pupils to choose between the arts and sport. Needless to say, it is important to be fit as a musician, so this can be counterproductive!

I have seen students pass through music college only to give up instrumental playing upon graduation, simply because they never really had a choice in their initial instrument.

Make your children feel it is their choice and let them pester you

I practically begged my parents to let me play the cello, so by the time I actually started learning, nothing could stop me because I was absolutely determined to play! A child's own emotional investment is priceless and sometimes a little inverse psychology can go a long way. Help your child to become excited at the prospect of playing an instrument – read about it together, listen to lots of examples of it being played, find pictures, look at Websites, make a collage or a project together. This will pay dividends when it is time to start studying.

Be imaginative and practical about the choice

Make sure that the instrument you choose together is appropriate for your child's physical size, fitness level, and lung capacity. Even string instruments require good breathing skills. Playing an instrument can be very physically demanding, but can also increase physical fitness levels through practice.

Don't just match instrument to perceived type – just because your daughter is delicate and sensitive, doesn't mean that she has to play the flute, she may enjoy the personality and power of a bass instrument! Less common instruments can lead to more playing opportunities later on – any school or youth orchestra is grateful for another viola, where there may already be a surplus of more common woodwind instruments. Don't just start your child on a certain instrument because it is already in the house.

Rent before you buy

Don't spend money until you are sure – look into the costs of renting instruments before committing to a costly purchase. Many music shops are happy to offer rent to own plans that are incredibly reasonable. Under such a plan you will have already paid for a proportion of the instrument if you decide to buy. If your child changes his or her mind about learning it, you will have only paid the rental costs.

In the pages that follow we have given each instrument a star rating to indicate how expensive they are. This takes into account the cost of a good quality beginner's instrument and the cost of lessons (with one star being the cheapest and six stars the most expensive).

Transferring

Your child may begin by studying one instrument and switch to another as they grow up. Be open to transferring instruments if it seems appropriate – the second instrument your child learns may be 'the one.'

Remember that the key musical skills and sensibilities learned on any instrument are totally transferable – the active technique will be different. For example, a recorder player may become a flute player or a saxophonist. (The recorder is an instantly gratifying instrument as everyone can make a sound the first time they pick it up – as discussed previously, it is vitally important that the instrument sounds good from the start.)

Here are a couple of examples of typical flows of instrumental learning:

• **Singing > recorder > clarinet > saxophone**

• **Singing > recorder > cornet >trumpet**

• **Singing > piano > violin > viola**

Teachers

Make sure you find a good teacher. A great teacher will probably have a waiting list, which can be frustrating if your child is really keen to get started, but if they're really good it will be worth the wait.

Most teachers will suggest an initial consultation lesson. This is mutually beneficial; a teacher may feel they cannot teach your child, or you may feel they don't relate to your child. Lesson prices can vary enormously depending on the experience, popularity, and professional profile of the teacher.

It is important to find the right teaching pattern. Is a weekly one-to-one session best or would a every two-weeks shared class be more effective? Some instruments can be taught in a group situation, others have to be studied one on one. A teacher will know what is best for your child and their choice of instrument.

USA
www.teachlist.com
A list of music teachers in the USA – 16,200 teachers featured to date

www.musicstaff.com

Examinations

There are different styles of graded examination that your child can take in their chosen instrument. Some children love the challenge of passing grades, whilst others find that exams make them nervous and take the fun out of playing altogether. I have no strong opinion on exams, except to say that they offer a clear pathway of repertoire and technical standards that is hard to beat. Also, some of the higher grades can later constitute part of the grade of an academic music qualification at school.

When you take an instrumental exam you are generally required to perform several specified pieces that you have selected from a shortlist. You are also required to play a piece of music by sight, and present technical material such as scales. The exams also feature aural tests to determine general musical skills.

Music theory

It is important that while learning instrumental techniques, your child also acquires a good working knowledge of music theory. This is essential for deeper comprehension of the music they are studying. Indeed, for some instrumental examinations it is mandatory for students to have achieved a certain level of skill before being able to enter the higher levels.

Maintaining interest

If your child does not want to practice an instrument, maybe the teaching style is not quite right for them. Every achievement should be rewarded with praise and they should feel they are developing their own musical voice.

Think about activities your child loves – it may be pitching a baseball, reading adventure stories, baking, or painting. All of these activities create their own rewards, they engender positive anticipation and immense satisfaction. Mix such activities together!

Of course, having good role models can help, so make sure your child is aware of leading, inspiring players. If your child finds the technical side of practice difficult and unstimulating, try to turn the exercises into more appealing activities. Even scales can be made to appear fun if approached in the right manner.

Practical considerations

Think very carefully about the practicalities of different instruments. For instance, if your child chooses to play the harp, you will probably need to purchase a van just to transport it!

• **Is it an instrument they can carry comfortably?**

• **Can they maintain it themselves and learn to take proper care of it if it is valuable?**

• **Is the instrument versatile with an interesting repertoire?**

If your child wants to play a noisy instrument, are there ways of muting it to preserve your own sanity and the goodwill of your neighbours?

Don't forget the hidden costs that come with instruments. Pianos need tuning, string instruments need spare strings and rosin, some woodwind instruments require reeds, and so forth. Then there is the cost of sheet music and exam entry fees.

Instrument families

This is by no means an exhaustive list, but may help you start to make choices of instrument with your child. Remember, the term 'startability' means how quickly and easily a child can make his or her first pleasing sounds on the instrument – the lower the rating the 'easier' it is.

Pianos and keyboards

Starting age:	6-7 years
'Startability':	★☆☆☆☆☆
Expense:	★★★★☆☆
Key facts:	Self-accompanying
	Not portable

Many households have pianos as part of the furniture, and so it can seem a logical step to start lessons when children are old enough. The piano is great as a solo instrument, but bear in mind that opportunities to play in an orchestra are rather limited later down the line when compared with a violin or clarinet. Keyboard skills are immensely useful though and have been shown to have positive effects on co-ordination skills and general neurological development. It is possible to start the piano from four years of age, but a teacher would normally recommend later, when reading skills, attention span, and hand size have developed.

Pianos are expensive and need regular maintenance; a tuner will need to come to your house to service the instrument. A cheaper alternative to a piano is a keyboard. Ths will probably have a wide range of sounds and effects, but be warned, you may tire of these rather quickly! Most keyboards do not accurately represent the playing action of a piano, which has weighted keys. If your child wants to learn the piano, a piano is the best thing to learn on!

There are also hybrid pianos available that look and sound like a normal instrument, but at the flick of a switch, can be made silent instruments with headphones for private practice.

The organ is a great instrument too – but has the added complexity of pedals to play with the feet. It is suitable for someone who is older who has already learned the piano.

Piano:
Gershwin	'Rhapsody In Blue'
Debussy	*Children's Corner*
Scott Joplin	'Maple Leaf Rag'
Beethoven	'Für Elise'

In the world of Jazz, you may want to listen to 'So What' by Miles Davis, or the soundtrack to the film *The Firm* by Dave Grusin. In rock and pop the piano has been used in a huge range of genres from rock 'n' roll (Jerry Lee Lewis, Little Richard), soul (Ray Charles), rock (Elton John) right through to current bands like Coldplay.

For further information try www.pianoeducation.org

Organ:
Bach	'Toccata & Fugue In D Minor'
Saint-Saëns	'Organ Symphony'
Poulenc	'Organ Concerto'
Widor	'Toccata'

Electric keyboard/organ
Jimmy Smith	'Organ Grinder's Swing'
Herbie Hancock	*Headhunters* (album)
Stevie Wonder	'Superstition'
Rick Wakeman	*The Six Wives Of Henry The Eighth* (album)

String instruments

String instruments can be started at a very early age, and come in a wide range of guises, either plucked or bowed. Most instruments are available in different-scaled sizes suitable for very young children up to adults. Instruments such as beginner violins or guitars can be bought or rented for a reasonable price – but be warned, even moderately good full-sized instruments can cost thousands of dollars! Instruments can be astoundingly expensive if your child progresses to a high level. As with any instrument there are some cost implications in addition to buying or renting the instrument: Bows need to be re-haired and strings can be surprisingly expensive.

Bowed string instruments can be fitted with practice mutes made of lead that make them almost silent for practice.

Violin

Starting age: 5 years

'Startability': ★★★★★☆

Expense: ★★★☆☆☆

Key facts: Most common orchestral instrument

The violin can be started from a very young age. Rent to own packages can be very cheap and include all the accessories the instrument requires. There are many highly effective systems for learning the violin either privately or in a class environment through methods such as Suzuki. The instrument is highly versatile and has a huge repertoire from many genres.

J. S. Bach	'Partitas'
Mendelssohn	'Violin Concerto'
Bruch	'Violin Concerto'
Vivaldi	*The Four Seasons* (Nigel Kennedy album)
Stefan Grapelli	Anything by the Hot Club de France Quintet
Vanessa Mae	*The Ultimate Vanessa Mae* (album)

Viola

Starting age: 7 years

'Startability': ★★★★★☆

Expense: ★★★☆☆☆

Key facts: Beautiful, dusky tone

The viola is slightly larger than the violin and makes a different colored sound. It is often a transfer instrument from the violin, and is always in demand in ensembles and orchestras.

J. S. Bach	'Brandenburg Concerto No. 6'
Telemann	'Concerto'
Mozart	'Sinfonia Concertante' For Violin And Viola
Berlioz	'Harold in Italy'

Cello

Starting age: 7 years

'Startability': ★★★★☆☆

Expense: ★★★★☆☆

Key facts: Has to be played sitting down

The cello is highly versatile, but it is bulky and can be difficult for small children to carry about. It is worth the trouble, though. The cello is very versatile and has a great repertoire.

J. S. Bach	'Suites for Solo cello'
Elgar	'Cello Concerto' (Dupre/Barenboim)
Tchaikovsky	'Rococco Variations'

Double Bass

Starting age: 10 years

'Startability': ★★★★☆☆

Expense: ★★★★★☆

Key facts: Very bulky

The double bass is even bulkier than the cello, but is always in great demand with an interesting, highly varied repertoire from classical to jazz to rock 'n' roll. There are specially adapted instruments for young players called minibasses – they make a great sound, are more suitable for small hands, and can be transported more easily than the traditional instrument.

Eberhart Weber   'Pendulum'
Any recordings featuring bassists Miroslav Vitous or Ray Brown.

Harp

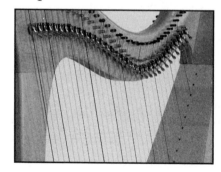

Starting age: 11 years

'Startability': ★★★☆☆☆

Expense: ★★★★★★

Key facts: Beautiful, but rent before you buy

The harp is a beautiful instrument that can be expensive and difficult to transport (depending on the size of harp, you may need to purchase a station wagon or van to transport it!). However, smaller beginner's instruments that fit on the back seat of a car are now available at much more reasonable prices. Technically, easier than the piano, though does requires good coordination.

Mozart	'Concerto For Flute And Harp'
Mahler	'Adagietto' (from 5th symphony)
Stevie Wonder	'If It's Magic'

Acoustic guitar

Starting age: 7 years

'Startability': ★★☆☆☆☆

Expense: ★★☆☆☆☆

Key facts: Easy and versatile
Portable

The guitar is a great instrument for children. The instruments come in small sizes for young players. It is probably a good instrument to start from the age of seven, and the techniques learnt on the acoustic guitar can be transferred to the electric guitar. Note that the classical guitar and the acoustic guitar are not the same thing. The classical guitar is a separate instrument, reserved for the classical repertoire and with its own technique. The steel-strung acoustic guitar is a larger instrument, usually associated with folk, pop, and rock.

There are many ways of learning the guitar: private or class lessons, from books, or even online. Guitar music can be represented by TAB charts, many of which are available on the Internet.

Rodrigo	'Concierto De Aranjuez' (Julian Bream)
The Beatles	'Blackbird'
Simon & Garfunkel	'Homeward Bound'
Eva Cassidy	'Somewhere Over The Rainbow'
Bob Dylan	'Mr. Tambourine Man'

| James Taylor | 'Sweet Baby James' |
| Rickie Lee Jones | 'Chuck E's In Love' |

Electric guitar

Starting age: 8 years

'Startability': ★★☆☆☆

Expense: ★★☆☆☆

Key facts: High 'cool' factor, which aids motivation

This is obviously a very appealing instrument for children as it has a very prominent profile in popular music, is relatively easy to learn, and is very loud. The electric guitar is obviously noisier than the acoustic, but can be used with headphones and can therefore be completely silent if desired. You should invest in some safe headphones for your child if you decide to go down this route. There are quite a few hidden costs to be considered: You will need to buy an amplifier and possibly a range of effects pedals.

The electric guitar is omnipresent is popular music, and your child may already have some favorite songs that feature the instrument; if not, here are a few guitar classics that may fire their imagination:

Chuck Berry	'Johnny B. Goode'
Jimi Hendrix	'All Along The Watchtower'
Jimmy Page (Led Zeppelin)	'Stairway To Heaven'
Carlos Santana	'Samba Pa Ti'
Pete Townshend (The Who)	'Pinball Wizard'
Keith Richards (The Rolling Stones)	'Brown Sugar'
Peter Green (Fleetwood Mac)	'Albatross'
George Benson	'On Broadway'

Other inspirational guitarists include The Edge (U2), Johnny Marr (The Smiths), Slash (Guns 'n' Roses and Velvet Revolver), Steve Vai, Angus Young (AC/DC) and George Harrison (The Beatles).

The bass guitar is often in demand as it's an essential part of most bands. It also comes in a version without frets – this is more difficult for tuning at first.

Flea (Red Hot Chili Peppers)	'Higher Ground'
Bernard Edwards (Chic)	'Good Times'
Sting (The Police)	'Walking On The Moon'
Mark King (Level 42)	'Running In The Family'

Other inspirational bassists include Jaco Pastorius, Stanley Clarke (try his track 'Lords Of The Low Frequencies'), Abe Laboriel, and Bootsy Collins.

Woodwind instruments

Instruments involving blowing (woodwind and brass instruments) should be introduced after the child's second set of teeth have grown through. Many woodwind instruments are easily portable – the flute, recorder, and oboe all fit into small cases – and are therefore easy for children to carry.

Recorder

Starting age:	5 years
'Startability':	★☆☆☆☆☆
Expense:	★☆☆☆☆
Key facts:	Inexpensive, easy, and popular

The recorder is an instantly gratifying instrument as anyone can make a sound the first time they pick it up. It is easily taught in a class situation and can be studied from fingering charts. The instrument does have its limitations, and is not often deployed in a very imaginative way.

Bach	Brandenburg Concerto No. 4
Vivaldi	Recorder Concertos

Flute

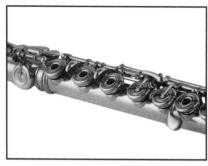

Starting age: 9-10 years

'Startability': ★★☆☆☆

Expense: ★★★☆☆

Key facts: Light, portable

The flute can be started from nine to ten years of age and is a popular instrument – it's relatively simple with an attractive sound and great repertoire. However, because it is popular, there may not be as many opportunities for ensemble work later down the line. 'Curved-head' models are available for younger players, which reduce the distance required to reach the end of the instrument.

Vivaldi	'Concerto For Flute And Strings in D Major'
Poulenc	'Flute Sonata'
Jethro Tull	*Aqualung* (album)

Oboe

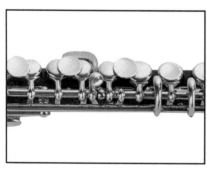

Starting age: 10 years

'Startability': ★★★★★★

Expense: ★★★★★★

Key facts: Difficult, double-reed instrument

The Oboe is quite hard for beginners because it is a 'double-reed' instrument that requires the player to compress the reeds together with lip (embouchure) pressure. The oboe is best considered after the age of ten.

Dvořák	'From The New World' Symphony, 3rd Movt.
Schumann	'Piano Concerto in A Minor'

Clarinet

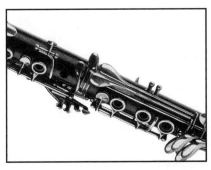

Starting age: 7 years

'Startability': ★★☆☆☆☆

Expense: ★★★☆☆☆

Key facts: Incredibly versatile gateway to the saxes

The clarinet is a good 'starter' instrument as it makes a satisfying sound and has a wide repertoire. Clarinets for beginners are constructed from modern plastics, and are therefore cheaper (and lighter) than many other instruments. The clarinet is prominent in many forms of music, from classical to folk and jazz and works well as both a solo and ensemble instrument.

Mozart   'Clarinet Concerto In A Major'
Weber   'Clarinet Concerto'
George Gershwin 'Rhapsody In Blue'
The Clarinet is also a prominent instrument in Trad Jazz (New Orleans-style jazz) and Klezmer (a Jewish musical tradition).

Saxophone

Starting age: 8-9 years

'Startability': ★★★☆☆☆

Expense: ★★★★☆☆

Key facts: High 'cool' factor Big family

If your child takes to the clarinet, they may want to try the saxophone too – the clarinet's close relation. This is a very popular instrument due to its versatility – not everyone realizes that it originated as a classical instrument. There is a whole family of instruments to choose from, but the larger instruments are more appropriate for older age groups, and cost more.

Soprano sax – this instrument is the highest of the commonly used saxophones, and is most like a clarinet in sound and feel, though it has a thicker, richer tone. Sometimes the soprano is long and straight, like a clarinet, and sometimes it is curled, which makes it look like a baby sax!

Alto sax – the instrument of Charlie Parker. Not as high in pitch as the soprano, yet still high enough to match the average pitch of a trumpet. Commonly found in wind ensembles and jazz bands, with a huge classical repertoire. This instrument is the easiest 'standard' sax for children because of its small size, though it does require a tighter embouchure (the formation of the muscles around the mouth) than the lower saxes.

Tenor sax – again this instrument is very common in wind ensembles and jazz groups, but less so in orchestras. There is, however, a huge repertoire of pieces for tenor saxes, both as solo instruments with piano accompaniment, and as part of small groups. It is larger and heavier than the alto, so therefore unsuitable for very young children.

Baritone sax – this honks the bass notes at the bottom of a brass section, or provides the fruity low-end sound in a big band. It is a large instrument that only mature children, with well-developed musculature, should attempt to play. It can also be very agile and has a very sweet sound in its upper register.

Most sax players play more than one type of sax (or even a combination of sax and flute, or sax and clarinet), and 'doubling,' as it is called, is very common in theater music and big bands. Often players come to the sax via the flute or clarinet, and then 'migrate' from alto or tenor to baritone. So, after a while most woodwind players who choose the sax will have had experience of most of the instruments mentioned above.

Recommended listening:

For soprano sax: Branford Marsalis
For alto sax: Charlie Parker
For tenor sax: Dexter Gordon
For baritone sax: Gerry Mulligan

It's also worth listening to some of the key saxophone ensembles such as the Apollo Quartet, the Quartz Saxophone Quartet, or the London Saxophone Quartet.

Bassoon

Starting age: 11 years

'Startability': ★★★★★★

Expense: ★★★★★★

Key facts: Double-reed
             Quite large

The bassoon has been unjustly neglected as an instrument for children. Modern student instruments are smaller and lighter than the conventional classical models and are available in mini-instrument forms, which sound great and are very affordable.

Vivaldi   'Bassoon Concertos'
Stravinsky   Introduction to 'The Rite Of Spring'
Servaille   'Introduction & Allegro Spiritoso'

Note that some woodwind instruments (clarinets, oboes, saxophones, and bassoons) require a regular supply of reeds, which can come as a surprise expense.

Brass instruments

Brass instruments should only be considered once the second teeth have grown through. The brass family of instruments is large and features very small instruments through to the positively huge.

There is a strong tendency for young players to change instruments within the brass family as they develop. This is made possible because the fingering systems on all three- and four-valve brass instruments is identical, with the honorable exception of the French Horn, which is a law unto itself. The trombone, having a slide instead of valves, is the other exception. This means that a player who starts on trumpet can easily make the switch to, say, euphonium, without having to learn a whole new regime of fingering. So don't get too hung up on whether your child starts with the trumpet or tuba – there's plenty of scope for change as they develop.

Trumpet

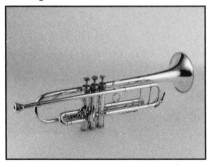

Starting age: 7–8 years

'Startability': ★★☆☆☆☆

Expense: ★★☆☆☆☆

Key facts: Loud, 'cool,' and versatile

The trumpet is a very versatile instrument that appears in almost every musical genre. It is dynamic, melodic, punchy, and yet expressive when in the right hands. There are some wonderful practice mutes available, some of which render the instrument silent to the outside world but enable the player to hear what they are doing through a pair of headphones. Trumpets come in a variety of sizes, from piccolo through to bass (which sounds more like a trombone). However, the most common is the B flat trumpet and this is the one that everyone starts on.

J. S. Bach	'Brandenburg Concerto No. 2'
Handel	'Music For The Royal Fireworks'
	'The Hallelujah Chorus' (from *Messiah*)
Haydn	'Trumpet Concerto'
Miles Davis	*Birth Of The Cool* (album)
Louis Armstrong	'Mack The Knife'
Dizzy Gillespie	'A Night In Tunisia'
The Beatles	'Penny Lane'

Cornet

Starting age: 7–8 years

'Startability': ★★☆☆☆☆

Expense: ★★★☆☆☆

Key facts: Key brass band instrument

The cornet looks like a stubbier version of the trumpet, but is in fact very different. It has a conical bore (i.e. the tubing gradually gets wider throughout the length of the instrument) whereas the trumpet has a straight bore, only flaring out as it gets nearer the bell. So, although it shares the same pitch and range as the trumpet, it has a far softer, much less penetrating sound. It is used mostly in brass bands and wind ensembles (which, interestingly, use both trumpets and cornets). It is a very agile instrument with a singing tone ideally suited to solo work.

> Bix Beiderbecke is the quintessential cornet player, but do also listen
> to traditional brass bands such as the Black Dyke Band to hear the
> distinctive tone of the instrument.

French Horn

Starting age: 11 years

'Startability': ★★★★★

Expense: ★★★★★

Key facts: The most difficult brass instrument

The French Horn is very difficult for young children (and professional players too!) and should probably only be studied from the age of eleven. However, it is a wonderful instrument to play, and is found in orchestras and wind bands, wind quintets, and all sorts of chamber music groups.

Handel	'Water Music'
Mozart	'Horn Concertos'
Strauss	'Horn Concerto'
Britten	'Serenade For Tenor, Horn & Strings'
The Beatles	'For No One'

Trombone

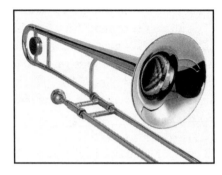

Starting age: 8-9 years

'Startability': ★★★★☆☆

Expense: ★★★☆☆☆

Key facts: Played with slide, not valves

Because of its size the trombone isn't suitable for very small children. It has a long slide that requires an arm-length not often found in children under the age of eight (though there are extenders that smaller children can use to get to the lower slide positions).

After the trumpet it is probably the most in-demand brass instrument, being found in orchestra, jazz groups, wind bands, and small ensembles.

The mouthpiece is quite large, and the instrument demands more air than the higher brass instruments, so decent lung capacity is needed.

> Gordon Jacob   'Concerto'
> Wagner   Overture to *Tannhäuser*
> In jazz, listen to recordings by players such as Frank Rosolino, J. J. Johnson, Bill Watrous and Mark Nightingale.

Euphonium / baritone

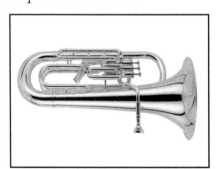

Starting age: 8-9 years

'Startability': ★★★☆☆☆

Expense: ★★★★★☆

Key facts: The cello of the wind and brass band

These are often referred to as the brass family's equivalent of the cello. The name euphonium means 'sweet-sounding,' and that's exactly what it is. Like the cornet it has a conical bore, which produces the softer sound. In the UK the difference between a baritone and a euphonium is that a baritone is usually slightly smaller, having only three valves, whereas the euphonium often comes with four. In the USA and other parts of the world the names are interchangeable.

You can get baritones with their bells rotated to point forwards, and these are common in American marching bands.

Tuba

Starting age: 10-11 years

'Startability': ★★★★★☆

Expense: ★★★★★☆

Key facts: Big, heavy, and beautiful

Tubas come in all shapes and sizes. The most common are the E flat and B flat bass tubas (though in professional orchestras you find tubas in C, F, CC, and so on). For beginners the E flat tuba is best, being the smaller of the two most common ones.

Although very large, it is possible to prop the instrument on your seat as you play, so it is not prohibitive to children of young ages, though it does require considerable lung capacity.

It can sound beautiful in its upper register (listen to the 2nd movement of the Vaughan Williams tuba concerto), and it has great power and depth in its mid- to-low registers. It is a very flexible instrument, appearing in orchestras, wind bands, jazz bands, and brass quintets.

Vaughan Williams   'Tuba Concerto'
Danny Kaye   'Tubby The Tuba'

For two contrasting examples of the way the tuba can be used, listen to some trad jazz followed by the Modern Jazz Tuba Project.

Other brass instruments

As well as the above, there are a number of other brass instruments, such as the flügel horn, a wider-bore trumpet commonly used in brass bands and jazz groups; the tenor horn is the brass band equivalent of the French horn, and it has the advantage of using the common three-valve system that other brass instruments use; the sousaphone is a tuba that wraps around the body of the player, making it easier to balance and therefore to march with. It is common in marching bands and trad jazz groups.

Drums/percussion

Starting age: 2 years

'Startability': ★☆☆☆☆☆

Expense: ★★☆☆☆☆

Key facts: Appeals to children's instincts

I believe everyone should study percussion in some form or another. It helps to develop true inner pulse and therefore forms a fundamental training stage for a musician. A lot of percussion instruments are very bulky – and you may find your garage becomes a practice studio! A drum kit occupies a great deal of space, is tricky to transport, and requires complicated transport arrangements. Again, you may need to look at what car you drive before considering kit drums!

In the world of jazz, these drummers are considered seminal:
Art Blakey
Bill Bruford
Billy Cobham
Buddy Rich
Jack De Johnette

Or, if your child shows more interest in rock and pop drumming then spend some time listening to recordings by the following drummers:

John Bonham (Led Zeppelin)
Ringo Starr (The Beatles)
Keith Moon (The Who)
Mick Fleetwood (Fleetwood Mac)
Stewart Copeland (The Police)
Meg White (The White Stripes)

These musicians will also inspire any prospective percussionists:

Trilok Gurtu
Evelyn Glennie
Paulhino De Costa
Talvin Singh
Tito Puente
Ensemble Bash

Formal vocal training

Starting age: 6-7 years

'Startability': ★★★★★★

Expense: ★★★★★★

Key facts: The one instrument we all possess!

The cheapest, most versatile, and possibly underrated instrument is, of course, your voice! Training the voice can and should begin from a very early age – there are many games and exercises in this book that may help. Another book you should look at is *Find Your Voice* by acclaimed vocal coach Jo Thompson. This provides a complete guide to vocal training for all types of singing and accompanying CDs of vocal exercises are also available.

In the book, Jo lists her ten favorite singers, and this is as good a place as any to start when trying to decide if your child would benefit from formal vocal training. Of course, they will have favorite singers of their own, but this list demonstrates the breadth of different styles of singing, from opera to pop:

Luciano Pavarotti
Stevie Wonder
Frank Sinatra
Eva Cassidy
Maria Callas
Cecilia Bartoli
Ella Fitzgerald
Aretha Franklin
Amy Lee (from *Evanescence*)
Take 6

Chapter 26

Music classes and formal training

Your child can attend music classes from before they are born! There is considerable evidence showing that the unborn baby can become familiar with musical concepts and specific repertoire from the third trimester of pregnancy. This is seen by some to be an opportunity for music education to start before birth. Consequently there are a multitude of classes for pregnant mothers to attend if they wish, in order to kick-start their unborn child's musical intelligence.

I feel the value of such classes lies in the opportunity for an unborn child to familiarize themselves with the characteristics of their parents' voice patterns. Those classes that espouse the playing of classical music at a loud volume with comments such as 'Isn't Beethoven marvelous?' – I'm not making this up – are probably best avoided.

Some classes focus on preparing the parents for the arrival of a child by teaching lullabies and basic composition skills. These classes make up for cultural traditions that may have disappeared – in the past, singing during daily activities may have been more commonplace than it is now. At best, a prenatal class will prepare your baby for the sound of your voice, and give you some clear ideas of how to interact musically with your baby once it is born.

Joining toddler music groups

You may be considering joining a toddler music group. As mentioned earlier. this can be a great way to introduce your child to a wide range of musical activities. A toddler music group can also be one of the best environments for your child to develop his or her social skills. Children at preschool age can be very shy, almost insular when around other young children, only when they reach school age do they really begin to open up and to view other children as 'friends.'

A good children's music group can also act as a catalyst for relating music to movement. The groups offer a chance for children to articulate themselves physically and emotionally within a playful environment.

Of course, there are good toddler music groups, and not so good. I have been to sessions where the leaders do not appear to know how to communicate with children, and one gets the feeling that it is just a business. A group should be highly professional yet highly interactive without being hysterical – after all, you don't want to come out of a session with a child who is so overexcited that they cannot be calmed down.

Look for creativity in the way the activities have been devised. Some groups use just taped music and little variation in the sequence of events from week to week. There should be a clearly discernible lesson plan and themes to follow during the term's activities. They should be active, not passive – even where listening activities are part of the sessions, these should be stimulating and interactive. The group leaders should have proper insurance, first aid training, and a background check where appropriate.

One of my favorite toddler groups is run by two former teachers. They use a clever combination of action songs, storytelling, and puppetry that keeps the children focused and entranced each week. They use a wide range of different instruments with the children, encouraging development of fine motor skills. By the end of the school year, the children have learned over 150 songs! The children have also become acquainted with other toddlers who are likely to be in the same nursery class when they start at the local school.

If there is no suitable group in your area, it is always worth starting your own informal group with other parents who have children of a similar age to your own. Any musical group activities at this age can have tremendous effects on your toddler's musical development, acquisition of vocabulary, and social skills that will benefit them for years to follow.

There are many high-quality, commercially franchised toddler music groups to consider. Some of the leading organizations are listed here:

KinderMusik

KinderMusik was founded in Germany in the 1960s and adapted in the 80s to be more inclusive. The core philosophies of the system are as follows:

- **Every child is musical.**

- **Every parent is the child's most important teacher.**

- **Home is the prime environment for learning.**

- **Music can help develop cognition, emotional growth, sociability, language skills, and general learning.**

- **Every child should experience the joy that studying music brings to life.**

The system is based on gentle guidance rather than by coaching. Prime elements are singing, moving, playing, creating, and listening. Classes are most effective with eight to 12 children participating at a time.

The Kindermusik system is usually split into three different stages; Curriculum One is for children aged 18 months through to four years, Curriculum Two is for three-and-a-half-year-olds to five-year-olds, and the third stage is designed for ages four to seven and is named KinderMusik for the Young Child.

There are more than 400 hundred registered, qualified teachers worldwide. You can find further information from: www.kindermusik.com
Telephone: 800-628-5687

Gymboree play and music
www.playandmusic.com
Sing and sign
www.singandsign.com

General musicianship classes and systems

The Jaques – Dalcroze system: Eurythmics

As mentioned earlier, Eurythmics stimulates and advances all the abilities and senses required for musicianship. These include aural, visual, and tactile sensitivity; knowledge and reasoning skills; and the ability to make informed, emotional, and intellectual judgements. These elements are co-ordinated by a kinesthetic sense – that is, the information flow between the mind and the body sent through the nervous system.

The student using the Dalcroze system is constantly strengthening key musical skills: the control of rhythm, dynamics, form, and tone. Eurythmics is founded on the notion that rhythm is the primary element of all music, and that the source of all rhythm is to be found in the human body.

The three main techniques covered in a Eurythmics session are Rhythmics (rhythm and dynamics through physical movement), Solfège (pitch, melody and harmony through the ear, eye and voice), and Improvisation (the combination of all elements).

The Core tenets of Eurythmics are as follows:

• **The beginning of music happens when human emotions are translated into musical motion.**

- Emotions are experienced physically.

- We feel emotions through our sensation of muscular contractions and releases.

- The human reveals internal emotions by movement, sound, gesture, and body shape.

- These are reflex actions, spontaneous actions, or conscious and considered actions.

- Internal feelings can be translated into music through breathing, singing, or the use of instruments.

- The primary instrument to be trained for music is the human body.

A skilled Eurythmics student will feel they are thinking with their body and physically flexing and performing with their mind. The method taps into bodily memory and seems to trigger deep-rooted coordination processes. I have taught students using Dalcroze methods, and have been able to help students to memorize complex chamber music accurately, without indulging in repetitive practice on the instruments.

The Dalcroze Society of America	www.dalcrozeusa.org
Institut Jaques-Dalcroze	www.dalcroze.ch

The Kodaly Method

'Music education should start nine months before the birth of the mother...' Zoltan Kodaly 1882–1967

Kodaly believed that all people who have language literacy have the capability to acquire musical literacy, and that music education must start at the youngest age possible to be most effective.

He believed that singing is the core foundation of all musicianship and that folk music should be the tool for all musical tuition, as it constitutes a musical and linguistic mother tongue. He was adamant that only the very best music should be used for education purposes and that music must be the core subject of any curriculum and the heart of education.

In the early stages of Kodaly training learning arises from enjoyable singing activities and is reliant on conscious thought processes at a later stage. Inner hearing, coordination, true intonation, and harmonic hearing are all developed at an early age. Singing provides a system of direct emotional expression and profound musical understanding.

The Kodaly technique uses a cycle of learning process:
Unconscious learning – conscious learning – reinforcement – acquisition of new skills – unconscious learning and so on...

The ability to internalize melody and rhythm is an essential skill for subsequent mastery of an instrument. The system uses lots of repetition and review techniques, which ingrain a lifelong command of musical concepts.

Songs are carefully chosen for their relevance to the participants. Great emphasis is placed upon folk music and works that fall well within the technical abilities of the students. The vocal cords should not be put under any strain – most Kodaly songs for children are within the range of D3 to B3:

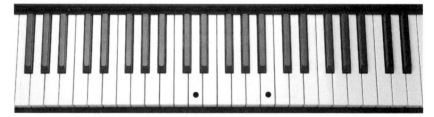

Songs used in the teaching method tend to avoid using close intervals (such as semitones) and have simple rhythm patterns. Songs have lyrics that trigger visual cues and assist in the development of creative play.

For further information, see:
www.oake.org
www.kodaly-inst.hu

Schulwerk

Devised by Carl Orff (1895–1982)

Carl Orff was one of the twentieth century's most influential and popular composers. *Schulwerk* is an incredibly effective system he devised to teach and learn music. It is an organic system that develops skills through activities that children naturally find enjoyable; namely singing, chanting rhymes, dance, body percussion, and instrumental percussion.

Orff's ideals are not very far removed from Plato's theories of ideal education, which combined athletic training with music study; indeed, Orff began his teaching at the Gunterschule which specialized in gymnastics and dance. Orff believed that reading and writing naturally grow out of direct experience of musical performance. *Schulwerk* is firmly rooted in the student's home musical traditions, as Orff believed that the acquisition of music skills should be built around music local to the participant – both geographically and culturally.

One of the central aims of the training is to lead children towards creating their own compositions. Orff knew that the process of learning only has meaning if it brings emotional satisfaction to the learner. True satisfaction comes from using acquired skills for creating new compositions. Children have an extraordinary level of pride when they feel they have created a piece of music – even a simple sequence of notes – that they own. This sense of ownership is a form of artistic pride and can build their confidence, self-identity, and emotional intelligence. Children have few opportunities to express opinions in modern life, and even fewer chances to have artistic opinions acknowledged and put into practice.

Orff believed that children should be given the opportunity to work with instruments that are rhythmic, melodic, and that sound beautiful. To this end, he was responsible for the promotion of metallophones, glockenspiels, and other tuned percussion instruments that now form the basis of most classroom instrument collections. The system has been translated into 18 different languages, each using music unique to the target country. There are more than 10,000 teachers of the *Schulwerk* system in the USA alone. For further information see The American Orff *Schulwerk* Association: www.aosa.org

The Suzuki Method

The Suzuki Method was devised by Dr Shin'ichi Suzuki (1898–1998). Suzuki was a great educator and Karate expert who realized that the way in which instrumental music is taught becomes much more effective when modeled on the patterns by which we acquire a mother tongue. Sounds should precede signs in the learning process and music technique and sensitivity can be learned through imitation and emulation.

He believed that the family should all participate in instrumental study, with parents initially taking lessons ahead of their children. He believed that every child has an infinite level of potential, and that talent is an artificial concept; all children can acquire the ability through a considered environment and careful training.

He believed that music itself should be studied to enrich life, and is a vehicle for spiritual and emotional development.

Suzuki's theories became widely associated with violin instruction, though the method has been successfully adapted for a range of instruments, including viola, cello, double bass, flute, piano, guitar, and voice among others.

The Suzuki method is often misrepresented in a somewhat diluted form, where the emphasis is on playing by rote and mass instrument ensembles and little space for personal expression. However, this is far from the original philosophies developed by Suzuki. When taught properly it is an incredibly effective method of instruction.

There are thought to be over 8,000 Suzuki teachers practicing today and over 250,000 students worldwide.

For further information, contact:
The Suzuki Association   www.suzukiassociation.org

Chapter 27

Conclusion

I hope that within the pages of this book you have found many ideas to help you engage in music with your child, and that you will soon see some of the many benefits resulting from active music-making. Only by really getting involved in the business of making music, not merely listening to it, will you see the most remarkable results.

In preparing this book, I have read a huge amount of scientific research on the effects of music on children's social, mental, physical, and neurological development. The vast majority of research focuses on the effects of hearing music, rather than the very different activity of making music.

Many of the scientific studies focus on the search for a kind of musical 'wonder drug' – one that will dramatically enhance numerical or linguistic abilities, or improve memory, or bestow any number of excellent qualities on our little darlings. This faddish pursuit of a mythical musical elixir is as unfocused as it is pointless – one month Mozart offers some magical answer, but a few weeks later Beethoven is the new craze. Many people are convinced that by exposing their children to a range of weighty, hardcore classical music CDs they will create a Nobel prizewinner of the future. You may have noticed that I remain very cynical about these claims! Music must be an active pursuit to have an effect on children.

In playing music, it is possible to stimulate all stages of the process of acquiring language while being able to go well beyond the boundaries of linguistic expression and even affect the very way our minds shape themselves.

Music bonds us all together in the past, present, and future, acting as a kind of social glue. Any significant social event is marked with some form of musical gesture. Such musical events help to articulate a sense of social cohesion, emotion, or change. Music goes way beyond language in its power and expression, and yet serves as the greatest tool for the acquisition of our mother tongue.

I believe music can positively affect a growing child by providing an outlet for expression, a place for confidence to flourish, and for the sense of self to be reinforced. This, in turn, enables children to be prepared for learning – and only when children are prepared to learn (in every sense of that phrase) can they begin to fulfill their potential.

There is a strong compulsion in humans to make music – we are born with a musical brain, and we respond strongly to rhythms, melody, and pulse. Yet as a society we insist on putting our musical abilities down. Many people are brought up believing they are not really 'musical,' whatever that means! I am certain that each of us is born with musical instincts and abilities. These enable us to interact with one another and to grow mentally and socially – even physically.

In my work developing new musical instrument technologies with a team of scientists at MIT (Massachusetts Institute of Technology, in Boston), any new idea, however complex, is initially tested in the lab with children's materials – sometimes with modelling dough or Lego bricks. The scientists believe that it should be possible to construct a model of any radical new concept from the simplest elements. Using the most basic building blocks encourages very articulate thought processes, stimulates creative play, and lateral thinking. The end product may be a piece of quantum nanotechnology, but it will still have begun life in the toybox!

Mozart developed a series of wordplays and dice games to help him compose some of his most revered pieces of music, and yet there exists a degree of snobbery around the idea of playing with music. I happily use many of the children's games in this book when composing music, as I believe they help me to manipulate as freely as possible the very building blocks of music. The end results are perhaps a little more sophisticated than when I first started out making music, but the initial processes behind composing remain the same – everything is based on simple improvisation games.

Making music should never be restricted to formalized training. Music is a living thing. It is practical, glorious, life-changing, noisy, relaxing, and energizing!

In writing this book I started out with a question – can music really have the wide range of beneficial effects many claim? To reflect the investigative nature of the challenge before me, the title of this book originally took the form of a question – *Can Music Make Your Child Smarter?* I didn't want to be too didactic about a subject that, it seemed to me, was open to interpretation in many ways.

However, during the many months of research, somewhere in the hundreds of interviews, and among the many thousands of words I've written for this book, that question became a statement – *Music Makes Your Child Smarter.* This change reflects the change in my attitude. Having read all the research and looked closely at the evidence I am convinced more than ever about the beneficial effects of music-making on your child.

I hope this book helps you unlock the potential of your child, and that you have many hours of fun and creative fulfilment over a whole lifetime of music-making with your children. And if you are in doubt about your own musical abilities just remember these two things: You are your child's first and best music teacher, and you are innately musical at a level that perfectly equips you for this most important role.

One last word: Music at this level is all about enjoyment, and shouldn't be approached in a serious or strict way. So take a deep breath, put a smile on your face and start making music!

Thanks and acknowledgements

Grateful thanks to:

Mike Sheppard and James Sleigh at Artemis for their patient support, guidance and expertise.

Tod Machover, Professor of Music and Media, and Diana Young at MIT Boston.

Professor Curtis Price, Jonathan Freeman-Attwood, Janet Snowman, and Ruth Byrchmore at the Royal Academy of Music.

Dawn Day and all the wonderful players at the Academy of St Martin in the Fields, Marianne at Oxford Cello School, Dorothea von Haeften and Arnold Steinhardt in New York for the hospitality and the chance to discuss the arguments in the book.

Roberta Guaspari and Lee Koonce and all my students at Opus 118 in Harlem.

Cathy and Charles Negus Fancey for their invaluable advice.

Dr Chrystalla Macedo for the medical expertise.

Sîan Davies for the expertise, friendship, and encouragement over many years.

My friends Maria K, Ant Genn, Tim Bird, and Roberto Borzoni for being there.

Most of all, my thanks and love to Belinda, Antonia, Elena, and Marilena (who arrived midway through the book).

The publishers would like to thank Besson Musical Instruments Ltd, Pilgrim Harps, Concord Group, Rosehill Instruments (Beaconsfield), Dawkes Music Ltd. (Maidenhead), and Sarah Lavelle.

Appendix

Research list and bibliography

Anvari, S. H., Trainor, L. J., Woodside, J., & Levy, B. A. (2002). 'Relations Among Musical Skills, Phonological Processing, And Early Reading Ability In Preschool Children.' *Journal of Experimental Child Psychology*, 83, pp. 111-15

Ball, G. F., and Hulse, S. H. (1998). 'Birdsong.' *American Psychologist* 53, pp. 37–58.

Bever, T. G., & Chiarello, R. J. (1974). 'Cerebral Dominance In Musicians And Nonmusicians.' *Science* 185, pp. 537–9.

Brown, K. (1999). 'Striking The Right Note.' *New Scientist*, 4 December 1999, pp. 38–41.

Butterworth, Brian. 'The Mathematical Brain.' *New Scientist* Opinion Interview: 3rd July 1999.

Chabris, C. F. (1999). 'Prelude Or Requiem For The Mozart Effect?' *Nature* 400, pp. 826–7.

Cytowic, Richard. *The Man Who Tasted Shapes*.

Cytowic, Richard (1995). Synaesthesia: Phenomenology And Neurophysiology.

Downing, A. T. (1995). *Music And The Origins Of Language*. Cambridge: Cambridge University Press.

Appendix

Elbert, T., Pantev, C., Wienbruch, C., Rockstroch, B. & Taub, E. (1995). 'Increased Cortical Representation of the Fingers of the Left Hand in String Players.' *Science* 270, pp. 305–7.

Fink, B. (1970). *The Origin Of Music.* Saskatoon, Canada: Greenwich Publishers.

Fraisse, Paul (1984). 'Perception And Estimation Of Time.' *Annual Review of Psychology* 35:1-36.

Fraisse, Paul (1982). 'Rhythm and Timing.' *The Psychology Of Music*, edited by D. Deutsch. New York: Academic Press.

Friederici A. D. (2003). 'Children Processing Music: Electric Brain Responses Reveal Musical Competence And Gender Differences.' *Journal of Cognitive Neuroscience* 15:5, pp. 638–93.

Gardner, H. (1987). 'Beyond IQ: Education And Human Development.' *Harvard Educational Review* 57:2, pp. 187–93.

Gardner, H. (1983). *Frames Of Mind: The Theory Of Multiple Intelligences.* New York: Basic Books, Inc.

Goldstein, A. (1980). 'Thrills In Response To Music And Other Stimuli.' *Physiological Psychology* 8, pp. 126–9.

Hepper, P. G. (1991). 'An Examination Of Fetal Learning Before And After Birth.' *The Irish Journal of Psychology*, 12, pp. 95–107.

Hofstadter, D. R., Goedel, Escher. *Bach: An Eternal Golden Braid*, NY: Basic Books, 1979.

Hofstadter, D. R., *The Mind's I: Fantasies And Reflections On Self And Soul*, together with Daniel C. Dennett, NY: Basic Books, 1981.

Hurwitz, I., Wolff, P. H., Bortnick, B. D., & Kokas, K. (1975). 'Nonmusical Effects Of The Kodaly Music Curriculum In Primary Grade Children.' *Journal of Learning Disabilities* 8, pp. 167–74

LaFuente, M. J., Grifol, R., & Segarra, J. *et al.* (1997). 'Effects Of The Firstart Method Of Prenatal Stimulation On Psychomotor Development: The First Six Months.' *Pre- and Perinatal Psychology Journal* 11, pp. 151-160.

Lamb, S. J., & Gregory, A. H. (1993). 'The Relationship Between Music And Reading In Beginning Readers.' *Educational Psychology* 13, pp. 19–27.

McDonald, K. L. & Alain, C. (2002). 'Automatic And Controlled Processing Of Melodic Contour And Interval Information Measured By Electrical Brain Activity.' *Journal of Cognitive Neuroscience* 14, pp. 1–13.

Moore, D. G., Burland, K., & Davidson, J. W. (2003). 'The Social Context Of Musical Success: A Developmental Account.' *British Journal of Psychology*

Motluk, A. (1996). 'The Big Chill.' *New Scientist* 150, pp. S17–S19.

Nantais, K. M., & Schellenberg, E. G. (1999). 'The Mozart Effect: An Artifact Of Preference.' *Psychological Science*, 10, pp. 370–3.

New Scientist Supplement: Emotions (1996).

Olsho, L. W. (1984) 'Infant Frequency Discrimination.' *Infant Behavior And Development* 7, pp. 27–35.

Panksepp, J. (1995). 'The Emotional Sources Of "Chills" Induced By Music.' *Music Perception* 13, pp. 171–207.

Panksepp, J. (1998). *Affective Neuroscience: The Foundations Of Human And Animal Emotions.* Oxford: Oxford University Press.

Panksepp, J., Normansell, L., Herman, B., Bishop, P. &Crepeau, L. (1988). *Neural And Neurochemical Control Of The Separation Distress Call. The Physiological Control Of Mammalian Vocalizations.* New York: Plenum Press.

Pascual-Leone, A., Amedi, A., Fregni, F. & Merabet, L. B. (2005) 'The Plastic Human Brain Cortex' *Annual Review of Neuroscience* 28, pp. 377–401.

Ramus, F. (2002). 'Language Discrimination By Newborns: Teasing Apart

Phonotactic, Rhythmic And Intonational Cues.' *Annual Review of Language Acquisition*.

Rauscher, F. H., Shaw, G. L. and Ky, K. N. (1993). 'Music And Spatial Task Performance'. *Nature* 365, p. 611.

Rauscher, J. H., Shaw, G. L. and Ky, K. N. (1995). 'Listening To Mozart Enhances Spatial-Temporal Reasoning: Towards A Neurophysiological Basis.' *Neuroscience*

Ratey John J., MD (2001). *A User's Guide To The Brain*. New York: Pantheon Books.

Richman, Bruce (1993). 'On The Evolution Of Speech: Signing As The Middle Term.' *Current Anthropology*.

Schellenberg, E. G., Trehub, S. E. (1996). 'Natural Musical Intervals: Evidence From Infant Listeners.' *Psychological Science* 7, pp. 272–7.

Schmithorst, V. J., Holland, S. K. (2003). 'The Effect Of Musical Training On The Neural Correlates Of Math Processing: A Functional Magnetic Resonance Imaging Study In Humans.' *Neurosci Lett* 354, pp. 193–6

Schmithorst, V. J., Holland, S. K. (2003). 'The Effect Of Musical Training On Music Processing: A Functional Magnetic Resonance Imaging Study In Humans.' *Neurosci Lett* 348, pp. 65–8.

Shahin A., Roberts L.E. & Trainor L.J. (2004). 'Enhancement Of Auditory Cortical Development By Musical Experience In Children.' *NeuroReport*, 15:12, 1917-21.

Shahin, A. & Roberts, L.E. (2003). 'Effects Of Musical Training On The Auditory Cortex In Children.' *Annals Of The New York Academy Of Sciences* 999, pp. 506–13.

Steele, K. M., Bass, K. E., & Crook, M. D. (1999). 'The Mystery Of The Mozart Effect: Failure To Replicate.' *Psychological Science* 10, pp. 366–9

Takeuchi, A. H., & Hulse, S H. (1993). 'Absolute Pitch.' *Psychological Bulletin* 113, pp. 345-60

Thompson, W. F., Schellenberg, E. G., & Husain, G. (2001). 'Arousal, Mood And The Mozart Effect.' *Psychological Science* 12, pp. 248–51

Thompson, W. F., Schellenberg, E. G., & Husain, G. 'Perceiving Prosody In Speech: Do Music Lessons Help?

Thorpe, L. A. & Trehub, S. E. (1989). 'Duration Illusion And Auditory Grouping In Infancy'. *Developmental Psychology* 25, pp. 122–7.

Trainor, L. J., & Heinmiller, B. M. (1998). 'The Development Of Evaluative Responses To Music: Infants Prefer To Listen To Consonance Over Dissonance.' *Infant Behavior and Development.*

Trehub, S. E., Bull, D. & Thorpe, L. A. (1984). 'Infants' Perception Of Melodies: The Role Of Melodic Contour'. *Child Development* 55, pp. 821-30.

Trehub, S. E, & Trainor, L. J. (1993). 'Listening Strategies In Infancy: The Roots Of Music And Language Development.' *Thinking In Sound: The Cognitive Psychology Of Human Audition*, edited by S. McAdams and E. Bigand. Oxford: Oxford University Press.

Trehub, Schellenberg, and Hill (1997). 'Origins Of Music Perception And Cognition: A Developmental Perspective.' *Perception And Cognition Of Music*, edited by I. Deliège and J. Sloboda. Hove: Psychology.

Trehub, S.E. & Thorpe, L.A. (1989). 'Infants' Perception Of Rhythm: Categorization Of Auditory Sequences By Temporal Structure.' *Canadian Journal of Psychology* 43, pp. 217–29.

Index

Index

Index

Index